永远的北朝

深圳博物馆北朝石刻艺术展

赵超　吴强华

文物出版社

图书在版编目（CIP）数据

永远的北朝：深圳博物馆北朝石刻艺术展 / 赵超，吴强华主编. -- 北京：文物出版社，2016.8
ISBN 978-7-5010-4653-9

Ⅰ.①永… Ⅱ.①赵… ②吴… Ⅲ.①石刻－中国－北朝时代－图集 Ⅳ.①K877.402

中国版本图书馆CIP数据核字(2016)第159871号

永远的北朝：深圳博物馆北朝石刻艺术展

主　　编：赵　超　吴强华
摄　　影：杨俊坡
封面题签：赖　非

责任编辑：谷艳雪
美术编辑：张希广
责任印制：张道奇
出版发行：文物出版社
社　　址：北京市东直门内北小街2号楼
邮　　编：100007
网　　址：http://www.wenwu.com
邮　　箱：web@wenwu.com
经　　销：新华书店
印　　制：雅昌文化（集团）有限公司
开　　本：889mm × 1194mm　1/16
印　　张：18.375
版　　次：2016年8月第1版
印　　次：2016年8月第1次印刷
书　　号：ISBN 978-7-5010-4653-9
定　　价：380.00元

Eternal Northern Dynasties

Stone Sculpture Artworks Exhibition of Northern Dynasties in the Shenzhen Museum

Zhao Chao & Wu Qianghua

Cultural Relics Press

出版说明

◎ 本书为2011年5月18日至2015年8月13日深圳博物馆“永远的北朝——北朝石刻艺术展”展览图录。

◎ 共收录展品及少量尚未公开展陈的藏品100件，以公元4～6世纪的北朝时期遗物为主，也包括一些隋唐时期的遗物。

◎ 石刻遗物80件，主要包括石床等墓葬遗物、佛造像等佛教遗物以及零星的道教遗物。其中佛教遗物种类丰富，包括佛像、菩萨像和供养人像，佛头、菩萨头、力士头和供养人头，造像底座，造像碑，飞天，护法狮，佛塔段，舍利函及器物等。此部分内容编排首先按照上述分类进行，并在分类的基础上分成北朝、隋唐两段，各段内以时代早晚为序。

◎ 金铜佛像20件，直接分成北朝、隋唐两段，各段内按照内容分类排序。

目　录
CONTENTS

图版目录
LIST OF PLATES

北朝石床与石屏风

——由深圳博物馆“永远的北朝——北朝石刻艺术展”谈起

赵　超

（中国社会科学院考古研究所 研究员）

中国古代社会中，始终存在着具有浓厚文化特色的丧葬礼仪。就现有的考古发现来看，远在旧石器时代的墓葬中就出现了带有宗教色彩的丧葬习俗迹象，新石器时代的墓葬中已经表现出了等级分明的随葬习俗，而在商周时期便有了系统地表现出社会等级制度的墓葬形制与陪葬品制度，说明作为社会意识形态重要组成部分的丧葬礼仪正式形成，并且由此产生了不同时代中不同形式的众多丧葬建筑和丧葬用品。由于古代墓葬是主要的考古发掘对象，出土材料十分丰富，对丧葬建筑与用品的研究必然成为考古学研究与文物研究中极其重要的组成部分，研究成果颇为可观，但是可深入研究的问题也俯拾皆是。这里要讨论的是一种以往介绍较少的特殊葬具。

在形制多样的中国古代丧葬用品中，有一种制作精美、意义丰富、但使用时期却相对短暂的特殊葬具——石床，前人一般称之为石棺床或石榻。

近百年来，得到妥善收藏与公布的石床材料并不太多，总数不过十余件。而我们现在却惊喜地看到，在深圳博物馆中一次就展出了五件北朝石床，可以说是国内北朝石床数量最多的一次集中展示。更可贵的是，这些石床均为藏家从海外收购回来的文物珍品，体现出富强发展起来的中华儿女对于祖先优秀传统文化的保护与珍视。这些珍品的展出，对提升深圳的城市文化品位必定会起到有益的作用，对于保护中华传统文化、了解古代艺术也颇具助力。现借此东风，以这些石床为主，对中国古代石床以及石屏风的概况做一点归纳与分析。

一　关于石床的定名与形制

在讨论石床这种重要的考古遗物之前，我们想先讨论一下这类遗物的定名问题。现有的考古发现表明：这类遗物最早见于北魏时期的北方墓葬中，以山西大同出土的北魏太和八年（484）司马金龙墓石床为代表[1]；下限至于北周时期，以在西安附近出土的北周天和六年（571）康业墓[2]与北周安伽墓石床[3]为代表。其形制相对较固定，均用石材制作成模仿实用木床的组合型葬具。其长度 2.2~2.5 米，宽度为 1 米以上，高度在 0.5 米左右。一般在正面（即面向墓室门）的床架与床足上雕刻各种纹饰图案，也有在四周床架和床足上均雕刻纹饰的，并已发现有多件石床在纹饰上描彩贴金，制作工艺十分华丽考究。在北朝墓葬中，与这些石床相配形成组合的还有由石板材构成的凹字形石屏风、小型石阙（包括围墙），以及石狮座等。石屏风一般由四件横向长的石板材构成，正面两件，两侧各一件，竖立围在石床的后、左、右三边。每件屏风构件朝向床内的一面上刻划有图像。小型石阙为两件，分为左右阙，摆放在石床上除安放石屏风诸边之外的第四边——前边。石狮座一般为两件，摆放在墓室中石床的前面。与石床相配的这些组件，并不是固定组合，已经发

[1] 山西省大同市博物馆、山西省文物工作委员会：《山西大同石家寨北魏司马金龙墓》，《文物》1972 年第 3 期。

[2] 西安市文物考古保护研究所：《西安北周康业墓发掘简报》，《文物》2008 年第 6 期。

[3] 陕西省考古研究所：《西安发现的北周安伽墓》，《文物》2001 年第 1 期。

现在墓室使用石床但没有石狮或没有石阙的状况，说明这种组合具有一定的随意性。

与此同时，在北朝墓葬中经常使用砖石与生土砌制棺床。这种棺床一般为长方形台子，也有些制作成须弥座样式，在上面安放棺木。这是一种延续时间很长，具有汉族丧葬特色的安葬方式。如果不深入考查，可能会把此类棺床与上述石床混为一类器物。但是详细比较下，我们认为在北朝时使用石床安葬显然是与使用砖石棺床安放棺木的普遍做法有所不同的特殊葬俗。其最显著的区别就是使用石床的墓葬中可能都不使用棺木装殓死者。石床这种葬具出现的数量较少，而且从目前所见资料分析，使用石床的墓葬主人可能主要是官职不太高的部分富有人士与粟特人后裔等西域来华人士。但是从它已经具有固定的式样、组合，常用的特有纹饰与图像等方面来看，石床已经成为一种独特的丧葬用具而被社会认同，并且其制作已明显地商业化了。

隋唐时期墓葬中仍存在有承放棺木的石棺床，是用石块砌成台子，有些做成须弥座式，有些在正面石块上雕刻出壸门装饰。它应该是延续了北朝墓葬中在墓室内砌制砖石棺床的习俗，但不像上述北朝石床那样仿照木床的形式单独制作，显然与北朝墓中使用的整体石床有区别。特别是隋唐墓葬中没有出现过与石棺床相配的石屏风、石阙、石狮等丧葬器物，应该是使用石葬具的习俗与礼仪制度已经有了重大的改变。因此，我们将石床及与之配套的石葬具组合确定为北朝时期特有的葬具。根据现有材料，北朝晚期，即北魏晚期与东魏、北齐、西魏、北周时期，使用这种葬具的情况较多。

以往的考古报告、简报与有关研究文章中，往往把北朝时期墓葬中所见的这组由四种器物组成的全套葬具统称作石棺床。也有人称之为石榻或围屏石榻，如韩伟在《北周安伽墓围屏石榻之相关问题浅见》一文中提出石棺床应该更名为围屏石榻[4]。郑岩则提出过应该是连榻[5]。

实际上，这些称呼并不科学。首先，我们看到考古发掘中出土的相当一部分石床上并没有安放棺木（或者没有遗留棺木的痕迹）。如在山西大同发掘出土的北魏太和元年（477）宋绍祖墓石床，河南固岸南水北调工程考古抢救发掘中出土的东魏武定六年（548）谢氏冯僧晖墓石床，以及西安北周天和六年康业墓石床[6]、安伽墓石床等。这些墓葬中的死者应该是没有使用棺木、直接安放在石床上的。此外还有很多类似情况，大同市考古研究所在《大同雁北师院北魏墓群》这一考古报告中指出：“在大同地区所发现的北魏墓葬中，有许多砖筑和石雕的棺床，但凡遗迹现象清楚的，大多使用的是尸体直接陈放在棺床上，而不用木棺的葬俗”[7]。这种葬法对于中原汉族人士来讲，似乎是当时称为“裸葬”的习俗。对于原籍西域的人士来讲，或许是在中亚宗教影响下的西域民族特有的葬俗。说明北朝流行的这类石床与用土与砖石块构建的、专门用于安放棺木的棺床有所区别，不宜混同为一类器物。

其次，石床、屏风、石阙、石狮座从各自独立的形制来说，应该是分别的四种器物，共同组合为一套葬具。但在已经科学发掘的有石床的墓葬中，并不是都同时出土有这四种器物，如山西大同地区出土的多件石床都没有石屏风和石阙等配件，河南固岸东魏武定六年谢氏冯僧晖墓中也没有石狮座的存在，说明它们只是多种器物的选择性组合，而不是一种固定的统称为“石棺床”的器物。就现有考古资料来看，最早的石床并没有与之配合的石屏风、石阙等，而很可能是像北魏司马金龙墓那样使用漆木屏风、丝绸帷帐等与石床配合。石屏风的出现要在北魏迁都洛阳以后。因此，我们认为，应该把这组葬具的各部分分别定名为：石床、石屏风、石阙模型与石狮座等。

至于将这些葬具称作“石榻”的说法。早在

[4] 韩伟：《北周安伽墓围屏石榻之相关问题浅见》，《文物》2001年第1期。

[5] 郑岩：《魏晋南北朝壁画墓研究》，第244页，文物出版社，2002年。

[6] 西安市文物考古保护研究所在《西安北周康业墓发掘简报》中称：“墓室中放石榻，上有尸骨，着锦袍，无其他陪葬品，无棺。”《文物》2008年第6期。

[7] 大同市考古研究所：《大同雁北师院北魏墓群》，第176~177页，文物出版社，2008年。

1979年，陈增弼在《汉、魏、晋独坐式小榻初论》一文中就对汉晋时期榻与床的区别做了专门的研究[8]，指出榻与床不同，是专门用于日常坐着待客的家具，其长度要小于床，不能用于睡眠。在现有的北朝线刻画中，多次出现这种专门用于坐着的短榻，如在河南固岸东魏武定六年谢氏冯僧晖墓石屏风上一幅孝子图画内就有放在屋外专门供老妇坐的榻，西安北周天和六年康业墓石屏风上的墓主人生活图中也有坐榻。所以，在墓葬中明显用于陈放墓主尸体的这类葬具不宜叫作榻，而应该叫作床，是在模仿日常生活中睡眠用的木床。这里还要指出，在一些石床的外侧四角发现有铁制的环，如山西大同南郊田村北魏墓中石床、日本和泉县久保惣纪念美术馆藏石床[9]与河南固岸东魏武定六年谢氏冯僧晖墓石床等。这些环应该是用来固定帐架的，说明与这套石葬具石床结合的还有竹木制的帐架和丝绸帐幕。山西大同南郊田村北魏墓中还出土有绘有彩色忍冬纹样的三段木杆，发掘者推测它们就是支撑帷帐的帐竿[10]。由此可见，墓葬中的石床完全是当时实际生活中使用的木质卧床的翻版，称之为专门用于坐着的“榻”是不正确的。滕磊在《一件海外回流石棺床之我见》一文中也认为“显然将其称为床更合适”[11]。石床与石屏风，郑岩曾认为应该就是古文献中所称的“连榻”。我觉得还是应该将其看作石床与石屏风两种器物的组合比较适当。周一良早就指出：“连榻当是可坐数人之榻，与独榻相对应而言。”[12]

附带提一下，对石床各部位的称呼，现在没有进行过统一，多为个人习惯叫法。为便于说明，我们将石床的构件分为上面平铺的床面与支撑床面石板的床架两部分。床架一般为三至四面，为雕有图案的竖立石板，每面的下部刻成二至三个床足。也有的仅在对着墓门的正面床架上雕刻图案。石屏风一般为四块以上的石板，呈倒凹字形竖立安插在石床左、后、右三边。石阙安放在石床的前边。本文中对石床等构件的称呼均以此为准。

二　有关石床的发现与流传情况

石床的发现与收藏迄今已有近百年。最早人们对它的时代与由来并不明晰，甚至把它叫作曹操床。以往，这类器物仅有零星被盗掘的传世品，经考古发掘出土的材料很少，因此也就更加被人们所珍视。现在可见的一些雕刻精美的珍品大多流散到海外各大博物馆，成为中华民族近代历史上的伤心往事。国内有关研究也比较少见。但是，近年来，随着国内北朝考古工作的进展，北朝墓葬中的石床陆续有所发现。特别是山西大同南郊、迎宾大道等多座北魏墓葬与北魏司马金龙墓中出土的石床葬具，以及河南安阳固岸南水北调工程中发掘的一座保存较好的使用石床作为葬具的北朝墓葬，给我们提供了北朝时期在墓葬中使用石床的具体例证。此外，西安北周天和六年康业墓和北周安伽墓，根据墓志的记载，墓主应该都是来自西域的民族人士，但都是使用石床作为葬具。这些发现使我们能够更深入全面地认识有关石床的丰富历史文化内涵。

这里主要讨论的是在深圳博物馆展出的五件保存完好的北朝石床。它们是新近由藏家自海外抢救回购的文物瑰宝。这批石床是目前国内石床数量最多最集中的收藏。它们形制多样，更充实了石床这类古代艺术雕刻文物的收藏宝库，为有关研究增添了重要的原始资料，是十分值得珍视的。

为了考察深圳博物馆展出的这些石床材料，我们先将以往的一些典型石床发现予以简要介绍。

较早受到世人关注的石床材料是据说1922年在安阳出土的一具北齐石床。因被不法奸商盗卖出国，其构件现散布在欧美各国，分别被美国华盛顿弗里尔艺术馆（Freer Gallery of Art, Washington D. C.）、美国波士顿美术馆（Museum of Fine Arts, Boston）、

[8] 陈增弼：《汉、魏、晋独坐式小榻初论》，《文物》1979年第9期。

[9]《久保惣纪念美术馆》，图13，内部发行，印行时间不详。

[10] 大同市考古研究所：《山西大同南郊区田村北魏墓发掘简报》，《文物》2010年第5期。

[11] 滕磊：《一件海外回流石棺床之我见》，《故宫博物院院刊》2009年第4期。

[12] 周一良：《魏晋南北朝史札记》，《南史札记》“香橙、连榻”，中华书局，1985年。

德国科隆东方艺术博物馆（Museum Für Ostasiatische Kunst, Cologne）、法国集美博物馆（Musée Guimet, Paris）等地收藏。姜伯勤曾撰文研究，将这些散布各国的构件组合起来，复原成一组“北齐时期的石棺床”。其中美国华盛顿弗里尔艺术馆存“台座上的二檐板”（即石床架的正面上部横架），最上方为椭圆形连珠纹，下面是莲瓣并列组成的饰带，再下面由透雕的壸门分出三个床足。左右两足浮雕手执三叉戟的袄教天神，足踏小型鬼怪及神兽；中央一足浮雕怪兽背负火坛，火坛的左右各有一名立在莲台上的合掌天女。壸门中凸雕莲花幢，幢左右各有一名头戴日月饰物的祆教神人，手托火珠。德国科隆东方艺术博物馆藏石床上的左右石阙2件。美国波士顿美术馆藏石床上正面石屏风2石。法国集美博物馆藏石床上侧面的石屏风10石。每石上雕刻一幅图画，采用减地浅浮雕手法刻绘出具有胡人风格的饮食、出行、狩猎与家居场面。姜伯勤认为“所描绘场景当是袄教节日，即汉文史料所谓的‘赛袄’”[13]。

另外，波士顿美术馆还收藏有一件石床，其纹饰与深圳博物馆展出的一件石床十分相似。该件为石床正面（长边），上部为一整条横栏，下部为三个直脚床足。由上至下分层雕刻纹饰：最上面为浮雕重叠莲瓣并列组成的横长条饰带；第二层为十五个正六角形与一个半边六角形组成的龟甲形纹样装饰带，六边形由直线与端点的圆形连续构成，在六边形内用平面减地浅浮雕刻画出图像纹饰，内容包括莲座火焰珠、青龙、白虎、凤鸟、畏兽等，神怪均面向中央，左右对称，六边形外装饰忍冬卷草纹样；第三层为绹纹装饰带；第四层为下垂的波浪纹饰带。左右两个床足浮雕侧立的狮子像，均正面像，一前足抬起，中央一足浮雕兽首。与之相配的有一组石门阙，上面浅浮雕人物形象。[14]

日本奈良天理大学附属的天理参考馆收藏有两件石床上的减地浅浮雕屏风石板，主要内容是表现墓主人日常生活出行的图像。[15] 1974年，美国弗朗西斯科美术馆公布了馆藏的两件石床上的屏风石板图像，并且推测这两件石板与日本奈良天理参考馆收藏品属于同一组石床。这一点可以根据两处石床构件上的图像刻画风格与伤残部位的痕迹得到证明。[16]

1971年，山东青州曾经发现一批画像石刻，经郑岩研究，认为是属于石床和石屏风组成的葬具中的构件，其内容表现家居、出行等生活场面，也带有一定的胡人艺术风格。[17]

1972年，沁阳县西向公社出土一套石床与石屏风，原简报称作棺床与石板围堵。石床正面最上方雕刻多方连续忍冬图案，下面为双阴线分割成的十六个方格。方格内减地阴线刻各种神异禽兽，包括凤鸟、畏兽、人面鸟、飞仙、鸟身怪兽等，左右两侧大多对应，均面向中央。石床有三足，左右两足均浮雕两名武士，穿长袍，戴小冠，右手托剑，中间一足浮雕一个半裸体侏儒，头顶熏炉，炉顶有莲花，莲蓬，两侧装饰忍冬与莲花。石屏风为四块石板，每块石板上雕刻四幅图画，共十六幅。图画内容主要是墓主夫妇的生活场面，以及侍女、侍从、牛车、骏马等图像。还有刻画男子跪拜等场面的。[18]

1977年，洛阳出土一套石床与石屏风，现在被洛阳古代艺术馆收藏。石屏风上面刻绘有十四幅图画，包括墓主人生活画像和孝子故事画，没有题榜。周到等人曾经在《中国画像石全集》第8卷《石刻线画》一集的说明中加以考证，参照北魏元谧石棺画像，认为其中包含有郭巨、丁兰、原谷、老莱子、眉间尺等人物的孝子故事。[19]此外，参照美国明尼

---

[13] 姜伯勤：《安阳北齐石棺床画像石的图像考察与入华粟特人的祆教美术——兼论北齐画风的巨变及其与粟特画派的关联》，《艺术史研究》第一辑，中山大学出版社，1999年。

[14] 据参观所见叙述。

[15] 水野清一监修：《天理参考馆图录·中国篇》，朝日新闻社，1967年。

[16] 林圣智：《北朝时代における葬具の图像と机能—石棺床围屏の墓主肖像と孝子传图を例として—》，《美术史》第154期，2003年。

[17] 郑岩：《魏晋南北朝壁画墓研究》，文物出版社，2002年。

[18] 邓宏星、蔡全法：《沁阳县西向发现北朝墓及画像石棺墓》，《中原文物》1983年第1期。

[19] 周到主编：《中国画像石全集》第8卷《石刻线画》，河南美术出版社，2000年。说明中所说丁兰、老莱子等图像与元谧石棺图像相同，实际上存在差别，仅可为参考。

阿波利斯美术馆所藏北魏孝子石棺上的孝子图题榜，可以判断洛阳古代艺术馆所藏的石屏风上还有伯奇的孝子故事。

1965年，山西省大同市博物馆发掘出北魏太和八年司马金龙墓。在墓室中出土一具石床，但没有石屏风。在墓室中清理出一组保存较好的漆木屏风，上面绘制有列女图等古代人物画，应该就是原来安放在石床上的配套器物，表现出这类葬具的早期形态。该石床由六块石板组成。正面的三个床脚上浮雕裸体力士，他们头顶卷发，项间挂珠链，肩上披帛带，腰间束帛；两侧床脚上各一名托举石床的力士，中间床脚上二力士，并且在这两名力士之间浅浮雕兽面。床檐板的边缘为两方连续卷草浮雕图案，中间的主纹以二方连续忍冬纹为骨干，在忍冬纹的空间“浮雕着龙、虎、凤、金翅鸟、人头鸟、伎乐等”。横列的伎乐人物一共十三人，中央为一舞者，舞者的两侧各有六名乐人，演奏着琵琶、排箫、横笛、箫、羯鼓、细腰鼓等乐器。最下层为多重波浪纹。[20]整体纹饰中带有浓厚的佛教艺术因素，或者说浓厚的西域文化色彩。

1982年，在甘肃天水石马坪文山顶发现了一套石床与石屏风。石床正面床座由二方画像石拼成。床座石面上凹雕上下两层各六个壸门；上层的壸门中雕刻乐伎，每个壸门中有一位乐伎，分别演奏着笙、钹、曲项琵琶、箫、腰鼓、竖箜篌等乐器；下层壸门中各有一个有翼畏兽。这些浮雕上饰以红黄彩色，蓝底色，并有贴金。床架外沿上减地浮雕两列连珠纹，两列连珠纹中间浮雕忍冬纹，并加饰金彩。石床前还有一对石狮和五件石刻伎乐人物俑。屏风共十一块画像石，上面刻画了门阙、游廊、殿堂、水榭、花园等建筑与正在进行饮宴、歌舞、狩猎与骑马出行等活动的人物。[21]原简报根据画像的内容，绘画风格、人物造型、乐器组合等方面的特点认为这批石刻是隋代至初唐时期的遗物，现在看来，也应该是北朝时期的石刻。

20世纪90年代，日本Miho博物馆购进了一批石屏风构件与一对门阙。屏风构件11件，上面用浅浮雕加彩绘贴金的形式刻画了大量反映西域民族生活和具有祆教文化特色的图像。[22]姜伯勤解读这些图像的意见是，其中包括墓主人宴乐、狩猎、出行、野营、盟誓、商队等生活场面，也有向娜娜女神献舞祭祀、祭司举行丧葬礼仪等祆教徒的宗教活动图像。[23]

日本和泉县的久保惣纪念美术馆也收购了一套石床、石阙与石屏风。石床正面最上方为双层莲花瓣并列组成的横条装饰带，下面是十三个方格组成的横装饰带。在方格内减地线刻各种神兽等图案，从右起依次为：尖喙鸟头畏兽、兽头鸟身神兽、狮面畏兽、鱼尾龙、口吐长舌的畏兽、鱼尾神鸟、莲座香炉与莲叶、独角兽头鸟身神兽、狮头畏兽、有翼神豹、兽面畏兽、象头鸟身神兽、狮头神兽，方格中的空隙处装饰忍冬叶瓣。最下面是波纹装饰。石床有三足，左右两足上浮雕畏兽图像，面向中央，中央一足上浮雕正向兽面。屏风由四块石板组成，共十二幅图画，包括墓主人夫妇坐像，侍女、侍从像，以及孝子故事图画，右侧三幅是郭巨埋儿的连续故事，左侧有原谷、丁兰等孝子故事。石阙素面无图饰。同出的墓志铭文为：“惟大魏正光五年（524）岁次甲辰十一月丁未朔，徐州兰陵郡赤县都乡里人匡僧安，名宁。在京士至殿中将军、主食左右。十月廿五日辞世。十一月十五日葬在洛阳西界北山中。墓记。”[24]

1995年，美国芝加哥美术馆入藏一套石床与石屏风。屏风上主要用线刻表现墓主生活和出行图。[25]

2000年，在西安大明宫乡炕底寨发现北周时期粟特人安伽的墓葬。墓中出土一套石屏风与石床（原

---

[20] 山西省大同市博物馆、山西省文物工作委员会：《山西大同石家寨北魏司马金龙墓》，《文物》1972年第3期。

[21] 天水市博物馆：《天水市发现隋唐屏风石棺床墓》，《考古》1992年第1期。

[22] Annette L. Juliano and Judith A.Lerner: “Cultural Crossroad: Central Asian and Chinese Entertainers on the Miho Funerary Couch”. *Orientations*, October 1997. Eleven panels and Two cate towers with relief carvings from a funerary couch, South Wing. Miho Museum 1997.

[23] 姜伯勤：《中国祆教艺术史研究》，生活·读书·新知三联书店，2004年。

[24] 根据《久保惣纪念美术馆》图录。

[25] 芝加哥美术博物馆藏品，未公开发表。转引自郑岩《魏晋南北朝壁画墓研究》，文物出版社，2002年。描述根据可见照片所作。

简报称作石榻）。石床正前方以及两侧的床架上用连珠纹勾画出椭圆形与方形边框，正前方刻有十七个边框，正中央为“正面狮头”，两侧各刻有八个边框，框内平面减地刻绘出动物头像，包括有鹰、鸡、象、狮、牛、马、龙、猪、犀牛等。床足上线刻畏兽（原简报称作力士承托图案）。石屏风上浅浮雕生活景象图画十一幅，并有彩绘贴金。这些图画中描绘的人物形象多为身着胡服、高鼻长髯的西域人士。原简报将这些画面归纳为：狩猎、车马出行、野宴、乐舞、居家宴饮、商旅、民族友好交往、出行送别等具有西方民族特色的生活场面。值得注意的是，该墓葬形制比较大，具有五个天井和五个过洞，砖砌甬道与墓室。在天井、过洞和甬道进口上方还有壁画，但是大部分已经毁坏。墓中还有石墓门、石狮门墩和墓志等。墓门门额也是石质，雕刻有祆教祭祀的图像。[26]

1998年至2002年间，在山西大同市南郊、迎宾大道、雁北师院等地发掘了大量的北魏墓葬，年代大致在北魏定都平城时期，下限在北魏迁都洛阳之前。其中有一些墓葬中出土了石床。例如大同雁北师院附近的北魏太和元年宋绍祖墓，墓室中有一座雕刻精美的殿堂式石椁，石椁内筑有“石棺床”。这件石床在石椁中占据大部分空间，仅椁门内一小部分没有石床，石床平面显示为倒凹字形。床架上浅浮雕一条横“S”形连续忍冬纹样，下面为连续波浪纹。床足为直脚，中央的床足上浅浮雕正面兽头铺首，左侧床足上浅浮雕忍冬花结，右侧床足上浅浮雕一只侧视蹲狮，其身上踏有另一只动物，可能是雌狮或幼狮。床上西部有两个石灰枕。[27]

又如大同南郊112号北魏墓葬，为一座长斜坡墓道土洞墓，出土一具石床，无屏风等配件。石床三足，床架上雕刻纹饰与宋绍祖墓石床相同，左右两侧的床足上各雕刻一个净瓶，内插忍冬花饰，中央床足上雕刻正面兽头铺首衔环，上面有两朵正面莲花。[28]

大同七里村14号北魏墓葬，是一座带有耳室的长斜坡墓道砖室墓。墓室中安放了呈直角相交的两座石床，耳室中还安放了一具石床。石床正面的床架上浅浮雕有一条横“S”形连续忍冬纹样装饰带，下面为连续波浪纹。床足为直脚，上雕刻正面兽头铺首衔环、莲瓣和人物形象。床上有石灰枕。墓中安放一男四女。[29]

大同南郊田村北魏墓，是一座长斜坡墓道砖室墓。墓室北侧安放了一具石床。石床正面的床架由两块石板组成，上面浅浮雕有一条横“S”形连续忍冬纹样装饰带，下面为连续波浪纹。床足为直脚，中央的床足雕刻正面兽头铺首衔环，两侧的床足各雕刻一枝忍冬。床上有两个石灰枕。[30]

以上这几座大同地区北魏墓葬，墓葬形制与随葬品形制均比较近似，石床的纹饰造型也基本一致，应该是同一时期墓葬。大同市考古研究所对大同七里村北魏墓群的研究意见是：“该墓群上限在建都平城的中后期，下限为迁都洛阳前后”。“墓葬形制和出土器物特征都较为一致，说明墓葬的年代十分接近。”[31]大同南郊112号墓与田村北魏墓、宋绍祖墓的年代也是这样。宋绍祖墓有明确的年代记录，这些有石床的墓葬年代大约都在太和元年前后，即北魏献文帝至孝文帝迁洛之前的二三十年内。

2004年，中国文物信息咨询中心征集到一件海外回流的石床，入藏首都博物馆。这件石床床架大部缺失，仅存正面一块，但保留有六块石屏风构件与两件石阙。床架上从上到下依次浮雕有莲瓣装饰带、变体龙纹装饰带与由十一只畏兽组成的横条装饰带。三个床足上各雕刻一只畏兽。石屏风上减地线刻有侍从人物、胡人牵马、牛车出行、墓主夫妇坐像与两幅孝子郭巨故事画，一幅为郭巨埋儿，一幅为郭巨夫妇供养老母，都是北魏晚期孝子故事画

[26] 陕西省考古研究所：《西安发现的北周安伽墓》，《文物》2001年第1期。
[27] 大同市考古研究所：《大同雁北师院北魏墓葬》，文物出版社，2008年。大同市考古研究所：《大同市北魏宋绍祖墓发掘简报》，《文物》2001年第7期。
[28] 大同市考古研究所：《大同南郊北魏墓群》，科学出版社，2007年。
[29] 大同市考古研究所：《山西大同七里村北魏墓群发掘简报》，《文物》2006年第10期。
[30] 大同市考古研究所：《山西大同南郊区田村北魏墓发掘简报》，《文物》2010年第5期。
[31] 大同市考古研究所：《山西大同七里村北魏墓群发掘简报》，《文物》2006年第10期。

的常见构图，并刻有题榜“孝子郭钜埋儿天赐金一父（釜）”，“孝子郭钜埋子府”。[32]

2007年在河南省安阳县永丰乡固岸村57号墓出土了一套石床、石阙与石屏风。根据墓中出土的墓志砖可以判定为东魏武定六年谢氏冯僧晖墓。该墓是一座带天井铲形墓，深13米多。床上有两具尸骨，没有棺木及棺木痕迹，其中北面一具尸骨面部向下，可能是后来迁入。石床正面最上方为莲瓣并列组成的横条装饰带，下面是十二个方格组成的横带，在方格内减地线刻各种神兽等图案。石床有三足，左右两足为浮雕畏兽，中间一足浮雕正向兽面。石屏风由四块石板组成，共十二幅图画，包括墓主人夫妇坐像，侍女、侍从、肩舆、牛车和男子牵马像，以及孝子故事图画。其中两幅是郭巨埋儿的连续故事，有一幅的构图与日本和泉县久保惣纪念美术馆的郭巨故事画十分相似，题榜为“郭巨夫妻埋儿，天赐黄金与之”与“孝子郭巨母祠（饲）孙儿时”。左侧有丁兰等孝子故事，有一幅题榜是“孝子丁兰□人□□”。石阙素面无图饰。值得注意的是，这件石床和石屏风的纹饰与构图与日本和泉县久保惣纪念美术馆的收藏品相类似，可能是源于同一个范本。[33]

2008年在西安出土有北周天和六年康业墓石床和石屏风，原简报称围屏石榻。石屏风内侧磨光，线刻图画十幅，局部贴金，两侧以及上部装饰了贴金的柿蒂纹。图画内容主要是男女主人日常生活场景，包括会见宾客、出行、仆婢随侍等，人物多为汉族衣饰。石床正面及两侧线刻图案，上下两侧为连珠纹，中间刻波浪形缠枝莲花纹，并在其中装饰了各种动物与神兽纹样，如山羊、骆驼、老虎、凤鸟、怪兽等。石床的正面三足圆雕为蹲踞的狮子形象，背面二足呈靴形。值得注意的是，在该墓的石门框上，上面刻有朱雀，下面刻有守门武士，均头戴小冠，身着宽袖长袍，穿尖头履，双手拄剑。墓室门口放置墓志一盒，称墓主名业，葬于北周天和六年十一月廿九日，为“康居国王之苗裔也”，曾任“大天主”，死后被追赠“甘州刺史”。[34]

另外，陕西西安碑林博物馆还收藏有一组石床，可能是在关中地区出土的。承碑林博物馆允许观察，该石床四周及床足上均有阴线雕饰，但是其装饰图案比较特殊，与现在见到的其他石床不同。两侧的床架上为一条横向装饰带，刻画了杂乱的卷曲纹样，可能是云纹，在云纹中夹杂有一些有翼天神和神兽。羽翼的形象与其他北朝图像中的神怪羽翼明显不同，是模仿展开的鸟翼，使得有翼天神的形象近似古希腊绘画中的天神，还有一些床架上的纹饰为类似葵花的连续纹样，由相对的波浪形纹组合成的宝相花结纹样等。单独的床足上线刻有畏兽的图样，与其他畏兽图像比较，应该是比较晚的造型。又据滕磊《一件海外回流石棺床之我见》文中介绍，2000年，美国曾拍卖一件北魏孝昌三年（527）的石床，为台湾私人所藏，石床前档上有刻铭“田阿敖”、“青州平原人”。[35]但具体图像不详。

三　石床与石屏风的图像纹饰特点和深圳博物馆展品

从以上图像装饰的具体内容来分析。石屏风与石床上面的图像存在着一定的区别与习见的绘画格套，从而反映出不同的文化内涵与民族特色，可以分别予以讨论。

现在已有的石屏风和石床材料，其图案装饰多采用平面减地浅浮雕加线刻手法雕刻，也有一些为浅浮雕，并在图像上涂彩色和贴金。这种刻画方式源于汉代画像石加工技艺，具有明显的中国传统美术特色。至于贴金的装饰方法则可能受到佛教艺术中造像工艺的影响。我们看到北朝晚期佛教盛行时，大量造像采用贴金彩绘的装饰手段，如山东青州窖藏北齐造像中就有多件贴金佛像出土。彩绘贴金应该是当时流行的石雕艺术品装饰方式。

石屏风的绘画内容和图案纹饰（以及部分石床

[32] 滕磊：《一件海外回流石棺床之我见》，《故宫博物院院刊》2009年第4期。
[33] 参见河南省文物考古研究所网站，2008年10月21日潘伟斌文《河南最大北朝墓地》。
[34] 西安市文物考古保护研究所：《西安北周康业墓发掘简报》，《文物》2008年第6期。
[35] 滕磊：《一件海外回流石棺床之我见》，《故宫博物院院刊》2009年第4期。

雕刻装饰）的文化风格可以分为两种主要文化类型。

第一种是以汉族传统文化内容为主的孝子图和墓主人日常生活出行图像。这一类的材料包括沁阳县西向出土石屏风、洛阳古代艺术馆藏洛阳出土石屏风、日本和泉县久保惣纪念美术馆收藏的石屏风、日本奈良天理大学附属的天理参考馆收藏的两件石屏风石板、美国芝加哥美术馆收藏的一套石床与石屏风、美国弗朗西斯科美术馆藏的两件石屏风石板以及西安出土的北周天和六年康业墓石屏风。新近在河南安阳固岸村出土的东魏武定六年谢氏冯僧晖墓中一组石屏风也是以孝子图为主的。

第二种是以表现火祆教宗教崇拜内容与粟特等西域民族生活场景为主的图像。其墓主大多可以确认为粟特族人等西方来华人士。这一类的材料包括1922年安阳出土的一具北齐石床，日本Miho博物馆收藏的一批石屏风构件与一对门阙，西安大明宫乡炕底寨北周时期粟特人安伽墓中出土的一套石床与石屏风等。此外，在山东青州傅家的一座北齐武平四年（573）墓葬中曾经出土一批石葬具，其中大批石构件被用于水库大坝建筑，当地博物馆仅收集到一批雕刻有图像的石板，从其形制与构图来看，应该是石屏风的残存。这些图像也属于具有粟特等西域民族文化特色的生活场景。[36]在甘肃天水石马坪文山顶发现的石屏风图像中，楼台亭阁等图像似乎更像是反映中原人士的家居生活，饮宴、歌舞、狩猎与骑马出行图像中也仅有部分人物衣着类似胡服。但是姜伯勤解读其中部分图像，根据有叵罗、来通等西方酒器和日月形象等，认为它里面表现了祆教徒进行饮酒的豪摩祭、日月神祭等祭祀场面，还把一座桥上的人物看作是密特拉神在离别之桥接引义人前往天国的场面。[37]这些看法，还需要有其他类似的图像资料予以更确定的证明。

现在见到的材料中，北朝石床装饰纹样及图案的布局比较固定。在大同地区出土的早期石床均为连续横“S”形忍冬纹样装饰带。其他地区出土的石床一般多在石床架正面上部凸雕横条装饰带，该装饰带由并排的莲瓣组成。装饰带下面的图案多表现为三种格式：

第一种是由方格连续图案组成的横条装饰带。横条由一组连续的用直线或连珠纹分割的方格组成。在每个方格内减地浅浮雕各种神异动物，如畏兽、人面鸟、龙、兽首鸟身的神怪等，或者在每个方格内减地浅浮雕伎乐人物。有些方格内还用连珠纹构成圆环，在环内减地浅浮雕神异动物等图形。如深圳博物馆展出的藏品（图版9、11、12）。

第二种是用六边形组成的龟甲纹装饰带。每个六边形的外边框刻成连珠纹或直线。在六边形中雕刻各种神异动物或伎乐人物。如深圳博物馆展出的藏品（图版10）与波士顿美术馆藏品。

第三种是横向一直贯穿的直线，与这一直线结合的是盘绕龙纹或其他神兽的缠绕形态图案。

石床的长边每侧一般有三只床足，在正面雕刻图像。这些床足上的图像大致有五种类型：

第一种：两侧为侧立的狮子形象，中间为怒目圆睁、张口咆哮的正面兽面铺首。

第二种：两侧为站立的畏兽形象，中间为兽面铺首。

第三种：两侧为裸体力士，中间为兽面铺首或畏兽。

第四种：两侧为执仗剑的武士，均头戴小冠、身穿宽袖长袍或袴褶服，中间为兽面铺首或畏兽。该组合或变换为两侧兽面铺首或畏兽，中间为仗剑武士。

第五种：具有祆教特色的神王和祭司、火坛等形象，如两侧为手执三叉戟的神王，中央为祆教火坛以及祭司、天女等图像。

这些纹饰图案，表现出丰富的文化特色，从源于汉代艺术的汉民族传统文化、来自西域与印度的佛教造型艺术、直到祆教美术因素，不仅能借以区分前后不同的历史阶段，也可以帮助我们深入了解各种外来文化因素进入中原的时间与具体影响程度，

---

［36］山东省益都县博物馆夏名采：《益都北齐石室墓线刻画像》，《文物》1985年第10期；夏名采：《青州傅家北齐画像石补遗》，《文物》2001年第5期。

［37］姜伯勤：《中国祆教艺术史研究》，生活·读书·新知三联书店，2004年。

特别是在了解祆教艺术方面独具价值。

姜伯勤《安阳北齐石棺床画像石的图像考察与入华粟特人的祆教美术——兼论北齐画风的巨变及其与粟特画派的关联》一文中，归纳出北齐石床所见入华粟特人的祆教美术与粟特画派的关联表现，包括四个方面：

1. 连珠—莨苕纹样的伊朗—粟特风格，见于响堂山样式及石棺床装饰。

2. 人物造型“其体稠叠，衣服紧窄”，“衣服贴体，如出水中”。

3. 世俗性乐舞宴饮场景与宗教性赛祆祭场景的和谐统一。

4. 波斯—中亚粟特祆教图像及祆教美术的中国化。这些中国化的表现有以下六点：a. 粟特祆教美术以圆拱龛表现天神所在的天宫。在敦煌北凉及西魏壁画中，我们已看到以穹形圆拱及汉式天阙交错使用，到安阳画像石中，已演变为汉式天阙。b. 在伊朗—粟特祆教美术中，多有翼神兽，如有翼羊、有翼骆驼、有翼马等。在中国神话美术中，自汉代已有“畏兽”。在北齐画像石天阙形象中多次出现托天的“畏兽”，这种有翼兽头人身的“畏兽”在响堂山石窟中已形成北齐的范式，这种从中国神话母题中借用的有翼畏兽图像，成为北齐入华粟特人祆教美术中的天神图像。c. 在粟特壁画中，神鸟常有相当于中国传统装饰艺术中的“戴胜”，……如安阳石棺画像石中的神鸟图像，多有“戴胜”。又，粟特美术中所见玉璜流苏一类的宴饮大厅装饰，在安阳画像石中演变为中国礼制画像中的玉璜羽葆。d. 安阳石床画像石在图画的构图上，采取了中土流行的屏风式手法，这种手法与粟特壁画中以连珠花纹分割画面的手法结合起来而演变为有中国气派的屏风或画屏。e. 安阳石床在建筑图像上，又将中国风的亭台楼阁、天阙建筑图像，与印度式的石柱图像、塔式图像和火珠装饰图像结合起来。f. 安阳石床画像石是一组浮雕，但其所依据之粉本应为线描，透过浮雕，可以看出其粉本以线描表现人物、坐骑和树木花卉等图像在技法上的进步。[38]

以上所总结的北朝石床艺术雕刻特点，在深圳博物馆展品上都得到了充分的体现。不仅如此，我们还可以在深圳博物馆展品中看到一些在以往北朝石床上没有出现过的图案纹饰与构图形式，极大地补充了北朝石床雕刻纹饰的内容，有利于对石床发展演变与分期的研究。下面就简要地介绍一下深圳博物馆展出的五件石床与一组石屏风。

第一件（图版9）：该件为分体雕刻的石床正面（长边）。上部为横栏，下部为三个直脚床足，在横栏两端各有一只铁环。由上至下分层雕刻纹饰。最上面为一条由浮雕莲瓣并列组成的横长条饰带。第二层为用直线划分开的十三个方格组成的装饰带，方格中用平面减地浅浮雕与线刻结合的手法刻画出图像纹饰，从左向右依次为畏兽、女人头鸟身马蹄足神怪、白虎、凤鸟、畏兽、牛角羊头鸟身马蹄足的神怪、左右有莲叶护持安放在莲座上的火焰珠、驼头鸟身马蹄足的神怪、畏兽、凤鸟、青龙、男人头鸟身鸟爪神怪、畏兽，神怪均面向中央，左右对称。第三层为下垂的波浪纹饰带。三个床足上，左右两侧足高浮雕侧面的狮子像，均面向中央，一足抬起；中央一足高浮雕正向的兽面。与此石床结合的还有一套石屏风（图版15~18），绘制墓主生活图与孝子故事画，详见下文。

第二件（图版10）：该件为分体雕刻的石床正面（长边）。上部为一整条横栏，下部为三个单独的直脚床足，残存有彩绘与描金。由上至下分层雕刻纹饰。最上面为一条横条装饰带，平面减地浅浮雕横“S”形连续卷草纹。第二层为由浮雕重叠莲瓣并列组成的横长条饰带。第三层为十七个正六角形与两个半边六角形组成的龟甲形纹样装饰带，六边形由直线与端点的圆形连续构成，在六边形内用平面减地浅浮雕与彩绘结合的手法刻画出图像纹饰，六边形外装饰忍冬卷草纹样。六边形内的图像

[38] 姜伯勤：《安阳北齐石棺床画像石的图像考察与入华粟特人的祆教美术——兼论北齐画风的巨变及其与粟特画派的关联》，《艺术史研究》第一辑，中山大学出版社，1999年。

包括莲座火焰珠、青龙、白虎、凤鸟、畏兽等，神怪均面向中央，左右对称。第四层为缠枝忍冬纹横条装饰带。第五层为下垂的波浪纹饰带。左右两个床足浮雕侧面的狮子像，均面向中央，一足抬起；中央一足浮雕正向蹲踞的裸体畏兽。

第三件（图版11）：该件为整体雕刻的石床正面（长边）。上部为横栏，下部为三个直脚床足。由上至下分层雕刻纹饰。最上面为一条由浮雕莲瓣并列组成的横长条饰带。第二层除中央床足以上部位外，左右各为用直线划分开的四个方格组成的装饰带，方格中用平面减地浅浮雕与线刻结合的手法刻画出图像纹饰，从左向右依次为白虎、凤鸟、驼头鸟身马蹄足的神怪、女人头鸟身马蹄足神怪、男人头鸟身兽爪神怪、兽头鸟身的神怪、凤鸟、青龙，均面向中央，左右对称。第三层为下垂的波浪纹饰带。三个床足上，左右两侧足浅浮雕正面畏兽像；中央一足与其上部横栏中连贯，中央浮雕一根圆柱，柱顶安放火焰珠，柱两侧各浮雕一名仗剑武士，身着裤褶服，头戴小冠。火焰珠两侧刻有"兴和四年（542）七月廿日亡人朱洛石洑冥记"的字样。

第四件（图版12）：该件为整体雕刻的石床正面（长边）。上部为横栏，下部为三个撇脚床足，左右两床足外侧各有一个铁环。由上至下分层雕刻纹饰。最上面为一条由浮雕莲瓣并列组成的横长条饰带。第二层为用直线划分开的十个方格组成的装饰带。方格中用平面减地浅浮雕与线刻结合的手法刻画出图像纹饰，从左向右依次为白虎、马尾马蹄足独角兽、鸟喙畏兽、牛角驼首驼蹄鸟身的神怪、雌狮子、雄狮子、独角兽头马蹄鸟身的神怪、手执锤钻的畏兽（可能是雷公形象）、马蹄足有翅独角兽、狮身有翅独角兽。所有神怪均面向中央，左右对称。三个床足上，左右两侧足平面减地浅浮雕畏兽像；中央一足平面减地浅浮雕两个裸体人物托举的莲座火焰珠。在图像的空隙中补充刻有草叶纹饰。

第五件（图版13）：该件为整体雕刻的石床正面（长边）。上部为横栏，下部为三个直脚床足。由上至下分层雕刻纹饰。最上面为一条由缠枝忍冬纹组成的横条装饰带。第二层为一幅通栏的长幅画面，用平面减地浅浮雕加线刻的手法刻画出大量山峦树木，在山峦树木中间穿插安排了众多人物图画，可以归纳为五组。第一组有一间房屋，屋内坐有一位老妇人，屋前跪着一位冠服男子。男子身后还站着两人，一个头戴笼冠，另一个用幅巾包头。第二组也是一座房屋内坐着一位老妇人，身边坐着一个小儿。屋前站立两人，一位用幅巾包头，另一位梳高髻，应该是一对夫妇。第三组在石床中央部位，有一男一女并列站立，他们右侧还有两人站立，最右边的一位似乎手中持有一只悬有流苏的长杖。第四组为一个妇人抱着一个小儿，右侧有一男子手中持一铁锹，似在挖地。第五组是一间房屋，屋内坐一位老妇人和一个小儿，屋外有两个男子侍立，右侧又一女侍持伞盖，一女子捧盒。右边还有一个男子牵着一匹鞍鞯齐全的骏马。这些图像中应该包含一些常见的孝子故事画与墓主人生活场面。参照其他孝子故事图画资料，推测可能有表现郭巨、丁兰等人的故事画。第三层为绹纹。第四层为下垂的波浪纹。左右床足上刻画畏兽，中央床足刻画正向的兽面。

此外，与第一件石床结合的还有一组具有墓主人生活场面与孝子图画的石屏风。全部屏风由四块石板组成，正面两块，左右各一块。每块石板上有三幅画面，正面六幅，两侧各三幅，共有十二幅屏风画，排成凹字形，形成一个从左、右及后面三面包围石床的立体屏风。图画采用平面线刻为主的雕刻手法，形象生动，线条流利精细。各幅图画的内容从左向右依次为：

1. 树下有三位侍女侍立。2. 二男仆牵一牛车。3. 三位侍女侍立。4. 一位老妇坐在屋内榻上，榻前摆放猪头、牛头。羊头等。屋前一个武士怒目奋髯，右手拔剑，题榜为"王寄日煞三生犹为不孝"。5. 一对老夫妇坐在屋内榻上。屋前一个长须男子头戴三角形装饰的帽子跪在地上，题榜为"老［莱］子欢孩"。6. 女主人正面坐像，两侧各一侍女侍立。7. 男主人正面坐像，两侧各一侍女侍立。8. 一个老妇在屋内坐榻上与一个幼儿玩耍，屋外一对夫妇侍立，题榜为“孝子郭钜”。9. 一个男子在挖坑，一个女子抱着幼儿立在旁边，题榜为“孝子郭钜煞儿养母”。10. 四位侍女捧器皿侍立。11. 一人牵马，马后有二侍女侍立。12. 二男仆抬舆，后有一男子跟随。

这套图画的表现方式与孝子故事内容与上述的洛阳古代艺术馆藏品、日本久保惣纪念美术馆藏品、安阳固岸东魏武定六年谢氏冯僧晖墓中石屏风等十分相似。其内容包含了以儒家孝义思想为代表的汉民族传统文化意识与丧葬礼仪，同时在人物造型服装等方面表现出明显的北朝文化艺术色彩。

四 有关石床的分期断代情况及几点总结

纵观以上所见的北朝石床情况，我们可以得出一些大体上的概念。

首先，北朝石床的装饰纹样与图像内容应该是与北朝墓葬中的整体装饰理念及其所反映的宗教思想相一致的。

在北朝墓葬中，虽然具有壁画装饰或者在葬具上加以图案纹饰装饰的个例不算太多，但是它们仍然能够反映出当时存在着对墓葬及葬具进行雕刻绘画装饰的习俗，这应该是从汉代和魏晋时期的墓葬习俗中延续下来的汉族丧葬礼仪宗教思想的表现。这种对墓葬及葬具的装饰，以前学者们有过深入的讨论，在其反映出汉族人士的宗教方术思想与宇宙观这一点上具有共识。墓葬中与葬具上的一切图像纹饰，都应该是在为死者营造一个安宁稳固的地下小宇宙空间，以驱逐邪魔鬼怪，保护死者魂灵安宁，在另一个世界中享受富贵生活，同时保护其子孙生者平安昌盛。所以，这些图像中包括各种宗教中的天神、祥兽以及象征吉祥的纹饰图案，如中国传统宗教中的东王公、西王母、青龙、白虎，佛教中的天王、力士、莲花、迦陵频伽，祆教的穆护、森莫夫、翼兽及连珠纹等等。制作者利用这些图像表现出神灵聚集的天堂景象，那是亡灵乐于前往的未来世界。墓主人的生活图像表现出对于富裕奢华生活的追求。孝子图画则反映了汉族文化中强调的孝义思想，并具有一定的宗教护佑意义。与此相同，表现祆教祭祀崇拜和西域民族生活的图像也反映了对于神灵和天国的尊崇，以及他们的丧葬礼仪观念。

在北朝墓葬中能够表现出时人丧葬礼仪与宗教思想的材料主要有墓室壁画与葬具、随葬品等。北魏早期重要的遗存，有宁夏固原雷祖庙出土的北魏描金彩绘漆棺[39]、大同智家堡出土的北魏石椁[40]、大同雁北师院北魏宋绍祖墓出土的石椁、大同湖东北魏一号墓中出土的漆画木棺[41]、沙岭 7 号北魏太延元年（435）壁画墓[42]、和平二年（461）梁拔胡壁画墓等[43]。北魏晚期的壁画墓有洛阳北向阳村的元乂墓[44]、洛阳孟津北陈村王温墓[45]、洛阳洛孟公路东侧的元怿墓等[46]，这一时期的重要石葬具有美国波士顿美术馆藏北魏孝昌三年宁懋石室[47]、美国明尼阿波利斯美术馆（The Minneapolis Institute of Arts）藏北魏正光五年元谧石棺[48]、美国纳尔逊·阿特金斯美术馆（The Nelson-Atkins Museum of Art）藏北魏孝子图像石棺[49]、开封市博物馆藏升仙画

[39] 宁夏固原博物馆：《固原北魏漆棺画》，宁夏人民出版社，1988 年。
[40] 王银田、刘俊喜：《大同智家堡北魏墓石棺壁画》，《文物》2001 年第 7 期。
[41] 大同市考古研究所：《大同湖东北魏 1 号墓》《文物》2004 年第 12 期。
[42] 大同市考古研究所：《山西大同沙岭北魏壁画墓发掘简报》《文物》2004 年第 12 期。
[43] 张庆捷：《大同南郊北魏墓考古新发现》，《2009 中国重要考古发现》，第 106~111 页，文物出版社，2010 年。
[44] 洛阳博物馆：《河南洛阳北魏元乂墓调查》《文物》1974 年第 12 期。
[45] 洛阳市文物工作队：《洛阳孟津北陈村北魏壁画墓》，《文物》1995 年第 8 期。
[46] 徐婵菲：《洛阳北魏元怿墓壁画》，《文物》2002 年第 2 期。
[47] 黄明兰：《洛阳北魏世俗石刻线画集》，第 95~105 页，人民美术出版社，1987 年。
[48] 黄明兰：《洛阳北魏世俗石刻线画集》，第 30~39 页。
[49] 黄明兰：《洛阳北魏世俗石刻线画集》，第 1~10 页。

像石棺[50]、山西榆社河洼村出土的北魏神龟年间（518~520）墓主人像石棺[51]、洛阳古代艺术馆藏北朝神兽石棺[52]等。可资参考。这些墓葬壁画与葬具雕刻的图像内容中，保存有比较多的汉代以来的墓葬装饰内容因素，例如：东王公、西王母、青龙、白虎、孝子故事图画、墓主人生活图、升仙图像、星空与云气等。这些图像内容，在上述的一部分石床与石屏风雕刻中有所反映。

其次，石床的装饰图像内容表现出比较明显的阶段性变化，可以在现有资料基础上做一些分期判断的工作。

上述北朝石床资料中，有几件具有比较可靠的年代记录，如大同出土北魏太和元年宋绍祖墓中石床和北魏太和八年司马金龙墓中石床，日本和泉县久保惣纪念美术馆藏北魏正光五年石床，河南省安阳县永丰乡固岸村57号墓出土的东魏武定六年谢氏冯僧晖墓中石床、石阙与石屏风，西安出土北周天和六年康业墓石床与深圳博物馆展出的东魏兴和四年朱洛石床等。在山西大同发掘的北魏墓中，出土石床的几座墓葬，根据当地北魏墓葬发掘的情况判断，也应该是孝文帝迁洛以前的墓葬。

在这里面，山西省大同市博物馆发掘的北魏太和元年宋绍祖墓中出土石床与北魏太和八年司马金龙墓中石床时代最早。值得注意的是，它们的图像中表现出浓厚的佛教艺术因素。如司马金龙墓中石床的足上浮雕裸体力士，他们头顶卷发，项间挂珠链，肩上披帛带，腰间束帛。床架上浮雕着龙、虎、凤、金翅鸟、人头鸟、伎乐等。其造型大多可以在同时期的佛教造像中找到原型。与之相配的漆屏风以列女图为主，是汉族传统文化孝义礼仪思想的反映。目前在这一阶段的墓葬中还没有发现与石床相配的石屏风，可能还是采用漆木屏风与石床共用。这也是这一时期石床葬制的特点。

而在北魏晚期与东魏的石床上，雕刻的神兽中出现了畏兽、翼兽、鸟身人面像等，表现出一些新兴起的祆教等外来宗教文化色彩。与之相配的石屏风中，则比较多地采用了墓主人生活图像与孝子故事画。如日本和泉县久保惣纪念美术馆藏北魏正光五年石床，河南省安阳县永丰乡固岸村57号墓出土的东魏武定六年谢氏冯僧晖墓石床、石阙与石屏风。

郑岩曾经指出："北魏葬具的画像装饰前后有一定的继承关系和阶段性特点。固原雷祖庙的画像可以为洛阳北魏晚期葬具图像上的许多图像找到先例，如前者的孝子故事、两侧的小窗和龟背纹的装饰等在洛阳石葬具上均可以见到。而前者的鲜卑服饰到晚期则为褒衣博带的服装所代替，前者出现的明显受佛教美术影响的题材在晚期也不再流行。"[53]这与我们对北朝石床的分期观察是相似的。

固原雷祖庙的北魏漆棺图像十分丰富，孙机先生曾认为该漆棺的制作年代在太和八年至十年之间（484~486）[54]。即与司马金龙墓中石床的时间近似，属于北魏孝文帝迁洛之前。这一时期的北魏文化中还存在有较多的鲜卑文化色彩，同时继承了一定的汉族传统文化因素。从绘画技法上讲，是以线条勾勒为主，人物造型与面部形状具有典型的汉民族特征。显然画工主要为汉族工匠，沿袭着汉代以来的中原传统绘画方式。但是画中人物的衣着服饰则是鲜卑特色，显示了当时鲜卑统治者的文化倾向。这应该是北魏早中期艺术的特点。

而在孝文帝迁洛之后，大力推行汉化政策，改服装，定礼仪，接受了大量从南朝传来的汉文化影响。墓葬壁画与葬具装饰中的汉化因素也随之增多，在绘画与雕刻的人物形象上，服装的时代变化尤为明显，成为褒衣博带、飘逸清雅的南朝式样汉装。这一时期的减地线刻图像，人物造型修长俊逸，树木山石的画法具有明显的南朝绘画艺术特点，画面充实，纹饰繁缛，刻画细致入微，线条纯熟流畅，具有突出的时代特色，与南京地区发现的镶嵌砖画等艺术作品画风相似。流失海外的元谧石棺线画、宁懋石室线画以及上面介绍的洛阳古代艺术馆藏石

[50] 黄明兰：《洛阳北魏世俗石刻线画集》，第24~29页。
[51] 王太明、贾明亮：《山西榆社县发现北魏画像石棺》，《考古》1993年第8期。
[53] 郑岩：《魏晋南北朝壁画墓研究》，第106页，文物出版社，2003年。
[54] 孙机：《固原北魏漆棺画》，见《中国圣火——中国古文物与东西文化交流中的若干问题》，辽宁教育出版社，1996年。

床和石屏风、首都博物馆收藏石床和石屏风、深圳博物馆展出的第一件石床与石屏风藏品等，都是这一时期艺术风格的代表作。

北魏晚期，随着疆域的扩大，与西域各国及北方草原民族的交通往来日益频繁，信奉祆教的粟特人以及其他西域民族人士在中原经商往来与定居的现象越来越多。东魏时杨衒之记录北魏晚期各国各民族来中原交往的盛况，曾经是“自葱岭已西，至于大秦。百国千城，莫不款附。商旅贩客，日奔塞下。所谓尽天地之区已。乐中国土风，因而宅者，不可胜数。是以附化之民，万有余家”[55]。这种情况使得西方流行的一些宗教思想在中原流行开来，其信仰的神祇形象也随之被中原人士所熟悉。从而直接造成祆教的宗教图像及带有中亚、西域文化色彩的纹饰图像也进入了中原的建筑与墓葬中。

北齐、北周时期的石床纹饰中，具有祆教等外来宗教文化色彩的纹饰图像更加突出，出现了祆教的天神与祭司、火坛等形象，现存的这一时期石屏风也有表现西域人士生活与宗教活动的图像。鉴于目前可以明确年代的北周石床均为粟特人士的墓葬中出土，与之相近似的北齐石床应该也大多是粟特人士的葬具，但是我们还不能完全确定这一时期的石床图案是以表现祆教及西域民族生活的图像为主，因为在这一时期的石床装饰中也还有采用墓主生活图像的例子，如北周天和六年康业墓石床等。但是至少可以看到，这些表现西域人士生活与宗教活动的图像不会早到东、西魏时期。这样，就可以把北朝石床的发展变化基本划分为三个阶段，即：北魏孝文帝迁洛之前（493 年前），北魏迁洛至东魏末年间（493~550），北齐与北周期间（551~588）。

依照上述阶段划分，参照有关的标准器物，我们觉得，深圳博物馆展出的石床基本上都是属于第二阶段，即北魏晚期到东魏晚期之间的。有些可能早一点，属于北魏制品，如第一件、第二件。从早期石床中佛教艺术因素影响较大的情况看，它们床足上面用狮子装饰的做法似乎要早于用畏兽图案的做法，第二件石床上面的龟甲纹装饰纹样也保存着固原雷祖庙北魏漆棺的传统。有些可能晚一点，如第五件，它的图案采取整体连贯的大型构图形式，而不是分割性的单元连续图案。这种做法在北魏晚期的石棺雕刻中经常采用，如北魏正光五年元谧石棺等。元谧石棺的两帮前部和底部刻画孝子故事，后部刻两位仙人骑马云游。各个孝子故事画面之间用山林、树木、流云等填补空白并加以区分，就是和这里相似的画法。显然，这件石床的时代要与元谧石棺相近或略晚一些。第四件石床中大量采用了成熟的畏兽与带有西域神兽特色的怪禽异兽纹样，可能是北魏晚期到东魏时期的作品。它们充实了这一阶段的文物资料，为我们更深入地了解丰富多样的北朝文化与灿烂的中国古代艺术提供了可贵的实物证据。

最后，附带谈一下中国古代“裸葬”的思想渊源与北朝石床的关系。

早在汉代文献中，就明确地表现出社会上存在着提倡“裸葬”的思想意识，这是与大肆耗费人力财力的厚葬形式针锋相对的，既表现了有识之士敢于以身作则，反对浪费社会资源、标志贫富分化的厚葬风俗，又反映了通达明哲的思想境界。它可能是西汉初年黄老思想流行影响下的产物，也影响着在东汉时期形成的道教思想宗旨。值得注意的是《汉书》中专门设立了《杨王孙传》，记录了一个普通平民杨王孙的身世。杨王孙与这部官修史书收录的其他人物身份地位极其悬殊，能够列入正史中，完全是凭借他大力主张的“裸葬”思想。可以说，《汉书》的作者班固也是这种思想的拥护者，《晋书・皇甫谧传》引皇甫谧《笃终》一文云：“杨王孙亲土，《汉书》以为贤于秦始皇”[56]。可见这种思想在汉晋时期的士人中颇具影响，才会在正史中完整地宣扬了杨王孙的主张。

《汉书・杨王孙传》载：“杨王孙者，孝武时人也。学黄老之术，……及病且终，先令其子，曰：‘吾欲裸葬，以反吾真，必亡易吾意。死则为布囊盛尸，入地七尺，既下，从足引脱其囊，以身亲土。’”杨王孙在给其友人祈侯的回信中清晰地说明了他的思想：“吾是以裸葬，将以矫世也。夫厚葬诚亡益

[55] 杨衒之：《洛阳伽蓝记》，见杨勇《洛阳伽蓝记校笺》，中华书局，2006 年。

[56]《晋书》卷五十一，第 1417 页，中华书局点校本。

于死者，而俗人竞以相高，靡财单币，腐之地下。或乃今日入而明日发，此真与暴骸于中野何异！且夫死者，终生之化，而物之归者也。归者得至，化者得变，是物各反其真也。反真冥冥，亡形亡声，乃合道情。”[57]

历代都有统治者提倡过薄葬，尤其是在经济凋敝的社会动乱时期，所以“裸葬”的思想一直有所传袭，史书中不乏实例。《后汉书·樊宏传》载樊宏“卒。遗敕薄葬，一无所用，以为棺柩一藏，不宜复见，如有腐败，伤孝子之心，使与夫人同坟异藏”[58]。这种做法甚至得到汉光武帝的赞许，称“吾万岁之后，欲以为式”[59]。《三国志·魏书·裴潜传》载裴潜“正始五年薨，追赠太常，……遗令俭葬。墓中惟置一坐，瓦器数枚，其余一无所设”[60]。《晋书·皇甫谧传》载皇甫谧“著论为葬送之制，名曰《笃终》，曰，‘……故吾欲朝死夕葬，夕死朝葬，不设棺椁，不加缠敛，……气绝之后，便即时服，幅巾故衣，以籧篨裹尸，麻约二头，置尸床上。择不毛之地，穿坑深十尺，长一丈五尺，广六尺，坑讫，举床就坑，去床下尸。平生之物，皆无自随，惟赍《孝经》一卷，示不忘孝道’”[61]。这些历代文献中的记载，反映了“裸葬”思想与其实际做法从西汉到晋代始终存在于汉族社会生活之中。

北朝使用石床葬具的情况则表现出，在社会动荡、异族统治交替变化，各种思想文化并存的北朝数百年间，中原汉族传统文化思想中具有较大影响的“裸葬”习俗仍有传承。上文已经介绍，考古发掘中出土的相当一部分北朝石床上并没有安放棺木，正说明这些墓葬中的死者是没有装殓入棺木，而直接安放在石床上的。这种葬法对于中原汉族人士来讲，应该是延续了秉承黄老思想和道教精神的反真做法，可以体现自己的民族文化传统，对于北方游牧民族来说，可能是比起儒家繁缛的丧礼更容易接受的一种丧礼形式，从而使之在异族统治下的北朝时期存留并沿袭下来。而后，对于原籍西域的民族人士来讲，这种“裸葬”与祆教的天葬形式或许有些相似之处，使得他们也接受了使用石床埋葬的习俗。众多的民族文化集中到一种流行的葬具上，才使得北朝石床上闪烁出如此丰富多彩的文化、艺术、思想之光。

[57]《汉书》卷六十七，第740页，中华书局点校本。
[58]《后汉书》卷三十二，第1121页，中华书局点校本。
[59]《后汉书》卷三十二，第1121页，中华书局点校本。
[60]《三国志》卷二十三，第673页，中华书局点校本。
[61]《晋书》卷五十一，第1416~1418页，中华书局点校本。

Stone Beds and Stone Screens of the Northern Dynasties

On the "Eternal Northern Dynasties: Stone Sculpture Artworks Exhibition of Northern Dynasties" in the Shenzhen Museum

Zhao Chao
(Research Fellow, the Institute of Archaeology, Chinese Academy of Social Sciences)

Among various forms of ancient Chinese grave goods, *shichuang* (stone bed), was elaborately manufactured and embodied with diverse meanings, but endured a comparatively short history of use. In previous scholarship, it was generally called "*shiguanchuang*" (stone coffin bed) or "*shita*" (stone couch).

In the past hundreds of years, only about a dozen of stone beds have been well collected and published, quite small in terms of numbers. Therefore, it is very surprising and delightful for us to see the 5 pieces of stone beds from the Northern Dynasties at once presented by the Shenzhen Museum, which can be the most inclusive domestic exhibition of the extant Northern Dynasties stone beds. More significantly, the fact that these stone beds are important cultural relics purchased from abroad by a private collector exemplifies the awareness and efforts of the Chinese people to cherish the cultural traditions inherited from ancestors while our nation is undergoing prosperous development. Moreover, such display of treasures will certainly improve the cultural image of Shenzhen, and it will be very beneficial to preserving Chinese cultural traditions and to the learning of ancient arts. Taking this occasion, this article centres on the exhibited stone beds and sets out to analyse and summarise the features of ancient Chinese stone beds and stone screens.

I. On the Naming and Structure of Stone Beds

Before discussing the important archaeological remains of stone beds, let us first look into the problem of naming. Past archaeological reports, briefs, and related research papers tended to use a general term "*shiguanchuang*" to refer to the Northern Dynasties funerary furnishings consisting of 4 parts: a stone bed, a half-enclosed stone screen made up of stone panels, small-scale stone tower and enclosure components, and stone lion caryatids. Sometimes, they were also called "*shita*" or "*weiping shita*" (stone couch with screen enclosure); for instance, Han Wei in his "Some Ideas on Stone Couches with Screen Enclosure from the Tomb of Anjia in the Northern Zhou" argues that "*shiguanchuang*" should be re-named as "*weiping shita*",[1] while Zheng Yan contends that it should be "*lianta*" (linked couch).[2]

Actually, none of these names are appropriate. First, from a considerable number of archaeological excavations, no coffins (or vestiges of coffins) are found placed on stone beds, as seen in the tomb of Song Shaozu dated to the first year of Taihe in the Northern Wei (477 CE) excavated at Datong, Shanxi; the tomb of Xie Shi and Feng Senghui dated to the sixth year of Wuding in the Eastern Wei (548 CE) from the salvage

1 Han Wei, "Some Ideas on Stone Couches with Screen Enclosure from the Tomb of Anjia in the Northern Zhou", *Wenwu [Cultural Relics]*, iss. 1, 2001.
2 Zheng Yan, *Research on Wei, Jin, Southern, and Northern Dynasties*, Cultural Relics Press, 2002, p. 244.

archaeological excavation during the "South-to-North Water Diversion Project" in Gu'an, Henan; the tomb of Kangye dated to the sixth year of Tianhe (571 CE) at Beizhou, Xi'an;[3] the tomb of Anjia and so forth. Occupants of these tombs were placed directly on the stone beds instead of into coffins, which seems to be the "*luozang*" (naked burial) custom described by Han people in Central China. It was probably formed under the influence of Central Asian religions and peculiar to the ethnical groups from the western frontiers which was later practiced by their descendants living in China. However, *guanchuang* (coffin bed) were constructed with clay, bricks, or stones to position coffins, and they are distinct from the stone beds popular during the Northern Dynasties, so it is not appropriate to confuse them as the same mortuary object.

Besides, stone beds, screens, stone towers with enclosure components, and lion sculptures each have their respective structure, so they should have been four different objects that compose a set of funerary furnishings. Nevertheless, not all of the 4 objects are found among the tombs that have been scientifically excavated. For example, several stone beds unearthed at Datong, Shanxi are not attached with stone screens or stone towers; lion caryatids are not found in the tomb of Xie Shi and Feng Senghui, which indicate that the combination of objects were selective rather than being fixed that can be generalised as a single structure of "stone coffin bed". From the available archaeological materials, the earliest funerary stone beds were not combined with stone screens or stone towers, but very likely to be matched with lacquer screens and silk curtains as found in the tomb of Sima Jinlong in the Northern Wei Dynasty. Current archaeological evidence shows that stone screens did not appear until the capital of the Western Wei was moved to Luoyang. We thus hold that each object in the set of furnishings should be specifically named as stone beds, stone screens, stone towers and stone lion caryatids.

With regard to the name of stone couch, Chen Zengbi, in as early as 1979, conducted a research in his "A Preliminary Discussion on Single-seat Couch in the Han, Wei, and Jin Dynasties" on the differentiation between *ta* (couch) and *chuang* (bed) in the Han and Jin periods.[4] He points out that ta, as opposed to chuang, was especially used as sitting furniture for guests, and its length was shorter than chuang, so it was not designed for repose. Extant linear engravings of the Northern Dynasties preserved quite a few this form of short couch. Moreover, iron rings are found on four exterior corners of some stone beds, such as the stone bed from a tomb of Northern Wei excavated at Tian Village, southern suburbs of Datong, Shanxi; the stone bed in the Kuboso Memorial Museum of Arts, Izumi; and the one from the tomb of Xie Shi and Feng Senghui. They could have been used to fix the curtain railings, which also suggests that bamboo railings and silk curtains were also attached to this furniture. At Tian Village, southern suburbs of Datong, Shanxi, three pieces of wooden poles painted with acanthus patterns were found in a Northern Wei tomb, and the excavators postulate that they were used to support curtains and canopy.[5] It can be concluded that the stone beds in tombs were replicas of the wooden beds used in daily life, and it would be rather erroneous to name them as couch which were particularly used for sitting and conversing.

II. On the Finds and Acquisitions of Stone Beds

This article focuses on the 5 well-preserved stone bed carvings of the Northern Dynasties exhibited at the Shenzhen Museum – cultural treasures recently acquired from overseas. This is so far the biggest collection of stone beds in China and they deserve to be cherished,

3 Xi'an Institute of Cultural Relics Conservation and Archaeology in "Excavation Brief of Kangye Tomb of the Northern Zhou in Xi'an" describes "there is a stone couch in the tomb chamber, a body in silk robe is placed on it, with no other mortuary objects, no coffin". See *Wenwu [Cultural Relics]*, iss. 6, 2008.

4 Chen Zengbi, "A Preliminary Discussion on Single-seat Couch in the Han, Wei, and Jin Dynasties", *Wenwu [Cultural Relics]*, iss.9, 1979.

5 Datong Institute of Archaeology, "Excavation Brief of Northern Wei Tombs in Tian Village, Southern Suburbs of Datong, Shanxi", *Wenwu [Cultural Relics]*, iss. 5, 2010.

because their formal diversity not only constitutes the relics treasury of such ancient carving art, but also adds important original materials to academic research.

To better study the stone beds exhibited at the Shenzhen Museum, we will first briefly introduce some typical examples of stone bed finds.

The earliest stone bed that caught attention is said to be excavated in Anyang in 1922. It was robbed and sold abroad by illegal dealers, and now its components are dispersed in different countries in Europe and America, collected by the Freer Gallery of Art in Washington D. C., Museum of Fine Arts, Boston, Museum of East Asian Art, Cologne, and the Guimet Museum in Paris. Jiang Boqin wrote an article suggesting that if put together, these parts would form a set of "stone bed of the Northern Qi period". On the top of the "two panels on a base" in the Freer Gallery, there are linked pearl patterns with a continuous band of lotus petals beneath. Further down below are three open-work carvings of *kunmen* (arched niche) which form three bed feet. On each side, a Zoroastrian deity in relief holds a trident and stands on small spirits and mythical animals. In the middle, a beast carries on its back a fire altar with two heavenly maiden standing on lotus pedestals with two palms pressing against each other. In the *kunmen*, a rilievo lotus pillar is flanked by two Zoroastrian deities with sun and moon decorations around their heads, holding fire balls. Two gate towers on two sides of the stone bed are collected by Museum of East Asian Art, Cologne; two screens in the front are collected in Museum of Fine Arts, Boston; ten screens on the side are collected in Guimet Museum, Paris. Each slab depicts in bas-relief feasting, outing, hunting and household scenes of the Sogdian people. Jiang Boqin argues that these scenes are from Zoroastrian festivals, which is referred to as "*Saixian*" (festive and contest scenes of the Zoroastrians) in the Han literature.[6]

Museum of Fine Arts, Boston has another stone bed whose decorations are very similar to one of the exhibits at the Shenzhen Museum. This item is the front side (longer side) of a stone bed. Its upper part is a horizontal panel, and the lower part three straight bed feet. Multi-tier compositional strategy was employed in its carving decorations: a continuous band of lotus petals cross the top; the second tier is a frieze of tortoise shell patterns made up of 15 hexagons and one half-hexagon, and pictorial bas-reliefs inside the hexagons include lotus pedestals with fire balls, green dragons, white tigers, phoenixes, *weishou* (mythical creatures that avert evil spirits); the third tier is a frieze of rope patterns and the fourth pendent waves. Two semi-frontal lion sculptures constitute two side bed feet, each with one front paw lifted. The middle bed foot is a monster head relief. The bed is accompanied by a group of stone gate towers carved with human figures in bas-relief.

Tenri University Sankokan Museum in Nara, Japan has two screen slabs carved in bas-relief with daily life and excursion scenes of the tomb owner.[7] In 1974, Asian Art Museum of San Francisco published images of two screen slabs from its collection, and suggested that these two and Sankokan Museum slabs were from the same set of stone bed. This presupposition has been confirmed by their similar pictorial carving style and matching broken parts.[8]

In 1971, a series of pictorial stone carvings were found in Qingzhou, Shandong. After research, Zheng Yan identifies them as components from a set of funerary furnishings of a stone bed and a stone screen. The content is also about daily life scenes of household and outing, with a certain western nomadic artistic style.[9]

In 1972, a set of stone bed and stone screen were excavated at Xixiang Commune, Qinyang. In the original

---

6 Jiang Boqin, "A Study of the Images on the Pictorial Stones of the Stone Coffin Bed of the Northern Qi at Anyang and Zoroastrian arts of the Sogdian Immigrants to China, with a Discussion on the Connection between the Dramatic Changes of the Northern Qi Painting Styles and Sogdian Painting Genres", in *Art History Research*, vol. 1, Sun Yat-Sen University Press.

7 Mizuno, Seiichi, ed., *Catalogues of Tenri University Sankokan Museum: China*, Asahi Shimbun, 1967.

8 See Lin Sheng-chih, "The Iconography and Function of Mortuary Objects during the Northern Dynasties", *History of Art*, iss. 154, vol. 52 (2), 2003.

9 Zheng Yan, *Research on the Mural Tombs of the Wei, Jin, Southern, and Northern Dynasties*, Cultural Relics Press, 2002.

brief, they were referred to as "*guanchuang*" (coffin bed) and "*shiban weidu*" (stone panel enclosure). The front top of the bed is carved with multiple scrolls of acanthus. The space below is divided into 16 squares by double lines. Inside each square, there are linear engravings of various mythical creatures including phoenixes, *weishou*, birds with human faces, flying divinities, monsters with bird bodies. This bed has three feet. Each foot on both sides comprises two guard reliefs in long robes and small hats, holding a sword in the right hand. In the middle, a half-naked dwarf carries an incense-burner on his head. On the top of the incense-burner there are lotuses and seedpods. There are also acanthus and lotus decorations on both sides. The screen is made up of four stone slabs, and each depicts four images and altogether 16 images. The subject matter of the images includes daily life scenes of the owner couple of the tomb and their maids, servants, oxcarts, and horses.[10]

In 1977, a set of stone bed and screen were unearthed at Luoyang, and collected by Luoyang Museum of Ancient Arts. 14 carvings on the screen showcase the life scenes of the tomb owner and Paragons of Filial Piety, but with no inscriptions. Zhou Dao and other scholars compared them with the pictorial elements on the sarcophagus of Yuan Mi in the Northern Wei Dynasty, and identified these narratives as filial piety stories about Guo Ju, Ding Lan, Yuan Gu, Laolaizi, Meijianchi.[11]

In 1981, Museum of Datong, Shanxi excavated the tomb of Sima Jinlong dated to the eighth year of Taihe of the Northern Wei Dynasty (484 CE). A stone bed was also disinterred, but no stone screen was found. Instead, there was a set of lacquer screen in fairly good conditions painted with ancient figures such as "exemplary women". It is very likely that the screen was placed on the stone bed as an earlier structure of this type of funerary furniture. The stone bed is made up of 6 slabs. Three front feet are carved with naked warrior reliefs, and on the middle foot, there is a monster head bas-relief between two warriors. The edges of the bed cornice are embellished with two continuous leaf scrolls in relief. On the panel, two continuous acanthus scrolls play a skeleton role of the composition, which are filled with "dragons, tigers, phoenixes, golden-wing birds, birds with human heads, and musicians carved in relief". 13 musicians are arranged in a horizontal row playing different string and percussion instruments such as *pipa, paixiao, hengdi, xiao, jiegu,* and *xiyaogu*. On the lowest there are wave patterns in multiple layers.[12]

In 1982, a set of stone bed and screen were found at the top of Mt. Wen in Shimaping, Tianshui, Gansu. The front base of the bed is made up of two pictorial stone panels. The base surface is divided into two tiers and 6 *kunmen* intaglios are carved on each tier. There is a musician inside each upper *kunmen* as inside and they altogether play various instruments namely *sheng, bo, quxiang pipa, xiao, yaogu*, and *shu konghou*, while a winged *weishou* inside each lower *kunmen*. The exterior edges of the bed frame are carved with two lines of linked pearl reliefs with gilded and painted acanthus patterns in between. In front of the bed there are a pair of stone lion sculptures and 5 musician figurines. The screen comprises of 11 pictorial stones displaying a plethora of architecture and human activities: gate towers, verandas, halls, waterside pavilions, and gardens as well as feasting, dancing, hunting, and riding horses.[13]

In the 90s of the 20th century, Miho Museum in Japan purchased a few stone screen components and a pair of gate towers. 11 screen components are bas-reliefs gilded

10 Deng Hongxing and Cai Quanfa, "Tomb and Sarcophagus with Images of the Northern Dynasties Discovered at Qinyang", *Zhongyuan Wenwu*, iss. 1, 1983.

11 Zhou Dao, ed., "Eight: Stone Linear Engravings", in *The Complete Collections of Chinese Arts Categories: The Complete Collection of Chinese Pictorial Stones*, Henan Fine Arts Publishing House, 2000.

12 Museum of Datong, Shanxi and Shanxi Committee of Culture Relics, "The Tomb of Sima Jinlong of the Northern Wei at Shijiazhai, Datong, Shanxi", *Wenwu [Cultural Relics]*, iss. 3, 1972.

13 Tianshui Museum, "A Tomb with Screens and Stone Coffin Beds of Sui and Tang Periods Discovered at Tianshui", *Kaogu [Archaeology]*, iss. 1, 1992.

and painted and they represent in details lifestyles of the western ethnic groups and of Zoroastrian cultural characteristics.[14] Jiang Boqin interprets these images as tomb owner feasting, hunting, outing, encamping, vowing, and caravan-trading; there are also Zoroastrian religious activities, such as dance sacrificing Goddess Nana and priests performing funerary rituals.[15]

The Kuboso Memorial Museum of Arts also acquired a stone bed, stone towers and a screen. Two horizontal bands of lotus-petals cross over the uppermost front of the bed. Another horizontal band below is made up of 13 squares cartouches, with linear engravings of various mythical creatures and acanthus leaves as backgrounds. The bottom is decorated with wave patterns. Two bed feet on each side are *weishou* reliefs both turning to the middle foot in form of a frontal monster head reliefs. The screen is composed of 4 slabs, and altogether 12 images of seated portraits of the couple tomb-owners, their maids and servants and the Paragons of the Filial Piety. On the right, one sees the series narratives of the story "Guo Ju burying his son"; on the left, stories about filial sons Yuan Gu and Ding Lan. However, the stone towers are undecorated. The tomb epitaph says, "on the fifth year of Zhengguang of the Great Wei Dynasty, 1st November; Xuzhou, Lanling, Chi County, Duxiang township, Kuang Seng'an, given name Ning. [He] reached the post of 'general in the palace' in the capital and obtained the responsibility for the Emperor's dining on his side. [He] deceased on the 25th October and was buried on 15th November in the Northern Mountain in western Luoyang. [This is] an inscription inside a tomb".[16]

In 1995, the Art Institute of Chicago acquired a set of stone bed and a screen. Linear engraving was the main technique on the screen depicting living and outing scenes of the tomb owner.[17]

In 2000, a tomb of a Sogdian named Anjian of the Western Zhou period was found at Kangdizhai, Daminggong, Xi'an. There were a set of stone screen and stone bed ("stone couch" in the original brief). Oval- and square-shaped cartouches are outlined with linked pearls on the front and two sides of the bed. The centre cartouche of the 17 on the front side is a frontal lion head. There are 8 cartouches on each side with animal head engravings, including eagles, roosters, elephants, lions, oxen, horses, dragons, boars, and rhinoceros. Linear engravings of *weishou* ("warrior-carrying motif" in the original brief) can be found on the bed feet. On the screen, 11 gilded and painted bas-reliefs represent life scenes mainly of peoples from the western regions in foreign costumes and with high nasal bridges and long beards. The lintel of the tomb entrance is also made of stone and carved with Zoroastrian sacrifice scenes.[18]

Between 1998 and 2002, a large amount of Northern Wei tombs were excavated in the southern suburbs, Yingbin Avenue, and Yanbei Normal College in Datong, Shanxi, and they were made during the period when the capital was still in Pingcheng, no later than the move to Luoyang. Stone beds were found in some of the tombs, such as the tomb of Song Shaozu at Yanbei Normal College dated to the first year of Taihe of the Northern Wei Dynasty (477 CE). In the tomb chamber, inside an elaborately carved and palace-like stone *guo* (outer coffin) there is a "*shiguanchuang*". This stone bed has a concave surface. The base is decorated with a horizontal band of S-shaped acanthus scrolls and continuous wave patterns below. Bed feet are straight. The centre one is a knocker-holder of a monster head bas-relief. The foot on the southeast corner is carved with acanthus flower

14 Annette L. Juliano and Judith A.Lerner, "Cultural Crossroad: Central Asian and Chinese Entertainers on the Miho Funerary Couch". *Orientations*, October 1997. "Eleven panels and two gate towers with relief carvings from a funerary couch, South Wing", Miho Museum, 1997.

15 Jiang Boqin, *Research on Zoroastrian Arts in China*, Joint Publishing, 2004.

16 See the catalogues published by the Kuboso Memorial Museum of Arts, Izumi.

17 This collection of the Art Institute of Chicago has never been published. References from Zheng Yan, *Research on the Mural Tombs of the Wei, Jin, Southern, and Northern Dynasties*, Cultural Relics Press, 2002.

18 Shaanxi Institute of Archaeology, "Tomb of Anjia of the Northern Zhou Discovered in Xi'an", *Wenwu [Cultural Relics]*, iss. 1, 2001.

medallions while the one on the southwest is carved in bas-relief a squatting lion looking sideways. There is another animal standing on the body of the lion, probably a lioness or a baby lion.[19]

Another Northern Wei stone bed was excavated in Tomb 112 at the southern suburbs of Datong. It has three feet but no screen or other accessories. The carving on the bed base is similar to that of the Song Shaozu tomb. Each foot on two ends is respectively carved with a *jingping* (a kind of funerary vase) holding acanthus flowers. The middle foot is carved with a knocker-holder in form of a frontal monster head holding a ring in its mouth. Above there are two lotuses.[20]

In Tomb 14 of the Northern Wei at Qili Village in Datong, two stone beds are placed diagonally and intersect at a right angle; another stone bed is placed in a side chamber. The fronts of their bases are decorated with a horizontal band of S-shaped acanthus scrolls and continuous wave patterns below. On each straight foot there are carvings of a frontal monster head holding a ring in its mouth, lotus petals, and figures.[21]

Another stone bed was found in the north side of the chamber of a Northern Wei tomb at Tian Village, southern suburbs of Datong, Shanxi. The front base is composed of two stone panels and similarly decorated in bas-relief with a horizontal band of S-shaped acanthus scrolls and continuous wave patterns below. Bed feet are all straight and the middle one is carved with a frontal monster head holding a ring in its mouth. One each side foot, there is a carving of a branch of acanthus.[22]

The aforementioned Northern Wei tombs in Datong area and their burial objects have similar structures, so are the decorative styles of their stone beds. Therefore, they should have been constructed during the same period. The Qili village cemetery, according to the research conducted by the Datong Institute of Archaeology, "was constructed between mid- and late-period when the capital was in Pingcheng to around the time when the capital was moved to Luoyang; the tombs have similar structures and burial objects, so they are from around the same time".[23] This conclusion also applies to the tomb 112 at the southern suburbs, Tian village tomb and Song Shaozu tomb. In particular, the last one was dated, so these tombs with stone beds can be dated to around the first year of Taihe (477 CE), that was twenty to thirty years before the move of capital to Luoyang under the reigns of Emperor Xianwen and Emperor Xiaowen.

In 2004, China Cultural Heritage Information and Consulting Centre acquired a stone bed back from overseas and it is currently in the collection of the Capital Museum. The base endured considerable loss of stone with only the front slab extant. However, 6 screen components and two stone towers have been preserved. From top to bottom of the base, there are bas-relief friezes of lotus petals, stylised dragons, and 11 *weishou* in horizontal row. *Weishou* are also carved on the three bed feet. Linear engravings on the screen display attendants, nomadic people leading horses, oxcart expeditions, seated portraits of tomb owners and two stories of the filial son Guo Ju. One is about Guo Ju burying his son and the other Guo Ju and his wife providing for their aged mother, both common compositions in the late Northern Wei. The inscription reads "the filial son Guo Ju buried his son; the Heaven bestowed on him a full pot of gold", "Guo Ju buried his son".[24]

In 2007, a set of stone bed, stone towers, and screen

---

19 Datong Institute of Archaeology, *Northern Wei Tombs at Yanbei Normal College, Datong*, Cultural Relics Press, 2008; and "Excavation Brief of Song Shaozu Tomb of the Northern Wei at Datong", *Wenwu [Cultural Relics]*, iss. 7, 2001.

20 Datong Institute of Archaeology, *Northern Wei Cemeteries at Southern Suburbs of Datong*, Science Press, 2007.

21 Datong Institute of Archaeology, "Excavation Brief of the Northern Wei Cemeteries at Qili Village, Datong, Shanxi", *Wenwu [Cultural Relics]*, iss. 10, 2006.

22 Datong Institute of Archaeology, "Excavation Brief of a Northern Wei Tomb at Tian Village, Southern Suburbs of Datong, Shanxi", *Wenwu [Cultural Relics]*, iss. 5, 2010.

23 Datong Institute of Archaeology, "Excavation Brief of the Northern Wei Cemeteries at Qili Village, Datong, Shanxi", *Wenwu [Cultural Relics]*, iss. 10, 2006.

24 Teng Lei, "My Opinions on a Stone Coffin Bed Returned from Overseas", *Journal of the Palace Museum*, iss. 4, 2009.

were excavated in tomb 57 at Gu'an Village, Yongfeng, Anyang, Henan. The epitaph brick inside the tomb indicates that this is the tomb of Xie Shi and Feng Senghui on the 25th April in the sixth year of Wuding of the Eastern Wei (548 CE). On the front of the bed, a continuous band of lotus petals cross the uppermost part, beneath there is a horizontal frieze made of 12 squares cartouches with linear engravings of various mythological creatures inside. Two side feet are *weishou* reliefs and the middle is a frontal monster head relief. The screen is composed of four slabs with 12 images depicting tomb owners' seated portraits, maids, servants, palanquins, oxcarts and men leading horses, and the stories of Filial Piety. Two images form a series of "Guo Ju burying his son". One of them has a very similar composition to that on the Kuboso stone bed, and its inscription reads "Guo Ju and his wife buried their son; Heaven bestowed gold on them" and "the filial son Guo Ju's mother feeding the grandson". On the left there are narratives of filial sons, such as Ding Lan, with an inscription "filial son Ding Lan x people xx". The gate towers are undecorated.[25]

In 2008, a stone bed and a screen dated to the sixth year of Tianhe of the Western Zhou Dynasty (571 CE) were unearthed from the tomb of Kangye. The inner side of the screen is polished and carved with 10 images in fine lines which are partially gilded with gold. Its two sides and the upper part are embellished with gilded persimmon-stem patterns. The subject matter of the images are daily life scenes of the couple owners of the tomb, such as entertaining guests, outing, attendance of servants and maids. Figures are mainly clad in Han attire. The front and two sides of the bed are engraved with fine lines. The uppermost and lowest are decorated with linked pearl designs, and between them there are spiral interlocking lotus scrolls. Various realistic animals and hieratic animals are added to the space, such as goats, camels, tigers, phoenixes, and monsters. Three squatting lion caryatids constitute the frontal feet of the stone bed.[26]

Shaanxi Beilin Museum also has a set of stone bed, which was probably excavated at central Shaanxi Plain. Linear engravings spread around the bed and its feet. On each short side of the base, there is a horizontal frieze with a profusion of curlicues which resemble cloud scrolls and are interwoven with winged deities and hieratic creatures. With wings spread like a bird, the deities are analogous to the immortals in ancient Greek paintings. One can also find repetitive sunflower-like patterns and rosette medallions formed by confronting wave patterns. One bed foot is carved with *weishou* of a style developed later when compared with other *weishou* designs. Teng Lei in his "My Opinions on a Stone Coffin Bed Returned from Overseas" introduced a stone bed dated to the third year of Xiaochang of the Northern Wei Dynasty. It was from a private collection in Taiwan and auctioned in the US in 2000. The front side is said to be inscribed with "Tian E'she", "A man from Pingyuan, Qingzhou".[27] However, unfortunately no image is available to us.

III. Decorative Characteristics of Stone Beds and Screens and the Shenzhen Exhibits

The patterns and subject matters above demonstrate pictorial diversity and customised design patterns on screens and stone beds. They represent different cultural meanings and ethnic characteristics. The following will discuss about them in details.

Extant stone screens and beds materials show that their patterns and decorations mainly employ bas-relief combined with linear engraving techniques. There are some exceptions of bas-relief embellished with colours or gilded. This carving method was adopted from the

25 See the website of Henan Institute of Cultural Relics Archaeology, the article by Pan Weibin, "The Largest Cemetery of the Northern Dynasties in Henan".

26 Xi'an Institute of Cultural Relics Conservation and Archaeology in "Excavation Brief of Kangye Tomb of the Northern Zhou in Xi'an", *Wenwu [Cultural Relics]*, iss. 6, 2008.

27 Teng Lei, "My Opinions on a Stone Coffin Bed Returned from Overseas", *Journal of the Palace Museum*, iss. 4, 2009.

processing techniques of the Han pictorial stones and characteristic of traditional Chinese arts. Gilding was possibly influenced by the techniques in Buddhist art. When Buddhism prevailed in China during the late Northern Dynasties, we see an increasing amount of gilded and painted sculptures, for instance, at a hoard in Qingzhou, Shandong several gilded Buddha sculptures of the Northern Qi were found. Painting and gilding must have been a popular decorative technique of stone carving arts.

The pictorial subject-matter and decoration cultural styles of stone screens (and some of the stone bed carving techniques) fall into two categories.

The first category represents traditional Chinese culture, such as Filial Piety figures, daily life and expedition scenes of the tomb owners. Similar materials include the screen found at Xixiang, Qinyang, Luoyang; screen in the Ancient Art Museum of Luoyang; screen in the Kuboso Memorial Museum of Arts; two screen slabs in Tenri University Sankokan Museum; stone bed and screen in the Art Institute of Chicago; two screen slabs in the Asian Art Museum of San Francisco; the screen from the tomb of Kangye; and a screen recently found from the tomb of Xie Shi and Feng Senghui.

The second category is about Zoroastrian worship and nomadic life of the Sogdians and other ethnicities on the western frontiers. Most of the tomb owners were Sogdians who migrated to China. This kind of materials include a Northern Qi stone bed excavated in 1992 Anyang, several screen components and a pair of gate towers in the Miho Museum, a set of stone bed and screen in the tomb of Anjia. Besides, another group of funerary furnishings were found at Fujia, Qingzhou, Shandong in a tomb dated to the fourth year of Wuping of the Northern Qi. However, a lot of the stone components were appropriated to build reservoir dam, and the local museum only managed to collect a limited number of pictorial slabs. Judged from structure and composition, they should be remnants of a screen. These images also depict Sogdian and western nomadic lifestyle.[28] The Mt. Wen screen in Gansu seems more likely to depict household life in Central China owing to the architectural styles; moreover, in the scenes of feasting, singing and dancing, hunting and riding, only a small number of figures are in foreign costumes. However, according to Jiang Boqin's interpretation, the ancient Persian wine vessels and sun and moon imageries manifest the drinking sacrifice of haoma and the Sun and Moon gods. He also interprets figures on a bridge as Mithra guiding righteous people to the paradise crossing the Chinvat Bridge.[29] These opinions need to be confirmed by more definite pictorial materials.

Available materials show quite regular decorative patterns and pictorial compositions of the Northern Dynasties stone beds. Earlier beds found at Datong area all have continuous bands of S-shaped acanthus; finds in other regions usually have undercut horizontal bands of lotus petals on the front top of the bed bases. Under the bands there are mainly three kinds of designs:

The first is a horizontal band of repetitive square cartouches delineated by either lines or linked pearls. Each cartouche is carved in bas-relief various mythical creatures, such as *weishou*, birds with human faces, dragons, creatures with monster heads and bird bodies; musician bas-relief can also be found in the cartouche. Sometimes, between the cartouche rim and the bas-relief creatures, a ring appears circumscribed with linked pearls. Such as the artworks are exhibiting in the Shenzhen Museum (Pls. 9, 11, 12).

The second kind is a frieze of turtle-shell patterns made up of hexagon shapes. Each hexagon is delineated with linked pearls or lines and carved with all kinds of mythical creatures and musicians inside, such as the Shenzhen Museum exhibit (Pl. 10) and another one at the Museum of Fine Arts, Boston.

The third is continuous horizontal striations which are

---

28 Xia Mingcai (Yidu Museum, Shandong), "Linear Portrait Engravings in Tomb Chambers of the Northern Qi at Yidu", *Wenwu [Cultural Relics]*, iss. 10, 1985; and "A Supplement to the Pictorial Stones of the Northern Qi at Fujia, Qingzhou", *Wenwu [Cultural Relics]*, iss. 5, 2001.

29 Jiang Boqin, *Research on Zoroastrian Arts in China,* Joint Publishing, 2004.

combined with swirling dragons or other hieratic animals.

Generally, there are three bed feet on each long side with pictorial carvings on the front. These carvings can be classified into five programmes:

First, lions stand sideways on both ends; a knocker-holder of a frontal monster head glares with round eyes and growls with open mouth in the middle.

Second, *weishou* stand on both ends with a knocker-holder of a monster head in the middle.

Third, naked warriors on both ends; a knocker-holder of a monster head or a *weishou* in the middle.

Fourth, warriors hold swords on two ends in small hats and long robes with wide sleeves or in *kuxi* costumes; in the middle, a knocker-holder of a monster head or a *weishou*. Sometimes, their positions shift, that is, monster or *weishou* on two ends and a warrior holding a sword in the middle.

Fifth, Zoroastrian deities, priests, and fire altars are also adopted, for instance, hieratic gods holding tridents on each side, and in the middle there are fire altars, priests, and goddesses.

These patterns were of diverse provenances, namely the Han Chinese traditional arts, western and Indian Buddhist sculpture techniques and Zoroastrian art elements. By analysing them, we can distinguish their periodic styles and better understand when various cultures were transmitted to central plains and to what degree they influenced the indigenous culture. It is particularly valuable to understand Zoroastrian arts.

Now let us introduce the 5 stone beds and 1 set of screen exhibited at the Shenzhen Museum.

The first one is a discretely carved front side (long side) of a bed, composed of one horizontal panel on top of three straight feet. One iron ring is attached to each side of the panel. On the uppermost, there is a continuous band of lotus petals in relief. The second tier is divided into 13 squares cartouches. The cartouches combine bas-relief and linear engraving techniques and depict, from the left to right, *weishou*, mythical creature with woman's head/bird's body/horse hooves, white tiger, phoenix, *weishou*, mythical creature with ox horn/goat head/bird body/horse hooves, a fire ball on lotus pedestal flanked with lotus leaves, mythical creature with camel head/bird body/horse hooves, *weishou*, phoenix, green dragon, mythical creature with man's head/bird body/bird claws, and *weishou*. The third tier is a frieze of pendent wave patterns. Two lion high reliefs form the feet on each end, while a frontal monster head in high relief serves as the middle foot. A set of screen came with the bed, depicting life scenes of the tomb owner and Paragons of Filial Piety, whose details will be dealt with in later paragraphs. (Pls. 9, 15-18)

The second one is also a discretely carved front side (long side) of a bed, composed of one horizontal panel on top of three straight individual feet with remnants of pigment and gilding. There is a continuous horizontal band of S-shaped leaf scrolls on the uppermost of the base. The second tier is a horizontal frieze of overlapping lotus reliefs, and the third turtle-shell patterns made up of 17 hexagonal cartouches and two half hexagons. Each cartouche is formed with straight lines and dots on vertices, all carved with images inside, such as fire balls on lotus pedestal, green dragons, white tigers, phoenixes, and *weishou*. Outside the cartouches, the space is decorated with scrolls of acanthus. The fourth tier comprises a horizontal band of interlocking acanthus branches, and the fifth pendent wave patterns. Lion reliefs on two side feet both turn to the centre with one paw lifted; a frontal naked *weishou* squats in the middle foot. (Pl. 10)

The third one is a front side (long side) of a bed carved as a whole, composed of one horizontal panel on top of three straight feet. There is a horizontal band of lotus petal reliefs. The second tier is divided into two, and except for the central part above the middle foot, each side is further divided into four square cartouches. They altogether from the left to the right depicting white tiger, phoenix, mythical creature with camel head/bird body/horse hooves, mythical creature with woman's head/bird body/horse hooves, mythical creature with man's head/monster claws, mythical creature with monster head/bird body, green dragon. The third tier comprises pendent wave patterns. Two side feet are frontal *weishou* in bas-relief. The middle foot and the panel part above it are connected by a column relief. A fire ball is placed on its top, and on each side there is a guard relief holding a sword in *kuxi* costume and small hat. Both sides of the fire ball are engraved with the inscription which reads "The Year of Xinghe, twentieth of July, epitaph on the deceased Zhu Luo's stone bed". (Pl. 11)

The fourth one is a front side (long side) of a bed carved as a whole, composed of one horizontal panel on top of three curved feet. An iron ring is attached to the exterior of each side foot. There is a continuous band of lotus petal reliefs on the uppermost of the base. The second tier is divided into 10 square cartouches by lines, the images inside the cartouches, from the left to the right, are white tiger, unicorn with horse tail and hooves, *weishou* with a beak, a mythical creature with ox horn/camel head/camel hooves/bird body, lioness, lion, unicorn with monster head/horse hooves/bird body, *weishou* brandishing hammer drills (probably an iconography of *Leigong*, God of Thunder), winged unicorn with horse hooves, winged unicorn with lion body. Bed feet on two sides are *weishou* reliefs; the middle foot is formed by two naked figures carrying lotus pedestals with fire balls. The background is filled with leaf scrolls. (Pl. 12)

The fifth one is a front side (long side) of a bed carved as a whole, composed of one horizontal panel on top of three straight feet. A horizontal band of interlocking acanthus runs across the uppermost. The second tier is a continuous scroll of images of hills and trees with many figures travelling in between, which can be grouped into five narratives. In the first group, an old lady sits inside a house, and in front of house a man in formal costume with headgear kneels down. There are another two standing figures behind him, one wearing a high-crown headgear and the other wearing a kerchief around the head. The second group also illustrates an old lady sitting inside a house but with a young boy sitting next to her. Another two standing figures in the house seem to be a couple, as one wears silk hood around the head and the other has a high-rolled hair bun. The third group is engraved just above the middle foot, where a man and a woman stand next to each other, and there are another two standing figures to their right. In the fourth group, a woman holds a young boy in her arms; on her right a man holds an iron spade as if he was digging the ground. The fifth one depicts an old lady and a little boy inside a house; two men stand outside in attendance; to their right, a maid holds a canopy and another cups a box, and there is also a man leading a saddled steed. Inferred from extant pictorial materials of Filial Piety stories, these are narratives about exemplary characters such as Guo Ju and Ding Lan. The third tier on the whole panel is decorated with rope patterns and the fourth with pendent wave patterns. *Weishou* caryatids serve as two side feet and the middle foot is a frontal monster head. (Pl. 13)

There is also a stone screen accompanying the first stone bed which illustrates the life scenes of the tomb owner and Filial Piety stories. The whole screen is composed of four slabs, two on front long side, and one on each short side. They form a half-enclosed and three-dimensional wall for the stone bed. There are three linear-engraved images on every slab. Lines are smooth and fine and the depictions are vivid and lively. From left to right, they are:

1. Three maids standing in attendance under a tree. 2. Two male servants leading an oxcart. 3. Three maids standing in attendance. 4. An old lady sits on a couch in a house with a pig head, an ox head, and a goat head placed in front of the couch; a glaring warrior with swinging whiskers draws his sword by his right hand; the inscription reads "Wang Ji butchered three livestock in a day which is especially not filial". 5. An old couple sit on a couch inside a house; a man with long beard kneels down in the front wearing a hat with triangular decorations; the inscription reads "Lao[lai]zi a happy child". 6. Lady of the house sitting frontally with one maid standing on each side in attendance. 7. Man of the house sitting frontally with one maid standing on each side in attendance. 8. An old lady sits on couch in the house playing with a little child; a couple stand outside in attendance; the inscription reads "the filial son Guo Ju". 9. A man digs a hole and a woman carries a little child in her arms; the inscription reads "the filial son Guo Ju buried his child and provided for his mother". 10. Four maids carrying utensils and standing in attendance. 11. A man leading a horse with two maids standing behind in

attendance. 12. Two male servants carrying a palanquin with another man following behind.

IV. On the Dating of Stone Beds and Some Other Conclusions

After a survey of the above stone beds of the Northern Dynasties, we can draw the following conclusions:

First of all, the decorative patterns and subject-matters of the Northern Dynasties stone beds accord with the overall decorative ideas of the tomb and with the religious beliefs they embody.

Not many examples of murals or decorated funerary objects have been found from the Northern Dynasties tombs. However, they nevertheless provide evidence that there existed carving and painting customs to decorate tombs and funerary objects during that time. These funerary customs represent the Han Chinese funerary rituals and religious beliefs that had been passed on from the Han, Wei and Jin Dynasties. Scholars have had heated and in-depth discussion about the decorations in tomb and funerary objects, and they reached to an agreement on the preposition that they reveal the religious thoughts and cosmology views of the Han Chinese. All these pictorial elements were supposed to create a peaceful and stable little underground cosmos to drive away evil spirits, protect the ghost of the deceased, and ensure their wealth in another world; moreover, they preserved peace and prosper of the next generations. That is why these images include religious deities, auspicious animals and patterns, such as King Father of the East, Queen Mother of the West, green dragons and white tigers from traditional Chinese religion; Heavenly Kings, warriors, lotuses, and *Kalavinka* from Buddhism; *Moghan*, *sermurv*, winged animals and linked pearl designs from Zoroastrianism. With all these imageries, manufacturers illustrated a paradise where deities and gods assembled – a future world to which the deceased would be willing to entrust themselves. The life scenes imply tomb owner' pursuit of wealth and luxuries; narratives of Filial Piety stories indicate such value emphasised in Chinese culture and was also believed to gain religious blessings. In the same way, images of Zoroastrian rituals and worships as well as the life scenes of the western nomadic people express their reverence of deities and the Heaven, and their funerary ritual beliefs.

Chamber murals, funerary furnishings and objects are major materials from the tombs of the Northern Dynasties that can reflect contemporary burial ceremonies and religious beliefs. Some important relics of the early Northern Wei includes a lacquer coffin, gilded and painted, excavated at Leizu Temple, Guyuan, Ningxia; a stone guo in Zhijiapu, Datong; a stone guo from the tomb of Song Shaozu; a wooden coffin with lacquer paintings excavated at Tomb No.1 in Hudong, Datong; a mural tomb dated to the first year of Taiyan of the Northern Wei (435 CE) excavated in the No.7, Shaling; a mural tomb of Liang Bahu dated to the second year of Heping (461 CE). Mural tombs of late Northern Wei include tomb of Yuanyi found at Xiangyang village, northern Luoyang; tomb of Wangwen at Beichen village, Mengjin, Luoyang; tomb of Yuanyi at the east side of Luomeng Road in Luoyang. Important stone funerary furnishings of this period include a stone house of Ningmao dated to the third year of Xiaochang (527 CE) at the Museum of Fine Arts, Boston; a sarcophagus of Yuanmi dated to the fifth year of Zhengguang (524 CE) in the Minneapolis Institute of Art, a sarcophagus with Filial Piety images in the Nelson-Atkins Museum of Art, Kansas City; a sarcophagus carved with ascending deities in the Kaifeng Museum, a sarcophagus with tomb owner's portrait excavated at Hewa village, Yushe, Shanxi dated to the Shengui period in the Northern Wei; and another Shengui period sarcophagus with mythical creatures at the Luoyang Ancient Art Museum. Those are for the references of the interested readers. However, these murals and furnishing carvings preserved many pictorial elements from the Han tombs, such as King Father of the East, Queen Mother of the West, green dragons, white tigers, Filial Piety stories, life scenes of the tomb owners, ascending deities, starry sky and clouds, which can be found on stone beds and screens mentioned above.

Besides, the decorations and patterns of the stone beds show periodic changes, and dating can be conducted based on extant materials.

Among the aforementioned stone beds of the Northern Dynasties, there are a few with reliable dating records, such as the stone beds from the tomb of Song Shaozu (477 CE) and the tomb of Sima Jinlong (484 CE); the stone bed in the Kuboso Memorial Museum of Arts, Izumi dated to the fifth year of Zhengguang of the Northern Wei (524 CE); the stone bed, gate towers and screen in the tomb of Xie Shi and Feng Senghui on 25th April in the sixth year of Wuding of the Eastern Wei (548 CE) found at Tomb No.57 in Gu'an village, Yongfeng, Anyang; the stone bed from the tomb of Kangye (571 CE) and the stone bed of the deceased Zhu Luo dated to the 20th July in the fourth year of Xinghe of the Eastern Wei (542 CE) exhibited at the Shenzhen Museum. The stone beds of the Northern Dynasties found at Datong tombs can be dated as before Emperor Xiaowen moving the capital to Luoyang, a judgment based on local excavation results of the Northern Wei tombs.

The tombs of Song Shaozu (477 CE) and Sima Jinlong (484 CE) excavated by the Datong Museum are two earliest examples. It is noteworthy that they are deeply influenced by Buddhist artistic elements. In the tomb of Sima Jinlong, the naked warrior relief caryatids have curly hair with beads around the neck and silk around shoulders and waist. The bed base is carved in relief with tigers, dragons, phoenixes, birds with human heads, and musicians whose iconography can be traced to the prototype in contemporary Buddhism. The main motif of the accompanying lacquer screen is "exemplary women", which embodies the filial and righteous ideals in traditional Chinese culture. During this period, no stone screen has been found, so it was probably typical of the funerary programme that only lacquer screens were used with stone beds.

In the late Northern Wei and Eastern Wei, mythical creatures like *weishou*, winged monsters, and birds with human heads began to appear on the stone bed carvings, which externalised foreign religious influence such as the newly-risen Zoroastrianism. The screens mainly depict the daily life of the tomb owners or Paragons of Filial Piety, such as the Kuboso Memorial Museum of Arts collection (524 CE) and the set from the tomb of Xie Shi and Feng Senghui (548 CE).

Before Emperor Xiaowen of the Northern Wei moved the capital to Luoyang, Xianbei ethnic elements were still common in Northern Wei culture along with the Han Chinese traditions, which formed the artistic characteristics of the early and mid-period of the Dynasty.

After moving the capital to Luoyang, Emperor Xiaowen ardently implemented sinification policies. He embraced the Han Chinese culture from the Southern Dynasties and instituted social reforms in clothing and customs, thus increasing Chinese elements can be found in funerary murals and other objects. It is especially conspicuous in figure paintings and sculptures, where clothing turns into wide robes with wide ribbons, floating and elegant, typical style of the Southern Dynasties. The linear engravings of figures during this period are slender and elegant; drawing techniques of trees, mountains, and stones are characteristic of the southern painting, similar to the inlaid pictorial bricks found at Nanjing. Linear engravings on the sarcophagus of Yuanmi and tomb house of Ningmao (both transacted to overseas and current locations unknown), stone beds and screens in the Luoyang Museum, the Capital Museum, and the first stone bed and screen in the Shenzhen Museum are representatives of the artistic style of this period.

To the Northern Qi and Northern Zhou, Zoroastrian and foreign religious influences were more prominent in stone bed decorations; Zoroastrian gods, priests, and fire altars also emerged. On the screens, there are daily life and religious ceremony scenes of the western nomadic people. However, it is not certain yet whether or not this was the main motif of stone bed decorations during that period, because depictions of tomb owner's life have been found as well, for instance, on the bed from the tomb of Kangye. Nevertheless, as we can see, pictorial elements of western nomadic life and religion did not appear before Eastern and Western Wei. Therefore, the development of Northern Dynasties stone beds can be divided into three phases: before Emperor Xiaowen of the Northern Wei moving the capital to Luoyang (before 493 CE), between the move to the late Eastern Wei

(493-550 CE), and from the Northern Qi to Northern Zhou (551-588 CE).

By reference to the analysis and evidence above, we dated most of the stone beds exhibited at the Shenzhen Museum to the second phase, i. e. between the late Northern Wei to the late Eastern Wei. However, a few may have been earlier productions of the Northern Wei, such as the first and the second items. Lion caryatids rather than *weishou* of the two beds support this point, as in the early phase stone bed decorations were more influenced by Buddhism. The turtle-shell patterns on the second item also preserved the pictorial traditions on the Northern Wei lacquer coffin from the Temple of Leizu, Guyuan. Be that as it may, the fifth one is possibly later. Its composition is integrated and coherent instead of being separated into multiple units, a sarcophagus carving custom frequently used during the late Northern Wei. A similar compositional programme can be found on the sarcophagus of Yuanmi (524 CE), which suggests that the fifth stone bed was made during the same period or slightly later. On the front and lower part of each long side of the Yuanmi sarcophagus, various narratives of Filial Piety are separated by mountains, trees and clouds which meanwhile fill the background space; the rear of long sides is carved with deities riding horses through the clouds. The fourth stone bed is dated between the late Northern Wei to the Eastern Wei, as it lavishly employs much stylised *weishou* and mythical creatures of western features. These stone beds expand the culture relics of the Northern Dynasties, and they provide significant material evidence for us to better understand the periodic cultures and moreover the splendid arts of ancient China.

(Translated by Zhang Guoying, SOAS University of London)

深圳博物馆展陈的佛教石造像

李裕群
（中国社会科学院考古研究所　研究员）

在深圳博物馆“永远的北朝——北朝石刻艺术展”展陈的石刻中，佛教造像占了相当的数量。这批佛教造像有单体造像、背屏式造像和造像碑等不同类型。根据有纪年的造像铭文和造像风格，可以判断雕造年代为北魏晚期至隋唐时期。这批造像没有明确的出土地点，但应出自中原地区古代佛教寺院遗址中。造像所反映的地域特点较为显著，大致可以分为河北定州系汉白玉造像、山东青州造像、陕西西安北周佛像，还有一些造像可能出自其他地区。上述地区均是中原北方佛教兴盛、石刻造像发达的区域，尤其是6世纪北魏晚期以来，佛教泛滥，塔寺林立，凿窟造像达到了登峰造极的地步，除了都城洛阳、邺城、长安以外，在地方上形成了定州、青州为中心的佛像雕造地。这批展陈的佛像以6世纪为主，绝不是偶然的。

从数量来说，这批造像并不多，但也不乏雕刻精细者，而且有些造像有纪年铭文，保留了许多重要信息，颇值得关注。下面按照不同造像的区域特点，选择比较重要的造像予以解读。

一　河北定州系汉白玉造像

河北定州是古代中原北方经济、文化的重镇，雕刻工艺发达。定州曲阳盛产晶莹透亮的汉白玉，是雕造佛教造像的上乘材料。大约从北魏晚期开始，定州地区出现汉白玉的佛教造像，至东魏、北齐、隋唐，汉白玉佛像广为流布。

展陈的石刻中，汉白玉造像数量最多，主要以北朝造像为主，还有一些属于隋唐时期的。其中镌刻纪年铭文的造像主要有：东魏天平三年（536）东方文贵造半跏思惟菩萨像（图版27）、东魏兴和元年（539）比丘惠略造观世音菩萨像（图版28）、北齐皇建二年（561）刘道和造像座（图版52）、北齐武平□年（570~575）弥姐相宝造弥陀像座（图版55）、隋开皇四年（584）李普贤造释迦像（图版23）。这些纪年铭文造像颇为重要。

1. 东方文贵造半跏思惟菩萨像

此像为东魏天平三年雕造。菩萨腰以上残，下身着裙，左腿下垂，右腿盘起，架在左腿上，左手抚于右小腿上，半跏坐于圆形束腰藤座上。座两侧有从菩萨身上垂下的披巾，披巾与藤座间为镂空。座下为低的覆莲台，台下为方座。方座的正面和左右侧面均有彩绘图像，十分珍贵。正面彩绘剥落较为严重，但仍然可以看出，画面中心为一覆莲座。座上绘有一佛塔，单层圆形塔身，塔顶为中国传统建筑四角攒尖顶样式。塔顶四角垂铃铛，顶上为塔刹。画面左右各一覆莲座，座上绘有一尊跪着的供养菩萨像。菩萨头戴宝珠冠，下身着裙。方座的左侧面（思惟菩萨左侧下方）绘有三身男性人物像，居前者为主人形象，头戴冠，头微微低垂，身着宽袖大袍，双手前伸，足穿履。后二者为童子形象，身着窄袖胡服，腰系革带，袖手，足穿乌头尖靴。方座的右侧面绘有三身女性人物像，居前者为女主人形象，头梳发髻，右侧面像，微微低垂，脸庞清瘦，双目下视，一副虔诚恭敬的神态，身着曳地长裙，肩上披有披肩，身体修长。后二者为少年女性，居中者身着长裙，正回首顾盼；居后者为正面形象，头束双环髻，并且微微向左侧弯，身着长裙。男女供养人均以墨线勾勒涂彩，人物形象十分生动。居前者应为镌刻者夫妻礼拜供养像，居后者应为子女家眷。男女主人的谦恭，与家眷的活泼，形成了很大的反差。

背面镌刻发愿文：“天平三年岁次丙辰／二月壬申朔五日丙／子中山郡卢奴县人／东方文贵为一切众／生后为亡妻敬造白／石思唯像一区供养”。按《魏书》卷一百六《地形志》记载：定州中山郡辖有卢奴县。卢奴，为州、郡治所在，即三级地方行政结构同治定州（今河北定县）。可知这尊半跏思惟菩萨像属于定州汉白玉造像。单尊的思惟菩萨像一般可以定为释迦太子像。最为特殊的是佛座正面的二菩萨供养佛塔的图像十分罕见，与常见的正面雕博山炉、护法狮子、力士像明显不同，此图像应有特定的含义。

在定州系白石造像中，半跏思惟菩萨像最早出现于东魏时期，流行于北齐。此尊造像应属于东魏稍早的造像实例。

2. 比丘惠略造观世音菩萨像

这是一尊保存基本完好的背屏式造像，为东魏兴和元年雕造。菩萨发髻已残，长方脸型，双目下视，头两侧有宝缯下垂及肩。长长的发辫垂于臂外两侧。颈部粗短，双肩上各有一圆饼装饰，颈下戴桃尖形项圈，双肩敷搭的披巾于腹部交叉穿环。上身着僧祇支，下身着裙。右手上举，持莲蕾；左手下垂执锁状物。露足，立于覆莲台上。整个身躯已经显露出丰壮的趋势。造像下为长方形座。座正面雕两只举一爪的蹲狮。背面镌刻发愿文：“兴和元年／岁在己未十／二月十九日尹／氏寺比丘惠／略为亡祖父母／亡父现存内亲／敬造观世音／像一区供养”。

在定州系白石造像中，立式观世音菩萨造像最早出现于北魏晚期，流行于东魏、北齐。其中东魏观世音菩萨最多，这与定州观世音信仰的流行密切相关。如《续高僧传》卷二十九《兴福篇》记载：“又高齐定州观音瑞像及高王经者。昔元魏平定州募士孙敬德，于防所造观音像。及年满还，常加礼事。后为窃贼所引，禁在京狱，不胜拷掠，遂妄承罪，并处极刑。明旦将决，心既切至，泪如雨下，便自誓曰，……梦一沙门教诵观世音救生经，经有佛名，令诵千遍得免死厄。德既觉已……有司执缚向市，且行且诵，临欲加刑，诵满千遍，折刀下，折为三段，……怪以奏闻，丞相高欢，表请免刑，仍敕传写被之于世。所谓《高王观世音》是也。”而《妙法莲花经·观世音菩萨普门品》所宣扬的观世音菩萨能救人于危厄之中：“一心称名，观世音菩萨即时观其声，皆得解脱。若有持是观世音菩萨名者，设入大火，火不能烧。……若为大水所漂，称其名号，即得浅处。……若复有人，临当被害，称观世音菩萨名者，彼所执刀杖，寻段段坏，而得解脱。……”为观世音菩萨信仰的广泛流行奠定了基础。这是东魏、北齐时期，定州观世音造像大为发达的缘由。

3. 刘道和造像座

此长方形座为北齐皇建二年雕造。座上造像已不存。从残迹看，有镂空雕的双树作为背屏，座上中心残存覆莲座，主尊造像已经不存，主尊像前有两尊半跏坐的供养比丘像，现残存双腿。主尊两侧各有两个仰莲台，残存双足，可知主尊的胁侍像为二弟子二菩萨像。佛座的正面中心雕二比丘奉博山炉，炉两侧各绘一火焰宝珠八角柱。再外两侧各雕一蹲狮和力士像，力士头毁。正面诸像均有贴金彩绘。佛座的右侧面镌刻发愿文：“皇建二年四月廿日邑子／刘道和等十七人敬造白／玉像一区上为皇帝陛／下师僧父母所生父母／含生之类共同因果”。发愿文后面刻“邑人翟安都／ 邑人孙磨侯”，其间绘有二身身着胡服、足穿乌头尖靴的世俗供养人。

此造像做工讲究，雕刻精细。特别是正面雕刻，二比丘奉博山炉及二狮子、二力士的组合形式与1965年河北临漳县习文乡太平渠出土的北齐如来七尊像和弥勒七尊像的佛座十分相似；火焰宝珠八角柱也见于这两件雕刻中，不过位置在力士像外侧。[1]二比丘奉博山炉见于南响堂山第1窟中心柱正面，火焰宝珠八角柱见于北响堂中洞、南响堂第1、7窟外顶部覆钵两侧。[2]因此，该造像座很可能出自邺城地区。

4. 弥姐相宝造弥陀像座

这是一个雕刻精细的方形佛座，北齐武平年间雕造。方座上面雕一宝装莲瓣的覆莲座，座上主尊造像已无。但从莲座看，原有造像为单体立佛像。方座的正面雕二比丘奉博山炉，两侧各雕一护法狮子。座的左右侧面各开四个小龛，龛内各雕一神王像。右侧面分别雕龙神王、象神王、狮子神王、珠神王。左侧面分别雕火神王、风神王、树神王、山神王。背面为发愿文：“大齐武平／□年七月／廿六日佛／

[1] 东京国立博物馆编：《中国国宝展》，第208~211页，图版141、142，朝日新闻社，2000年。
[2] 邯郸市峰峰矿区文管所、北京大学考古实习队：《南响堂石窟新发现窟檐遗迹及龛像》，《文物》1992年第5期。

弟子弥姐／相宝仰为／亡考敬造／白石阿弥／陀像一区愿／一切法界／众生发菩／提心离苦／得乐俱时／作佛”。

佛座上雕刻的神王题材是作为佛陀的护法神出现的。神王题材广泛流行于北魏洛阳时期至北齐、北周雕造的石窟和单体造像中。一般以成组的形式出现，在石窟内雕刻于四壁壁脚或中心柱基座四面。在单体造像中一般雕刻于佛座四面。现存唯一有完整题名的神王像是东魏武定元年（543）骆子宽造像。神王像雕刻于佛座的左右后三面，共有十尊。左侧为：珠神王、风神王、龙神王；后面为：河神王、山神王、树神王、火神王；右侧为：狮子神王、鸟神王、象神王。[3]在北齐时期，雕刻有神王题材的造像主要集中在邺城地区的石窟寺中，如河北邯郸南北响堂山石窟[4]、安阳灵泉寺石窟和小南海石窟等[5]。在邺城地区出土的单体造像中，佛座上也常常雕刻神王。从现有的资料看，河北定州造像中尚不见神王题材出现，因此，该佛座可能出自邺城。或者说，造像石材虽然出自定州，但雕造地应在邺城。

根据发愿文可知，所雕主尊造像为阿弥陀佛立像。在定州地区，阿弥陀佛（包括无量寿佛）出现于北齐时期。但在邺城地区出现西方净土信仰却较早，如1997年在河北省邯郸市成安县城关镇南街村佛寺遗址中出土的北魏太和六年（482）雕造的释迦三尊像，背面为浅浮雕，正中雕无量寿佛[6]；北齐开凿的南响堂石窟第1、2窟前壁的西方净土变；安阳小南海中窟的观无量寿佛经变等。这表明，邺城地区净土信仰由来已久，到北齐时期则大为流行，此尊造像则为研究邺城净土信仰增添了新的实例。

根据发愿文还可得知，发愿雕造者为弥姐相宝。据考证，弥姐氏为羌人[7]。见诸文献的弥姐氏寥寥无几，南北朝时，仅见于《周书》卷二十七《蔡祐传》中提到：“及侯莫陈悦害贺拔岳，诸将遣使迎太祖。将赴，夏州首望弥姐元进等阴有异计。”夏州治统万城，即今陕西靖边县县城北55千米处，城址尚存。因此，弥姐氏造像发愿文，对于研究羌人在邺城的活动显得格外重要。

5. 李普贤造释迦像

此像保存基本完好，雕造于隋开皇四年，圆雕。佛像肉髻低平，面相浑圆，头后有圆形头光。颈部粗短，身体健壮。身着通肩袈裟，袈裟前襟上左右衣纹不连贯。右手上举，左手置左膝盖上，双足下垂，足下踩一覆莲台，倚坐于方座上。造像残留贴金彩绘。座正面雕刻一地神，作蹲状，左手托覆莲台，右手支撑在右膝盖上。佛座三面均镌刻发愿文。右侧面为“开皇四年／岁次甲辰／六月八日”，背面为“佛弟子李／普贤为父／母及祖父／母造释迦／像一／区”，左侧面为“佛弟子杨／和媚一心／供养佛”。

此尊造像与常见的隋初具有北齐佛像特征的造像具有明显的差异，如颈短，身体宽厚而粗壮，通肩袈裟的领口低垂，左右衣纹不连贯的做法与北周造像相似。可以怀疑，在隋初，定州造像开始受到来自长安北周造像的影响。按《隋书》卷三十九《豆卢勣附兄通传》记载：豆卢通于隋开皇元年（581）出任定州刺史，开皇九年（589）还尚在任上，豆卢通崇信佛教，在隋开皇元年赴定州，途径平定州时还雕造大型佛像[8]，定州任上，还参与七帝寺的重修[9]。因此，北周的造像样式有可能随着崇信佛教的京官到来，而开始影响到定州地区。

此倚坐姿的佛像与发愿文所提到的造释迦佛并不相符。倚坐佛从北魏云冈石窟就开始流行，如云冈第19窟二胁洞中的主尊倚坐佛。至迟从北魏晚期开始，倚坐姿的佛像已成为弥勒特有的坐姿，是表现弥勒下生，在龙华树下三会说法，普度众生的形

[3] 金申：《海外及港台藏历代佛像——珍品纪年图鉴》，第88~91页图，山西人民出版社，2007年。
[4] 水野清一、长广敏雄：《响堂山石窟》，京都，东方文化学院京都研究所，1937年。
[5] 河南省古代建筑保护研究所：《河南安阳灵泉寺石窟及小南海石窟》，《文物》1988年第4期。
[6] 邯郸市文物研究所编：《邯郸市古代雕塑精粹》，图版39、40，第218~219页图版说明，文物出版社，2007年。
[7] 姚微元：《北朝胡姓考》（修订本）外篇第五，羌族诸姓弥姐条，第360页，中华书局，2007年。
[8] 山西省古建筑保护研究所、北京大学石窟考古组：《山西平定开河寺石窟》，《文物》1997年第1期。
[9] 北京图书馆金石组编：《北京图书馆藏中国历代石刻拓片汇编》第9册，第25页，隋开皇五年（585）“惠郁等造像记”，中州古籍出版社，1989年。

象。特别是弥勒双足下有地神承托，不管是弥勒菩萨，还是弥勒佛都是常见的做法，而不见于释迦佛。因此，该造像可以确定为弥勒佛。至于发愿文所称释迦佛，应出自发愿者本人的意愿，与造像本身关系不大。[10]定州佛像雕刻素称发达，因此，在佛教造像方面，有可能出现商品化的产品，导致了尊像与购买者的诉求不同。

此外，属于定州系汉白玉还有北朝隋唐时期的佛头、坐佛像、菩萨头像，菩萨立像、双观世音菩萨立像、力士头像以及北齐镂空背屏上的飞天等，以及造像背光残件，背面绘有树下坐禅比丘像，十分精彩。

河北定州佛教源远流长，有着深厚的佛教文化底蕴[11]，这为佛教造像的出现和流行奠定了基础。1954 年在曲阳修德寺出土了 2200 余件[12]，以质地细腻的汉白玉石像为主，其中有造像题记者 247 件，包括北魏 17 件、东魏 40 件、北齐 101 件[13]。最早纪年造像为北魏神龟三年（520）上曲阳邑义廿六人造弥勒像。以后，定州周边地区也有许多汉白玉造像出土，如藁城县北贾同村出土的北齐汉白玉造像，雕刻之精美，胜过修德寺造像[14]。2012 年，在邺城遗址北吴庄佛教造像埋藏坑出土了多达 2800 余件的造像，其中大部分为北朝汉白玉造像。这样极大地丰富了定州系汉白玉造像资料。

从已发表的资料和上述诸造像的分析看，定州系汉白玉造像并非都是定州当地雕造。这里可举一个例子，2006 年在河北邢台南宫市后底阁遗址出土了一批造像，其中一件北齐汉白玉五尊像，在主尊立佛两侧各雕一条龙。[15]佛座上雕刻双龙是青州北朝造像的特征，此题材不见于定州造像中。南宫地近山东，此造像应是受到来自青州造像的影响，而不是来自定州的造像。更为重要的是，邺城地区出土的汉白玉造像，无论是雕刻技艺，还是造像题材都与定州汉白玉造像有较大的差异，雕刻工艺水平远在定州造像之上。由此可以看出，造像石材应由定州运抵邺城，并在当地进行雕刻。所以，研究定州系汉白玉造像，定州中心区以外出土的汉白玉造像就不能简单地都归入定州造像样式中，应注意它的地域性，以及定州与邺城佛教造像的关系。

二　山东青州造像

青州位居中原地区东部。东晋、宋为江南王朝所辖，北魏时归属。东魏、北齐时，与并州（今山西太原）并称为“霸业所在，王命是基”的重镇。经济发达、文化底蕴深厚，又地临南朝，深受江南文化的影响。大约从北魏晚期开始，青州地区兴起了雕造佛像的热潮，到北齐时达到了顶峰。与定州不同，青州盛产质地细腻的优质青石。因此，佛像的雕造，因地制宜，就地取材。

本次展出可以确认为青州造像有 2 件佛首（图版 36、37）和 1 尊菩萨像（图版 31）。

两件佛首均为细腻的青石雕造，属于北齐时代（550~577）雕造的作品。但造像样式分属于两种不同的类型。其一，肉髻低平，螺发。每个螺发宽大，扁如纽扣，以螺发中心旋出右旋发丝，面如卵形，鼓脸，弯眉，细长眼睛，鼻梁较高，嘴角上翘，露出笑容（图版 36）。此尊佛首样式也见于青州龙兴

[10] 在修德寺还有一件北魏正光元年（520）释迦倚坐像，也应该是弥勒佛（参见杨伯达：《埋もれた中国石佛の研究》，图版 8，东京美术，1985 年）。

[11] 杨泓：《论定州北朝石造像》，《保利藏珍》，第 182~185 页，岭南美术出版社，2000 年。

[12] 罗福颐：《河北曲阳县出土石像工作简报》、李锡金《河北省曲阳县修德寺遗址发掘记》，二文同刊于《考古通讯》1955 年第 3 期。据冯贺军：近年，修德寺地宫出土隋仁寿元年（601）舍利塔下铭，据铭文可知，修德寺前身为定州恒阳县恒岳寺，为隋文帝开皇元年（581）所立（参见冯贺军：《曲阳白石造像研究》，第 12~14 页，紫禁城出版社，2005 年）。

[13] 杨伯达：《埋もれた中国石佛の研究》第三章《纪年铭像による时代区分》，东京美术，1985 年。冯贺军：《曲阳白石造像研究》，附录三《发愿文总录》凡例，第 140–142 页，紫禁城出版社，2005 年。关于定州白石造像的综合研究，可参见李静杰、田军《论定州系白石佛像》（中山大学艺术史研究中心编《艺术史研究》第六辑，第 205~257 页，中山大学出版社，2005 年）。

[14] 程纪中：《河北藁城县发现一批北齐石造像》，《考古》1980 年第 3 期。

[15] 河北省文物研究所、邢台市文物管理处、南宫市文物保管所：《河北南宫后底阁遗址发掘简报》，《文物》2012 年第 1 期，第 21 页图四～六。

寺造像中，其螺发样式和面容，明显地受到了来自古代中印度秣菟罗造像样式的影响。其二，肉髻低平，细密螺发。但每个螺发较小而高，不见右旋发丝，面相清秀（图版37）。该像属于传统的汉地佛教造像样式。

菩萨像（图版31）保存头部和上半身，圆雕，头束圆发髻，发辫长披于肩外两侧，冠两侧扎宝缯，宝缯垂于肩上圆饼装饰上，这是青州造像菩萨宝缯典型的披法。面相清瘦，脸露微笑。颈下戴项圈，身披璎珞和披巾，上身斜披僧祇支，手残。身体清秀。这尊菩萨为东魏末至北齐初雕造。

青州造像之所以引人注目，是因为1996年在青州龙兴寺遗址发掘出土了400余件精美的石刻造像[16]，雕造工艺精湛，表面施以鎏金彩绘，光彩照人。龙兴寺是北朝青州地区著名的寺院。据北齐《临淮王碑》记载：临淮王娄定远在青州龙兴寺"爰营佛事，制无量寿像一区，高三丈九尺，并观世音、大势至二大士侠侍焉"。造像十分雄伟。龙兴寺造像一经出土就轰动了整个学术界，青州造像从此名扬于世。

事实上，青州造像早在20世纪初期就已发现，在1925年伦敦出版的 *Chinese Sculpture – from the Fifth to the Fourteenth Century* 一书中就著录几件青州造像，如山东省博物馆藏（原存青州）北魏正光四年（523）张宝珠造像[17]。20世纪70年代以来，除了龙兴寺外，青州还出土有北朝造像[18]，周边的博兴[19]、诸城[20]、临朐、广饶、无棣、高青、鄄城等地寺院遗址也陆续出土了一批石刻造像[21]。特别是1995年，在济南灵岩寺般舟殿遗址发掘中，出土了2件雕刻非常精美的佛头像和菩萨像，均属于青州样式的北齐造像[22]，可以看出青州造像系统涵盖的范围向西扩展到了齐州。

上述这些石刻造像大都与北朝寺院遗址有关。有些寺院大殿遗址上尚保留了不少"丈八大像"。如博兴兴国寺丈八石佛[23]、临淄西天寺遗址（现为临淄石刻馆）二尊5米余的丈八石像[24]。现藏青岛市博物馆的双丈八石佛像，原存淄川龙泉寺遗址。[25]

青州造像主要以北朝为主，从北魏孝明帝（约516）开始，延续到北齐时期。在造像题材、造型、服饰等方面，发展演变的脉络清晰，地域特色显著，自成体系。[26]

比如，造像题材，北魏、东魏以释迦、弥勒为主，与北魏龙门、巩县石窟相似，应受到来自洛阳的影响。北齐时期出现并流行《华严经》所尊奉的教主卢舍

[16] 青州市博物馆：《青州龙兴寺佛教造像窖藏清理简报》，《文物》1998年第2期。青州市博物馆：《青州龙兴寺佛教造像艺术》，山东美术出版社，1999年。中国历史博物馆、北京华观艺术品有限公司、山东青州市博物馆：《山东青州龙兴寺出土佛教石刻造像精品》，1999年，北京。

[17] Osvald Siren, *Chinese Sculpture – from the Fifth to the Fourteenth Century*, pp.54–61, pls.201~219, London, 1925.

[18] 夏名采、庄明军：《山东青州兴国寺出土石造像》，《文物》1996年第5期。青州市博物馆：《山东青州发现北魏彩绘造像》，《文物》1996年第5期。夏名采：《山东青州出土二件北朝彩绘石造像》，《文物》1997年第2期。青州博物馆：《山东青州出土北朝石刻造像》，《文物》2005年第4期。

[19] 常叙政、李少南：《山东省博兴县出土一批北朝造像》，《文物》1983年第7期。山东省博兴县文物管理所：《山东博兴龙华寺遗址调查简报》，《考古》1986年第9期。

[20] 杜在忠、韩岗：《山东诸城佛教石造像》，《考古学报》1994年第2期。

[21] 宫德杰《临朐县博物馆收藏的一批北朝造像》、临朐县博物馆《山东临朐明道寺舍利塔地宫佛教造像清理简报》，《文物》2002年第9期。惠民地区文物管理组：《山东无棣出土北齐造像》，《文物》1983年第7期。常叙政、于丰华：《山东高青县出土佛教造像》，《文物》1987年第4期。鄄城县文化馆路明：《山东鄄城发现一批北朝石造像碑》，《文物资料丛刊》10，文物出版社，1987年。房道国：《济南市出土北朝石造像》，《考古》1994年第6期。

[22] 李裕群：《灵岩寺石刻造像考》，《文物》2005年第8期。

[23] 刘凤君：《山东地区北朝佛教造像艺术》，《考古学报》1993年第3期。

[24] 中国美术全集编辑委员会：《中国美术全集·雕塑编·3·魏晋南北朝雕塑》，图版147，解说第57页，人民美术出版社，1988年。

[25] 时桂山：《青岛的四尊北魏造像》，《文物》1963年第1期，图二、三。

[26] 关于青州龙兴寺出土造像的分期，可参见夏名采、王瑞霞《青州龙兴寺出土背屏式佛教石造像分期初探》，《文物》2000年第5期。李静杰：《青州风格佛教造像的形成与发展》，《敦煌研究》2007年第4期。刘凤君：《青州地区北朝晚期石佛像与"青州风格"》，《考古学报》2002年第1期。杨泓：《关于南北朝时青州考古的思考》，《文物》1998年第2期。

那佛。卢舍那佛都以立佛形象出现，身着通肩袈裟，衣纹极少，有的身上绘出天上、人间、地狱，表示六道轮回的人物图案，如青州出土的、现已流入台湾的北齐造像即是比较好的实例[27]。这种题材的大量出现，与邺城地区地论宗的兴起有密切关系。

又如，北魏至东魏时期，佛、菩萨均身体清瘦，佛身着褒衣博带式袈裟或通肩袈裟，基本上承袭了洛阳龙门石窟的造像样式，属于典型的"秀骨清像"样式。进入北齐以来，佛、菩萨的造型大变，流行形体丰满健壮的形象。佛像的袈裟多为袒右或通肩。特别是中印度秣菟罗造像样式的传入，佛像流行单薄贴体，显露形体的袈裟，成为这一时期造像独特的风貌。

再如，背屏式造像背光上往往雕有龙的图像，主尊造像的佛座两侧流行姿态优美的龙的图像。这是山东地区极富地方色彩的题材，从北魏晚期开始一直到北齐都是极为流行的。但前后略有变化。早期主要背光上流行单龙样式，双龙形象则少见。到北齐时期，单龙罕见，而流行双龙护塔的形象。

关于青州西方样式的传入，宿白先生在《青州龙兴寺窖藏所出佛像的几个问题》一文作了精辟的论述[28]，认为：1. 南朝梁武帝奉请天竺佛像的影响；2. 葱岭东西诸胡和天竺僧众的影响；3. 高齐反对北魏汉化政策，提倡胡化。其实，后两点只是阐述了青州西方样式得以流行的历史背景，并不能解决青州西方样式的传入途径。由于在青州以西现存的北朝石窟和造像中，尚未见到类似的秣菟罗造像样式实例，因此这种西方样式的传入，恐怕与南朝萧梁有关。

正如宿白先生指出的："萧衍建梁（502~549 年在位），境内基本安谧近五十年，扶南、天竺沙门相继浮海东来，南朝寺刹之建斯时为全盛。对于佛像的供奉，似出现了重视天竺形制的迹象。"南朝梁武帝奉请天竺佛像的事迹很多，其影响不容忽视。《法苑珠林·敬佛篇·感应缘》卷十四"梁高祖等身金银像缘"记载："梁祖武帝以天监元年（502）正月八日梦檀像入国，因发诏募往迎……决胜将军郝骞谢文华等八十人应募……天监十年（511）四月五日骞等达于扬都，帝与百僚徒行四十里迎还太极殿。"扶南王还多次遣使送佛像到梁。《梁书》卷五十四《海南诸国传》记载：扶南国于"天监二年（503）……遣使送珊瑚佛像"。"十八年（519）复遣使送天竺旃檀瑞像"。"大同五年（539）……诏遣沙门释宝云随（扶南）使往迎之（佛发）。先是，三年（537）八月高祖改造阿育王寺塔，出旧塔下舍利及佛爪发。发青绀色，众僧以手伸之，随手长短，放之则旋屈为蠡形"。天竺样式的佛像，在江南地区还未发现实例，不过，成都地区梁代出现了新出现并流行的中印度秣菟罗佛像样式，比较典型的是梁中大通元年（529）鄱阳王世子造像，身体宽厚，着通肩袈裟，衣裙单薄，紧裹身体，透出健壮的躯体。属于秣菟罗佛像样式还有阿育王像，身着通肩袈裟，衣褶稠叠贴体，衣纹呈尖棱泥条状。鄱阳王世子造像头已不存，但这一类天竺式佛像必然是螺发，成都万佛寺还有不少螺发佛头。我们认为：萧梁时期天竺式佛像的传入，海路尤显重要，主要是经南海诸国首先传入中国江南地区，成都地区秣菟罗佛像样式和阿育王像都来自于建康。[29]

虽然我们没有直接的证据说明青州出现的秣菟罗佛像样式来源于江南，但青州造像受南朝的影响是可信的。比如，青州造像中龙的造型与崇拜应与南朝萧梁有关。据《续高僧传》卷 1《宝唱传》记载：梁武"帝以时会云雷，远近清晏，风雨调畅，百谷年登，岂非上资三宝，中赖四天，下藉神龙。……或建福禳灾，或礼忏除障，或飨接神鬼，或祭祀龙王"。梁承齐祚以来，随着南北方大规模军事冲突的停止，梁朝境内太平清晏，风调雨顺，五谷丰登，迎来了一片繁荣景象。梁武帝认为，这一切全靠佛法、神鬼、龙王的护持。因此，梁武帝十分重视祭祀龙王和鬼神。在南朝建康地区，南朝造像罕见，南京栖霞山石窟和浙

[27] 该像为台湾财团法人震旦文教基金会所藏（参见台北"故宫博物院"编《雕塑别藏—宗教编特别图录》，图版 29、29-1 至 29-8，台北，1997 年）。

[28] 宿白：《青州龙兴寺窖藏所出佛像的几个问题》，《文物》1999 年第 10 期。

[29] 李裕群：《试论成都地区出土的南朝佛教石造像》，《文物》2000 年第 2 期。

江新昌大佛和千佛院主要是南朝齐代雕造，洞窟内尚无龙的图像出现。四川出土的南朝梁代造像也不见龙的图像。1999年，在湖北襄樊谷城县肖家营发掘的一座南朝墓葬（M40），墓葬中的许多花纹砖，具有浓郁的佛教特色，花纹有手持净瓶的侍女、莲花净瓶、莲花瓦当、忍冬纹、双龙奉莲花。最重要的是带有背光的青龙和朱雀花纹方砖。从发表的图片看，青龙砖镶嵌在西壁，显然不是表示方位的。青龙砖为舟形火焰背光样式，背光中心部分雕刻盘龙图案，与山东佛像背光及单龙基本一致。背光是佛教造像所特有的，襄阳又是南朝佛教兴盛之地。因此，这个发现大概可以作为南朝萧梁时期崇拜龙的例证。[30]

三　陕西西安北周佛像

西安是西魏、北周的都城所在。近年来不断出土的北周造像，使我们认识到，长安是西部地区北周雕造佛像的中心，并对北周范围内的石窟造像产生巨大的影响。

展品中一尊佛首即是典型的北周造像（图版39）。佛首形体较大，从尺寸看，应属于等身像大小的佛像头部，质地为细腻的青石。虽然面部留下了一些磕碰的斑点，但整个头像保存完好，雕刻工艺极其精湛。佛像头顶有细密的螺发，每个螺发都刻出右旋的发丝，肉髻低平，面相近方圆，眉眼细长，嘴角微微上翘，露出微笑。颈部较粗。头后面有一小方孔，是为安装背光留下的。

这尊头像与近年来西安地区出土的北周造像较为相似，北周时期以青石造像为主。如2004年在未央区中查村出土的一批佛像，其中4号佛像和14号、15号佛头均为低平肉髻、螺发样式、面相方圆的佛像。[31]又如2004年在灞桥区湾子村出土的5尊青石造像也具有相同的特征，其中一尊有北周大象二年（580）发愿文。[32]2007年西安未央区窦寨村出土佛像9尊，其中佛头2尊，特点相同。[33]因此，这尊头像应出自西安汉长安城或城外附近区域。

过去，西安也曾陆续出土不少北周佛教造像，比较重要的，如1975年未央区李家街村出土北周汉白玉造像，多达17件[34]；1992年，未央区西查村出土3尊汉白玉贴金彩绘观音像[35]。

上述出土的北周造像雕琢精细，代表了长安北周雕刻工艺的最高水平。北周造像地域特征显著，如佛像头部比例大，面相近方圆，脸庞不如北齐造像清秀，身体明显偏胖，上身长，下肢偏短，身材比例不如北齐造像那样匀称。这种造像样式多发现于当时宇文氏统治的长安及附近地区，故被称为“陕西派”样式。[36]

公元534年，北魏分裂，东魏迁都邺城（今河北临漳县），西魏建都长安（即汉长安城），以后高氏和宇文氏分别取代元氏建立北齐、北周王朝。东、西魏及北齐、北周是两个相互对峙的政权。政治上的分裂，在一定程度上阻碍了东西部之间的政治、经济、文化的交流。东西部佛教造像艺术、雕刻工艺逐步走向不同的发展道路，形成了西魏、北周独特的造像样式。

如果说西魏尚保留着中原地区北魏晚期流行的“秀骨清像”样式，那么，到了北周则风格大变。这种变化的原因，固然与北齐、南朝梁，在经济、文化上存在的差异，和工匠雕刻工艺水平的高低有关，但可能更多的是政治上的原因。陈寅恪先生在《隋唐制度渊源略论稿》一书中对东西部文物制度有一段著名的论述：“洛阳文物人才虽经契胡之残毁，其遗烬再由高氏父子之收掇，更得以恢复炽盛于邺都。魏孝文以来，文化之正统仍在山东，遥与江左南朝

[30] 襄樊市考古队、谷城县博物馆：《湖北谷城县肖家营墓地》，《考古》2006年11期，第15~37页，图一三，3；图版壹2。
[31] 中国社会科学院考古研究所编著：《古都遗珍——长安城出土的北周佛教造像》，图版一六、三九、四二，文物出版社，2010年。
[32] 赵力光、裴建平：《西安市东郊出土北周佛立像》，《文物》2005年第5期。
[33] 西安市文物保护研究所：《西安窦寨村北周佛教石刻造像》，《文物》2009年第5期。
[34] 马咏钟：《西安文管会所藏北朝白石造像和隋鎏金铜像》，《文物》1979年第3期。西安市文物保护考古所：《西安北郊出土北朝佛教造像》，《文博》1998年第2期。
[35] 西安市文物局：《西安北郊出土北周白石观音造像》，《文物》1997年第11期。
[36] 松原三郎：《改订东洋美术全史》，第182页，东京美术，1981年。

并为衣冠礼乐之所萃，故宇文泰所不得不深思畏忌，而与苏绰之徒别以关陇为文化本位，虚饰周官旧文以适鲜卑野俗，非驴非马，藉用欺笼一时之人心，所以至其子（武帝）并齐之后，成陵之鬼馁，而开国制度已渐为仇雠敌国之所染化。然则当日山东邺都文化势力之广大可以推知也”[37]。宇文泰窃据关中后，为了笼络六镇武将、关陇豪右，与东魏、萧梁相抗衡，大搞关陇本位主义，仿周礼建立六官制度。[38]因此，北周造像，既不同于萧梁，又不同于北齐，与宇文泰的关陇本位、思想保守和复古思潮有一定的关系。[39]

这一点还反映在政治版图上，山西省博物院所藏多尊北周佛像，如北周天和四年（569）周亮智造释迦立像，均出自北周所辖的山西晋南地区（临汾以南区域）[40]，造像样式与长安佛像如出一辙。与晋南相邻的晋东南地区和晋中地区（包括太原）石窟造像，则为典型的北齐造像样式，二者泾渭分明。这种情况的出现，使人感受到佛教造像背后的强有力的政治推动力。因此，政治的因素是不能不考虑的。

这次展陈的还有一背屏式造像的背光残件（图版 21），疑出自邺城地区，也值得关注。

背光残件属于中型背屏式造像的上半部分，已断成数块，拼接而成。正面为火焰背光，表面残留有贴金彩绘痕迹。背光中心为圆形头光，头光中心残留有主尊造像头部的断痕。头光的内匝为单瓣莲花、五圈同心圆；外匝中心为莲花摩尼宝珠，其余均为藤蔓、忍冬和莲叶组成。莲叶有正面卷曲、张开的，也有背面样式，表现十分生动。头光外为舟形火焰纹，火焰中雕刻有四身供养天，之中一身为正面像，头束双环发髻，面相圆润，颈下戴桃尖形项圈，上身袒露，双手合十。左侧两身和右侧一身，形象相同，均束头束双环发髻，侧脸，面朝中心。

背面浅浮雕菩提双树。双树之间为太子思惟菩萨像，残存半个头部，头后有圆形头光。菩萨头戴火焰宝珠高冠，脸庞浑圆，头微微侧向左侧，左手食指支左腮。左侧菩提树之左为女供养人，残存两身，靠近菩提树的一身为女主人像，形体较大，头缠绕布，面部短圆，脸侧向菩萨，身着交领宽袖长裙，单领竖起，胸部束带，左臂下垂，右手上举，持一束莲花、莲叶和莲台。身后为女丫鬟，头梳双环髻，服饰与女主人相同。女主人头上有伞盖。伞盖上方有方形榜题，镌刻“故正平郡君裴”。右侧菩提树之右上方雕刻一莲花化生，化生有低平肉髻，面相浑圆，双手举于胸前。下方残存一身女供养人头部，头梳双环髻，面容为青春少女形。头上有伞盖和榜题，镌刻“亡女”二字。

整个背光正面雕刻较深，近似于透雕，有极强的立体感，表现了高超的雕刻技艺，堪称北齐佛教雕刻的上乘之作。根据榜题，可知礼佛供养的女主人是已故的正平郡君裴氏。按古代赐封制度，郡君之封始于晋。《晋书》卷二十五《舆服志》记载：“王妃、特进夫人、封郡君。”北朝沿袭了这种制度。根据文献和碑刻资料的记载：北齐时期诸王夫人封为郡君者很多。如东安王娄睿夫人杨氏被封为东安郡君，《娄睿华严经碑》有东安郡君杨氏的题名。[41]《北齐书》卷四十四《张景仁传》记载：“景仁出自寒微，本无识见，一旦开府、侍中、封王。其妻姓奇，莫知氏族所出，容制音辞，事事庸俚。既诏除王妃，与诸公主、郡君同在朝谒之例，见者为其惭悚。”可见，封郡君者身份地位很高。榜题中的正平郡，即今山西新绛县，《魏书》卷一百六《地形志二上》记载：正平郡辖闻喜、曲沃二县。所以，正平郡君裴氏应当出自河东名门望族闻喜裴氏家族。这件作品的出资镌刻者虽然不得而知，但其身份地位应是某位封王者，他是为已故妻、女祈福而雕造的。

[37] 陈寅恪：《隋唐制度渊源略论稿》，第 43 页，上海古籍出版社，1982 年。
[38]《周书》卷二《文帝纪下》，中华书局点校本。
[39] 李裕群：《北朝晚期石窟寺研究》，第 195~198 页，文物出版社，2003 年。
[40] 山西省博物馆编：《山西省博物馆馆藏文物精华》，图版 256，山西人民出版社，1999 年。周亮智造像出自稷山县，是北周的边境，与北齐接壤。又图版 264，北周释迦立像出自万荣县。
[41] 李裕群：《北齐娄睿华严经碑研究》，《考古学报》2012 年第 1 期。

Buddhist Statues on Display in the Shenzhen Museum

Li Yuqun
(Research Fellow, the Institute of Archaeology, Chinese Academy of Social Sciences)

A large number of the stone artifacts on display in the Shenzhen Museum are Buddhist statues. They fall into different types, such as standalone statues, niched statues, and image stelae. Although none of them has a known provenance, these objects may be assigned to the late Northern Wei to the Sui-Tang periods, based on dated inscriptions and stylistic analysis. Initially, they may have been installed in ancient Buddhist monasteries in the Central Plain. These stone objects have strong regional characteristics and can be classified into the following groups: marble statues of Ding Prefecture, Hebei; statues of Qing Prefecture, Shandong; and statues of Xi'an, Shaanxi. Other statues were probably made outside these areas. In the above-mentioned areas in the Central Plain, Buddhism thrived and stone sculpture was highly developed. Starting in the sixth century, the last phase of the Northern Wei, Buddhism became widespread. Numerous Buddhist pagodas and monasteries were set up as the building of cave temples and the creation of Buddhist statues reached their acme. In addition to the metropolitan cities such as Luoyang, Ye, and Chang'an, in the provinces centers of Buddhist sculptural art also took shape especially in Ding Prefecture and Qing Prefecture. It is no coincident that the statues on view in the Museum mainly date from the sixth century.

Although these sculptures are not great in number, quite a few of them are of excellent craftsmanship. Some bear dated inscriptions and contain much crucial information. In the following I will examine a select number of the more important ones, with a focus on their regional characteristics.

I. White Marble Statues of Ding Prefecture in Hebei

Ding Prefecture in Hebei was an economic and cultural center of the Central Plain where sculptural art was well developed. Quyang in Ding Prefecture was renowned for its translucent white marble, excellent for Buddhist sculpture. Approximately in the late Northern Wei, white marble Buddhist sculpture began to emerge in Ding Prefecture and became quite common in the following Eastern Wei, Northern Qi, and Sui-Tang periods.

Among the sculptures on display, those of white marble, predominantly of Northern Wei vintage, are most numerous. A few belong to the Sui-Tang period. Those with dated inscriptions include: The 536 semi-cross-legged contemplative bodhisattva statue by Dongfang Wengui (Pl. 27), the 539 Avalokiteśvara Bodhisattva statue by Bhikṣu Huilue (Pl. 28), the 561 statue plinth by Liu Daohe (Pl. 52), the square statue plinth of 570-575 (Pl. 55), and the 584 Śakyamunistatue by Li Puxian (Pl. 23).

1. The semi-cross-legged contemplative Bodhisattva Statue by Dongfang Wengui

The upper part of this 536 statue from the waist up is missing. The left foot is resting on the ground while the right leg is crossed over the left leg and the left hand is placed on the right ankle. The whole figure is sitting in a contemplative posture in a rattan seat. A stole is draping down both sides of the seat. The seat rests on a low overturned lotus base, and the lotus base is in turn placed on a square plinth. The front and the right and left sides of the square plinth are covered with colored paintings. On the front, much of the color paint has peeled off. But an overturned lotus base is still visible at the center supporting a single-story Buddhist pagoda with a round base and a pyramid roof topped by a finial in a traditional Chinese architectural style. From the four roof corners hang four bells. The pagoda is flanked by two overturned lotus bases. Kneeling on each of the bases is an offering bodhisattva wearing a bejeweled cap and a skirt. The painting on the left side of the plinth features three male figures. The one in front is apparently the main figure with his head slightly tilted and his hands stretched out. He wears a loose-fitting robe and shoes. Behind him are two boys, each of whom wears a caftan with narrow sleeves, a leather belt and black boots with pointed tips. The painting on the right side of the plinth features three female figures. The one in front is apparently the main figure. With her hair tied into a bun, she wears a long skirt that falls to the floor and a shawl on her shoulders. Behind her are two young girls wearing long skirts. The male and female donors are all vividly sketched in black ink and painted with colors. The two main figures are identified as husband and wife making offerings. Those behind them are identified as their offspring. The humility of the main figures contrasts greatly with the liveliness of their sons and daughters.

A votive text is inscribed on the back side of the square plinth. It reads, "On the fifth (a *bingzi* day) of the second month—the first day of the month is a *renshen* day—in the third year of Tianping, a *bingchen* year, Dongfang Wengui of Lunu County, Zhongshan Commandery, for the sake of the offspring of all creatures, and for the sake of his deceased wife, reverently sponsored the creation of one contemplative statue of white marble." According to Chapter 106, the "Treatise on Geography" ("Dixing zhi"), in the *History of the Northern Wei* (Wei shu), Zhongshan Commandery under Ding Prefecture had under its jurisdiction Lunu County (in present-day Dingxian, Hebei), and Lunu served as the seat of the county, the commandery, and the prefecture. From this we know that this statue of the contemplative bodhisattva is one of Ding Prefecture white marble. A standalone contemplative bodhisattva statue can usually be identified as that of the crown prince Śakyamuni. What makes this statue special is the Buddhist pagoda flanked by the two offering bodhisattvas, which distinguishes it from the usual imagery of the Boshan burner, Dharmapala lions and vajra-warriors.

2. The Avalokiteśvara Bodhisattva Statue by the Bhikṣu Huilue

This near-perfectly preserved "niched statue" dates to the first year of Xinghe of the Eastern Wei (539). The oblong-faced bodhisattva, wearing a hair bun (damaged), directs his gaze downward. Two silk bands drape down from the sides of the head to the shoulders. There is a ring on the neck. From the shoulders a stole hangs down. The bodhisattva, clad in a saṃkakṣikā (toga) over a skirt, is holding high a lotus bud in his right hand, and clutching a lock-shaped object in his left hand. With his feet revealed, he stands on an upturned lotus base. Overall, the statue presents a well-rounded image. It is placed on an oblong plinth. On the front of the plinth are carved two lions with a raised paw. On the back side of the plinth is inscribed the votive text, which reads, "On the 19th of the 12th month in the first year of Xinghe, a *jiwei* year, the Bhikṣu Huilue of the Yins' Monastery, for the sake of the surviving kin of his late grandfather, grandmother, and father, reverently sponsored the creation of an Avalokiteśvara Bodhisattva statue."

White marble standing bodhisattva statues made their first appearance in Ding Prefecture in late Northern Wei times, and became popular under the Eastern Wei and Northern Qi. They were especially common during the former period, a phenomenon closely linked to the spread of the Avalokiteśvara worship in Ding Prefecture. For example, Chapter 29, "Xingfu", in the *Sequel to the Biographies of Eminent Monks* (Xu gaoseng zhuan), records, "In addition there are the auspicious Avalokiteśvara statue of Ding Prefecture and the 'King Gao Sutra'. In the past, when the Northern Wei conquered Ding Prefecture it recruited the warrior Sun Jingde. Sun sponsored an Avalokiteśvara statue at his sentry post. After his tour of duty for about a year, he was due to return home. He had often performed rituals [to the statue]. Later he was implicated by robbers and thrown into the capital's prison. Under torture, he confessed falsely to his crime and was sentenced to death. On the following day, when he was about to face execution, his heart was filled with emotion as tears rolled down like rain. He swore to himself and said... He dreamed of a śramana teaching the Sutra on Avalokiteśvara Saving Lives. The śramana asked one to recite the Buddha's name in the Sutra one thousand times as a way to save oneself from death. When Jingde woke up... the officer in charge had him tied up and conducted to the market. En route, he kept reciting the name. At the time of the execution, he just finished reciting the name the one thousandth time. When the sword fell [on his neck], it broke into three pieces... The officer considered it a weird incident and reported it the court. Chancellor Gao Huan then submitted a memorial to request the exemption of Sun from execution. So the whole account was written up by an imperial edict and got spread in the world. This is the so-called King Gao's Avalokiteśvara [Sutra]." This passage testifies to the popularity of Ding Prefecture Avalokiteśvara statues in the Eastern Wei and Northern Qi.

3. The Plinth of the Statue by Liu Daohe

This oblong plinth is datable to the second year of Huangjian of the Northern Qi (561). The main statue is no longer extant. Surviving evidence suggests that in front of the main statue there were two semi-cross-legged bhikṣus statues, of which only the legs remain. The main statue was flanked by two upturned lotus bases on each side. Of the statues on the lotus bases only the legs remain. This informs us that attendant on the main statue were statues of the two disciples and the two bodhisattvas. At the center of the front of the plinth are carved two bhikṣus holding a Boshan burner. On either side of the burner is painted an octagonal pillar with a flaming pearl. Further away on each side are carved a lion and a vajra-warrior (with damage to the head). All the images in front are either gold-foiled or painted in color. On the right side of the plinth is inscribed the votive text, which reads, "On the 20th of the fourth month, in the second year of Huangjian, seventeen fellow countrymen including Liu Daohe and others reverently sponsored the creation of a white marble statue for the sake of His Imperial Majesty, their teacher-monks, fathers and mothers, birth fathers and mothers, and all beings, with the shared cause and effect." At the end of the votive text is inscribed "Countryman Zhai Andu, Countryman Sun Mohou." There are also the images of two donors wearing barbarian clothing and black boots with pointed toes.

This piece is of exquisite craftsmanship, especially the carvings on the front side. The combination of two bhikṣus holding a Boshan burner, two lions, and two vajra-warriors brings to mind the Tathāgataseven-figure statue, and the plinth of the Maitreyaseven-figure statue, both unearthed from Taipingqu, Xiwen Town, Linzhang County, Hebei, in 1965. These two statues feature octagonal pillars with flaming pearls as well. The image of two bhikṣus holding a Boshan burner is found on the front of the central pillar of Cave No. 1 in the Southern Xiangtangshan Caves. Octagonal pillars with flaming pearls are found in the Central Cave of the Northern Xiangtangshan Caves; and on the "upturned bowls" on top of Caves Nos. 1 and 7 in the Northern Xiangtangshan Caves. This may help provenance the plinth and its statue to the Ye City area.

4. The Plinth of the Amitabha Statue by Mijie Xiangbao

This square plinth of exquisite workmanship is datable to the Wuping period (570-575) of the Northern Qi. On top of the plinth is a richly decorated upturned lotus base. The main statue is no longer extant. Judging by the lotus base, the statue should be a standalone standing Buddha. On the front of the plinth is carved the image of two bhikṣus holding a Boshan burner. On each side of the image is a Dharmapala lion. On either side of the plinth are four small niches. Each niche features a god-king. Those on the left side are the Fire-god King, Wind-god King, Tree-god King, and Mountain-god King. Those on the right side are the Dragon-god King, Elephant-god King, Lion-god King, and Pearl-god King. On the back side of the plinth is the votive text, which reads, "On the 26th of the seventh month in the XX year of Wuping of the Great Qi, the Buddhist disciple Mijie Xiangbao reverently sponsored the creation of a white-marble Amitabha statue in honor of his late father and in hopes that all living beings in the Dharmadatu would bring forth the Bodhi mind, escape suffering, attain happiness, and simultaneously become Buddhas."

The god-kings as a carving motif are Dharmapala gods. As such they are widely seen in cave temples and on standalone statues of the Northern Wei, Northern Qi, and Northern Zhou. Usually, they appear as a group. In a cave temple, they are carved in the lower parts of the four walls or the four sides of the plinth of the central pillar. On a standalone statue, they are usually carved on the four sides of the plinth. The only surviving statue with god-kings accompanied by a complete inscription is the statue of the first year of Wuding (543) of the Eastern Wei by Luo Zikuan. There are ten god-kings carved on the right, left, and back sides of the plinth. On the right side are the Lion-god King, Bird-god King, and Elephant-god King; on the left side are the Pearl-god King, Wind-god King, and Dragon-god King; and on the back side are the River-god King, Mountain-god King, Tree-god King, and Fire-god King. In Northern Qi times, statues with the motif of god-kings were mainly concentrated in the cave temples in the Ye City area. For example, the Northern and Southern Xiangtangshan Caves in Handan, and the Lingquansi Caves and Xiaonanhai Caves in Anyang. On the plinths of standalone statues unearthed in the Ye City area are often carved god-kings. Judging by existing evidence, the motif of god-kings has not been found on statues in Ding Prefecture in Hebei. Thus, the plinth in question probably came from Ye City. In other words, although the stones were quarried from Ding Prefecture, the statue may have been created in Ye City.

The votive text informs us that the donor of the statue is Mijie Xiangbao. There is evidence that Mijie is a Qiang surname. Very few records of the Mijies survive in the sources. For the Northern and Southern Dynasties period, there is only one mention, in Chapter 27, the "Biography of Cai You" (Cai You zhuan), in the *History of the Northern Zhou Dynasty* (Zhou shu), "After Houmochen Yue killed Heba Yue, various generals sent their envoys to welcome Taizu (Yuwen Tai). When [Cai You] was about to go, [it was found out that] Mijie Yuanjin who was from a prominent clan in Xia Prefecture and others were planning a conspiracy." Xia Prefecture had as its seat Tongwancheng, about 55 kilometers north of present-day Jingbian County, Shaanxi. The site is still extant. At any rate, the votive text by a Mijie is highly important for studying the activities of the Qiangs in Ye City.

5. The Śakyamuni Statue by Li Puxian

This relatively well-preserved statue datable to the fourth year of Kaihuang of the Sui (584) is a sculpture in the round. The head is topped by a lowuṣṇīṣa (cranial bump). The countenance is plump. Behind the head there is an aureole. The neck is short and thick. The overall physique is robust. The body is clad in a sleeved cassock. The creases in the right and left parts of the front of the cassock look mismatched. The right hand is holding high while the left hand is placed on the left knee. The Buddha is seated on a square plinth, with both feet, resting on an upturned lotus base, pointing downward. There are remnants of gold foil and color paint. On the front side of the plinth is carved a squatting Earth-god, who is supporting the upturned lotus base with his left hand and resting his right hand on his right knee. The votive text is inscribed on the remaining three sides of the plinth. On the right side, it reads: "The eighth day of the sixth month, in the fourth year of Kaihuang, a *jiachen* year"; on the back side: "The Buddhist disciple Li Puxian sponsored the creation of a Śakyamuni statue for the sake of his father, mother, grandfather, and grandmother"; on the left side: "The Buddhist disciple Yang Hemei dedicates himself to sponsoring the Buddhist statue."

This statue is markedly different from those early Sui statues with Northern Qi characteristics. For example, the short neck, the stout physique, the sleeved cassock with a low neckline, and the mismatching of creases—they are reminiscent of Northern Zhou statues. It seems that some Ding Prefecture statues in early Sui times began to come under the influence of Northern Zhou statues in Chang'an. According to Chapter 39, the "Biography of Doulu Tong" (Doulu Tong zhuan), Doulu Tong took up position as prefect of Ding Prefecture in the first year of Kaihuang (581), a post he still held in the ninth year of Kaihuang (589). Doulu Tong was a devout believer in Buddhism. By the time he passed through the hamlet called Pingding Prefecture, a colossal Buddhist statue he had sponsored was still unfinished. As prefect of Ding Prefecture, he was involved in the renovation of the Seven Emperors' Monastery. Thus, the Northern Zhou style was probably brought to Ding Prefecture by Buddhist officials from the capital, which in turn exerted an influence on the area itself.

The sitting posture of the stature, however, is not appropriate for the Śakyamuni Buddha mentioned in the votive text. This type of sitting posture had become common in the Yungang Caves of the Northern Wei. For example, the sitting Buddha in the cave attached to Cave 19 of Yungang. Starting in the early Northern Wei at the latest, the sitting posture became the unique position of the Maitreya Buddha. It depicts how Maitreya, after his birth on earth, preached the Law under the ironwood tree at the Three Gatherings to bring deliverance to all creatures. A special characteristic of the iconography is the Earth-god supporting the two feet of Maitreya, which is common to statues of Maitreya whether as a bodhisattva or as a Buddha, and is never associated with the Śakyamuni Buddha. In view of this, we can identify the statue in question as that of the Maitreya Buddha. As for its identification with the Śakyamuni Buddha by the votive text, that is the wishful thinking of the donor himself, having little to do with the statue itself. Because Buddhist statue sculpture in Ding Prefecture was highly developed, it was likely that some of statues were produced for commercial purposes, and thus different from what customers wanted.

Among other Ding Prefecture white marble pieces of the Northern Dynasties to the Sui-Tang period, there are Buddha heads, sitting Buddhas, bodhisattva heads, standing bodhisattvas, the statue of the double standing Avelokiteśvara Bodhisattvas, vajra-warrior heads, and the Northern Qi statue niche with openwork apsaras. In addition, there is a remnant of an aureole, on the back side of which is skillfully painted a meditating bhikṣu under a tree.

II. Statues from Qing Prefecture in Shandong

Qing Prefecture was located in the eastern part of the Central Plain. During the Eastern Jin and Song, it was taken over by the Northern Wei. In Eastern Wei and Northern Qi times, it was considered, together with Bing Prefecture (based in present-day Taiyuan, Shanxi), a key area where "the base for the hegimon's cause was laid and the foundation for the kingly mandate was created." Not only did Qing have a prosperous economy and a highly developed culture, it was also subject to profound cultural influence from the South, being its immediate neighbor. Approximately starting in the late Northern Wei period, there arose in Qing Prefecture a craze for Buddhist statue sculpture, which peaked during the Northern Qi. The area differed from Ding Prefecture in its abundant supply of high-quality fine blue stone and its Buddhist statues were made from locally quarried stone.

On view in the Museum are two Buddha heads (Pls. 36, 37) and a bodhisattva statue that may be the Qing Prefecture provenance (Pl. 31).

The two Buddha heads are both made of fine blue stone, dating back to the Northern Qi dynasty (550-557). Stylistically, they fall in two different types. The first type has a low uṣṇīṣa (cranial bump or topknot) and spiral hair with wide and thin curls with right-turning hairs coming out of the center. The face is egg-shaped and bulbous. Under the arched eyebrows are the narrow eyes. The nose bridge is relatively high. The corners of the mouth are curving upwards, suggesting a slight smile. This kind of imagery is also seen in the statues of the Longxing Monastery in Qing Prefecture. The spiral hair and facial expressions were apparently influenced by the Mathura style in north India. (Pl. 36)

The second type has a low uṣṇīṣa and spiral hair with fine and dense curls. The curls are relatively small and tall. There are no right-turning hairs. The facial features are delicate. This must be a traditional Han statue style. (Pl. 37)

As for the bodhisattva statue, it is a sculpture in the round. Only the head and upper body remain. The head wears a round bun. Long hair braids cascade down the shoulders. Two silk ribbons drape down from the sides of the head to the round ornaments on the shoulders, as is typical of bodhisattva statues produced in Qing Prefecture. The slender face with delicate features reveals a slight smile. There is a jade-and-pearl necklace and a stole on the upper body. A saṃkakṣikā (toga) drapes diagonally across the shapely body. The hands are damaged. This statue is datable to the late Eastern Wei or the early Northern Qi period. (Pl. 31)

Qing Prefecture statues have attracted much attention thanks to the 1996 excavation of more than 400 stone statues from the site of the Longxing Monastery. Of exquisite craftsmanship, they are covered with gold foil and color paint adding to their brilliancy. The Longxing was a famous monastery in the Qing area under the Northern Dynasties. According to the "Stela on the Prince of Linhuai," Prince of Linhuai Lou Dingyuan at the Longxing Monastery "thus took part in Buddhist ritual, created a Amitayus Buddha statue, 3 *zhang* 9 *chi* in height, accompanied by the statues of the Avalokiteśvara and Mahāsthāmaprāpta Bodhisattvas." The excavation of the Longxing Monastery statues became a sensational event in academe, and was instrumental in making Qing Prefecture statues world famous.

In reality, however, the discovery of Qing Prefecture statues can be dated back as early as the early 20th century. Osvald Siren's *Chinese Sculpture: From the Fifth to the Fourteenth Century* (London 1925) catalogues a few Qing Prefecture statues. One example is the Northern Wei statue of the fourth year of Zhengguang (523) by Zhang Baozhu, now in the collection of the Shandong Museum. Since the 1970s, statues of the Northern Dynasties have come to light in Qing Prefecture other than those of the Longxing Monastery. Neighboring places such as Boxing, Zhucheng, Linqu, Guangrao, Wudi, Gaoqing, Juancheng, and others have also yielded a number of stone statues in monastery sites. Especially worth mention are two superbly carved pieces unearthed in the site of the Banzhou Basilica of the Lingyan Monastery, Jinan. One is a Buddha head, and the other a bodhisattva statue. Both are Qing Prefecture style Northern Qi pieces. They attest to the fact that by then the Qing Prefecture style had spread westward to Qi Prefecture.

From the Northern Wei to the Eastern Wei, statues of Buddhas and bodhisattvas were of slender physique. The Buddhas wear loose cassocks with wide girdles or sleeved cassocks, which inherits the statue style of the Longmen Caves at Luoyang—that of "slender physique and delicate facial features." Starting in Northern Qi times, Buddha and bodhisattva statues underwent a major stylistic change as the imagery of stout physique became popular. The cassock a Buddha statue wears often has two sleeves or reveals the right shoulder. Thanks especially to the influence of the Mathura style of north India, sensual cassocks of thin fabric are often worn on Qing Prefecture Buddhist statues, which is a unique period characteristic.

Furthermore, aureoles of niched statues are often carved with dragon images, whereas the right and left sides of the plinth often feature images of graceful dragons. These are highly regional motifs particular to Shandong with a wide currency from the late Northern Wei to the Northern Qi. However, there was a slight stylistic change as well. In the early phase, aureoles often featured single dragons, rarely double dragons. In the Northern Qi, this trend was reversed as single dragons became rare, replaced by double dragons in the role of pagoda guardians.

III. Northern Zhou Buddhist Statues in Xi'an, Shaanxi

Xi'an is the site of the Western Wei and Northern Zhou capital, Chang'an. In recent years, it has yielded a large number of Northern Zhou statues, affirming its position as the center of Buddhist statue sculpture in the western part of the Northern Zhou, with an enormous influence on temple caves within the realm.

The Buddha head on view in the Museum is a typical Northern Zhou sculpture (Pl. 39). Made of fine blue stone, the head, judging by its size, must have belonged to a life-size statue. In spite of dents on its surface, the head is well preserved. The craftsmanship is superb. On the top of the head there remain some slender, dense right-turning spiral hairs. The uṣṇīṣa is low and flat. The shape of the face is nearly square-round. The eyes and eyebrows are slender and narrow. The slightly upturned corners of the mouth suggest a slight smile. The neck is thickish. There is a small hole in the back of the head for installing the aureole.

This Buddha head is similar in style to Northern Zhou statues, mostly of blue stone, recently excavated in the Xi'an area. For example, in a group of Buddhist sculptures excavated in Zhongcha Village, Weiyang District, in 2004, the Buddhist statue No. 4 and the Buddha heads Nos. 14 and 15 all have a low and flat uṣṇīṣa, spiral hair, and a square-round face. The five blue stone statues excavated in Wanzi Village, Baqiao District, in 2004 share the same characteristics. One of them bears a votive text datable to the second year of Daxiang of the Northern Zhou (580). In 2007, nine Buddhist sculptures came to light in Douzhai Village, Weiyang District, Xi'an. Of these, two Buddha heads have the same characteristics as described above. Thus the Buddha head in question can be provenanced to Han Chang'an or an area nearby.

The exquisite craftsmanship of the Northern Zhou sculptures covered above represents the best Chang'an-based Northern Zhou sculptural art had to offer. Among the prominent regional characteristics of the Northern Zhou sculptures are the proportionately large head, the near square-round face, facial features not as delicate as those of Northern Qi statues, remarkably plump physique, the long upper body, and the short legs. In general, the body is not as well proportioned as that of Northern Qi sculptures. These characteristics are often found in statues from Chang'an and its environs under the rule of the Yuwens. Thus they are referred to as the "Shaanxi style."

The Eastern Wei-Northern Qi and the Western Wei-Northern Zhou were political rivals. The political division between the two to some extent hindered the exchange of political, economic, and cultural ideas between east and west. The Buddhist statue art and carving craftsmanship of the west took a different course from the east and developed the unique Western Wei-Northern Zhou statue style.

In the Museum there is a damaged aureole, probably from the Ye City area (Pl. 21), that is worth mention.

The piece originally belonged to the upper part of an aureole attached to a niched statue. It is reconstituted from several smaller pieces. The front is the aureole itself, where remnants of gold foil are still visible. At the center of the aureole is a circular halo where there is evidence that the head of the statue has been broken off. The inner ring of the halo is composed of single lotus petals and concentric circles in groups of five. The outer ring is made up of a Mani pearl, vines, palmettes, and lotus leaves. Outside the halo are flames, among which are four offering gods. The one at the center presents a frontal view. The head wears a double bun. The face is smooth. There is a ring with a pointed tip on the neck. The upper body is naked. The two hands are folded together. The two gods on the left and the god on the right have similar characteristics as the central figure. All wear a double bun. But they face the central figure, presenting a profile view.

On the back of the aureole is a double bodhi tree in bas-relief. Between the two trees is the image of the contemplative crown prince as bodhisattva. Only half of the head remains. Behind the head is a circular halo. The bodhisattva wears a high crown set with a flaming pearl. He lifts his left index finger to support his left chin. To the left of the bodhi tree on the left is the female donor and her maid. Both images are damaged. The donor wears a long dress with loose sleeves. A band is tied around the chest. The left arm hangs down; the right hand is holding high a lotus flower with leaves resting on the lotus throne. Behind her is the maid with a double bun. Her clothing and ornaments are similar to those of the donor. Over the head of the donor is a canopy. On top of the canopy is a colophon with the inscription, "The late Commandery Mistress of Zhengping Pei." To the right of the bodhi tree on the right is carved a lotus reincarnation with a low uṣṇīṣa and a round face. The two hands are held up in front. Below is the remnant of the head of another female donor, topped by a double bun. Over the head are a canopy and a colophon with the inscription "deceased daughter."

The carving on the front of the aureole is so deep it almost produces an openwork effect with a strong three-dimensional feel to it. The superb craftsmanship in carving makes it one of the best carved Buddhist pieces in the Northern Qi. According to one of the colophons, the donor/offerer is the late Commandery Mistress of Zhengping Pei. In the ancient investiture system, the title of "Commandery Mistress" was first conferred in the Jin dynasty. Chapter 25, the "Treatise on Carriages and Dress" (Yufu zhi), in the *History of the Jin Dynasty* (Jin shu) states, "Consorts of princes, wives of lords specially advanced, and commandery mistresses ride in small carriages." Evidently, the recipient of the title "commandery mistress" was of very high status. The Northern Dynasties continued the practice. The "Zhengping Commandery" in the colophon had as its seat present-day Jiangxian County, Shanxi. Chapter 106, the "Treatise on Geography, Part I," in the *History of the Northern Wei Dynasty* (Wei shu) records that Zhengping Commandery had under its jurisdiction Wenxi and Quwo Counties. The Commandery Mistress of Zhengping Pei in question must have been a member of the Wenxi lineage of the Pei clan, a prominent clan in Hedong. There is no way of knowing the sponsor of the piece. But his rank must have been that of a prince. He created this piece to offer blessings to his deceased wife and daughter.

(Translated by Victor Cunrui Xiong, Western Michigan University)

北朝葬具孝子图的形式与意义

郑　岩
（中央美术学院 教授）

深圳博物馆“永远的北朝——北朝石刻艺术展”中展示了一批精美多样的北朝石棺床（以下简称“深圳展出北朝石棺床”）等葬具，其中包括一套完整的石屏风，具有很高的文物价值与历史考古价值。这套石屏风上面以减地浅浮雕加线刻的形式雕刻了多幅人物画像，有反映墓主人生活的场面，也有表现孝子故事的图画。这种画像在北朝墓葬石雕艺术品中颇具代表性，尤其是有关孝子故事的图画，值得深入研究。

在儒家思想作为主流意识形态的古代中国，孝子孝行题材的绘画、雕刻等（以下简称“孝子图”）数量极多，特别是在精英艺术以外的世俗与宗教艺术中，这类作品更为习见。如元代以降，《二十四孝图》等成套的孝子图就曾被大量复制，广泛传播。考古发现还揭示出这类艺术题材在丧葬艺术中传承的历史，其中资料最为丰富的是汉代及辽宋金元时期[1]，此外，许多北朝葬具上的孝子图也引人注目。北朝葬具多为石质，主要有棺和棺床两种，其中棺又分为殿堂式和匣式，棺床以上三面立屏风。石葬具上带有贴金彩绘的阴线刻画像，常见墓主像、鞍马牛车等出行仪仗、孝子图和升仙图等。《魏书·穆观传》所提到的“通身隐起金饰棺”[2]，可能就属于此类葬具。20世纪初以来，北朝石葬具曾大量流散于海外，近年来，经过多方努力，又有多批回归国内。[3]这篇小文试图在前人研究的基础上[4]，结合近年来新公布的一些材料，对北朝葬具上的孝子图作些补充。

这些带有孝子图的石葬具，年代多属于北魏洛阳时代（493~534），2007年河南安阳固岸东魏武定六年（548）谢氏冯僧晖墓出土石棺床则是纪年较晚的一例[5]。另外，在宁夏固原雷祖庙北魏墓出土的

[1] 关于“二十四孝”及《二十四孝图》源流的研究，详赵超《“二十四孝”在何时形成》，《中国典籍与文化》1998年第1期第50~55页、第2期第40~45页。关于墓葬艺术中孝子图研究的成果较多，汉代墓葬艺术中的孝子图最具有代表性的两项分别见于山东嘉祥东汉武梁祠和内蒙古和林格尔小板申东汉墓，相关研究，见：巫鸿《武梁祠——中国古代画像艺术的思想性》，第181~201页，柳杨、岑河译，生活·读书·新知三联书店，2006年；陈永志、黑田彰主编《和林格尔汉墓孝子传图辑录》，文物出版社，2009年。关于辽宋金元墓葬中孝子图的研究，见：邓菲《关于宋金墓葬中孝行图的思考》，《中原文物》2009年第4期，第75~81页；万彦《宋辽金元墓葬中女孝子图像的解读》，《艺术探索》2009年第5期，第17~19页。

[2]《魏书》第664页，中华书局，1974年。

[3] 比较集中的资料报道，见：郭玉堂《洛阳出土石刻时地记》，大华书报供应社，1941年；王子云《中国古代石刻画选集》，中国古典艺术出版社，1957年；黄明兰《洛阳北魏世俗石刻线画集》，人民美术出版社，1987年；王树村主编《中国美术全集·绘画编·石刻线画》，上海人民美术出版社，1988年；周到主编《中国画像石全集》八《石刻线画》，山东美术出版社、河南美术出版社，2000年。有关综述，见：贺西林《北朝画像石葬具的发现与研究》，巫鸿主编《汉唐之间的视觉文化与物质文化》，第341~376页，文物出版社，2003年。此外，近年来出土的多批北齐、北周至隋代入华西域人的墓葬中，也见有类似结构的石葬具，但图像内容大多与北魏以来的传统有所区别，更不见孝子图，故不在本文的讨论范围中。

[4] 关于北朝葬具孝子图的主要研究成果，见：长广敏雄《六朝時代美術の研究》，（东京）美术出版社，1969年；Eugene Y. Wang, Coffins and Confucianism–The Northern Wei Sarcophagus in The Minneapolis Institute of Arts, *Orientations*, vol.30, no.6, June 1999, pp. 56~64；林圣智《北朝时代における葬具の图像と机能—石棺床围屏の墓主肖像と孝子传图を例として—》，《美术史》总第154期（2003年），第207~226页；赵超《关于伯奇的古代孝子图画》，《考古与文物》2004年第3期，第68~72页；邹清泉《北魏孝子画像研究》，文化艺术出版社，2007年。

[5] 河南省文物考古研究所：《河南安阳固岸墓地考古发掘收获》，《华夏考古》2009年第3期，第19~23页，彩版15~20。

描金彩绘漆木棺上也有孝子图[6]，其年代在太和八年至十年之间（484~486）[7]。同时期南朝墓葬画像砖中也见有孝子图[8]，可以与之对比。

这时期孝子图流行的大背景是世风的变化。南北朝王朝更迭频仍，赵翼慨叹“六朝忠臣无殉节者”[9]。近人蒙思明指出，魏晋以后家族地位压倒国家，孝亲比忠君更为重要，而“畸形的孝道”无非是为了维护和强化世族的地位。[10]唐长孺也谈到，除了门阀的经济与政治利益，司马氏夺取晋室政权，并不符合儒家传统“忠”的道德，这也促进了亲先于君、孝先于忠的观念的形成。[11]此外，还有学者从北魏宫廷制度入手，讨论了北魏孝子图流行的背景。[12]

与丧葬相关的孝行，以及部分墓葬、葬具、壁画、随葬品等物质遗存，是孝的思想观念、道德规范的体现，反过来也积极、能动地形塑了这种意识形态。我们应致力于寻找现象和意义之间具体的链接方式，需要对图像做出历史的解释，而不只是建立在其他研究基础上的判断。在这个方向上，所思考的问题应包括：在当时特定的丧葬环境中，制作这些画像的意图何在？图像以何种方式体现其意图？孝子图的意义是否严格控制在儒家思想的范围内？诸如此类的问题虽然与社会史和思想史相关，但其核心却是图像本身，所涉及的基本概念是图像的题材、形式、意义。基于这样的认识，本文以郭巨和蔡顺两种孝子图为例，作些尝试性的讨论，其中既包括对于图像内部视觉元素的观察，也涉及针对图像外部的礼仪环境。

一

目前已经发现的北朝葬具上的郭巨画像数量较多，可以支持我们对其表现方式加以比较。郭巨故事的文本早在西汉已比较完整，刘向《孝子图》曰：

> 郭巨，河内温人。甚富，父没，分财二千万为两，分与两弟，己独取母供养。寄住邻，有凶宅无人居者，共推与之，居无祸患。妻产男，虑养之则防供养，乃令妻抱儿，欲掘地埋之，于土中得金一釜，上有铁券，云赐孝子郭巨。巨还宅主，宅主不敢受，遂以闻官，官依券题还巨，遂得兼养儿。[13]

这个故事颇不符合近人的观念[14]，但在南北朝时期却十分为流行。例如，在《宋书·孝义列传》中，郭巨的事迹被移植到他人身上：“郭世道……家贫无产业，佣力以养继母。妇生一男，夫妻共议曰：‘勤身供养，力犹不足，若养此儿，则所费者大。’乃垂泣瘗之”[15]。山东长清孝里铺孝堂山东汉早期石祠，在北朝被误认为纪念郭巨的祠堂[16]，从中也可以看到郭巨在当时的影响。

---

[6] 宁夏固原博物馆：《固原北魏墓漆棺画》，宁夏人民出版社，1988年。

[7] 关于该墓年代的讨论，参见孙机《固原北魏漆棺画》，氏著《中国圣火——中国古文物与东西文化交流中的若干问题》，第122~138页，辽宁教育出版社，1996年。

[8] 河南省文化局文物工作队：《邓县彩色画象砖墓》，文物出版社，1958年；襄樊市文物管理处：《襄阳贾家冲画像砖墓》，《江汉考古》1986年1期，第16~33页；杨一：《襄城区麒麟村南朝画像砖赏析》，《襄樊日报》2009年2月13日B3版。

[9] 赵翼：《陔余丛考》卷十七，第322~324页，商务印书馆，1957年。

[10] 蒙思明：《魏晋南北朝的社会》，第128~131页，上海人民出版社，2007年。

[11] 唐长孺：《魏晋南朝的君父先后论》，氏著《魏晋南北朝史论丛续编·魏晋南北朝史论拾遗》，第235~250页，中华书局，2011年。

[12] 邹清泉：《北魏孝子画像研究》，第76~116页。

[13] 李昉等撰：《太平御览》卷四一一，第1898~1899页，中华书局，1960年。邹清泉统计，郭巨故事还见于宋躬《孝子传》（《太平御览》卷八一一、《初学记》十七）、佚名《孝子传》（《法苑珠林》四十九），也见于敦煌本《孝子传》及日藏阳明本、船桥本《孝子传》（邹清泉：《北魏孝子画像研究》，第124~125页）。另外，还见于晋干宝《搜神记》（干宝撰、汪绍楹校注：《搜神记》卷十一，第136页，中华书局，1979年）。

[14] 如鲁迅对郭巨故事就有严厉的批评，见《朝花夕拾·二十四孝图》，《鲁迅全集》，第2卷，第258~264页，人民文学出版社，2005年。

[15] 《宋书》，第2243页，中华书局，1974年。

[16] 蒋英炬认为将孝堂山祠堂视为郭巨墓祠的说法始于北齐武平元年（570）胡长仁《陇东王感孝颂》（蒋英炬：《孝堂山石祠管见》，南阳汉代画像石学术讨论会办公室编：《汉代画像石研究》，第206页，文物出版社，1987年）。林圣智则根据其中“访询耆旧”一语，认为胡长仁只是记录了流传于当地民间乡里的传说（林圣智：《北魏宁懋石室的图像与功能》，台湾大学美术史研究集刊编辑委员会编：《美术史研究集刊》第十八期，第48~49页，台湾大学艺术史研究所，2005年）。

图一　宁夏固原雷祖庙北魏墓描金彩绘漆木棺郭巨画像

（采自宁夏固原博物馆：《固原北魏墓漆棺画》，拉页线描图之三）

目前所知最早的郭巨故事画像见于固原雷祖庙北魏墓出土的描金彩绘漆木棺。[17]在这具已经残破的漆木棺左侧上部横长的区域内，以三角形的火焰纹区隔，绘各种孝子图，其中至少用了三个单元表现郭巨故事（图一），似为自左而右展开。现存第一单元描绘郭巨掘地得金，有榜题曰“□衣德脱私不德与”；第二单元为郭巨夫妇并肩而立，有两则榜题，分别为“相将□土冢天赐皇今（黄金）一父（釜）”、“以食不足敬□曹（？）母”；第三单元描绘二人并坐于屋宇下，应为郭巨母与郭巨子，有榜题曰“孝子郭距（巨）供养老母”。汉代画像大多用单幅画表现一个故事，除了抓取故事高潮外，还努力将不同时空的情节集中在一起。[18]以多个连续画面表现同一个故事，可能受到佛教艺术中故事题材绘画的影响。在这种新的形式中，文字叙事的顺序转换为画面上线性展开的结构，它要求观者的目光按照特定的顺序依次在画面上移动，就像钟表的指针逐一扫过表盘上的数字，无形的时间变得“可见”。

美国纳尔逊·阿特金斯美术馆（The Nelson-Atkins Museum of Art）所藏早年洛阳出土北魏石棺（以下简称为“纳尔逊孝子棺”）左侧中央的郭巨画像延续了三幅式的结构，但画面不是生硬地一一平列，郭巨掘地得金的情节位于画面左下部，与郭巨夫妇抬金釜回家的部分前（下）后（上）排列，顺着郭巨夫妇行走的方向，可以看到右部供养母亲和孩子第三部分，这三个部分之间的山石、树木，既起到了区隔的作用，又起到了联系的作用，“幅”的概念变得较为模糊（图二）。画像上部榜题曰“□子郭巨”，似是故事的标题，而不是对于情节或人物身份的说明。这一画像的构成形式相当成熟，对于第三维度的表现令人印象深刻。日本大阪府和泉市久保惣纪念美术馆藏北魏正光五年（524）匡僧安墓石棺床右侧屏风也用三幅画面表现郭巨故事（图三）[19]，有榜无题，每一幅的内容都可以与纳尔逊孝子棺郭

[17] 宁夏固原博物馆：《固原北魏墓漆棺画》，拉页线描图之三。此前有研究者认为，河南登封太室山南麓东汉延光二年（123）启母阙之西阙东面第五层的画像“似为郭巨埋儿的故事”（吕品：《中岳汉三阙》，37、69页，图124，文物出版社，1990年），证据恐不充分。这幅画像刻一人坐于树下，另一人手执长物，似在耕作。画面中缺少郭巨妻、郭巨儿、金釜等必要的指标，如果是一幅孝子图的话，那么释为董永故事，亦无不可。

[18] 刘敦愿：《美术考古与古代文明》，第49页，人民美术出版社，2007年；邢义田：《格套、榜题、文献与画像解释》（修订本），氏著《画为心声——画像石、画像砖与壁画》，第106~110页，中华书局，2011年。尽管学者们常举汉代山东嘉祥东汉武氏祠荆轲刺秦王画像作为讨论汉代单幅式故事画的例子，但值得注意的是，建立在时间概念上的图像序列已经出现，如在武梁祠中，从西壁开始，经北壁（正壁）到东壁，由上而下，依次描绘了从人类诞生到武梁本人的整部历史（有关分析，见巫鸿《武梁祠——中国古代画像艺术的思想性》，第161~167页），只是这个“非虚构类”的“大故事”不同于文学性的故事而已。

[19] 《久保惣纪念美术馆》，图13，内部发行，印行时间不详。

图二　纳尔逊孝子棺郭巨画像

（拓片反相，采自黄明兰：《洛阳北魏世俗石刻线画集》，第7页，图9）

图三　久保惣纪念美术馆藏北魏匡僧安墓石棺床屏风郭巨画像（郑岩绘图）

巨画像对应，只是细部略有些差别：如第二幅“回家”一节，郭巨肩扛金釜，而未与其妻分担；最后一幅郭母端坐在房内，与雷祖庙漆木棺画像所见一致。

在其他几套石棺床的屏风中，郭巨画像多为二幅式：第一幅为郭巨掘地得黄金的一刹那，郭妻怀抱小儿立于一侧；第二幅刻郭母坐于床上与孙子戏耍，郭巨夫妇立于堂下，省去了夫妇抬金釜还家的环节。如2004年入藏首都博物馆的一套石棺床的屏风中，第一幅榜题为：“孝子郭钜埋儿天赐金一父（釜）”，第二幅的榜题“孝子郭钜埋子府”刻于建筑上。[20]深圳展出北朝石棺床屏风上两幅榜题分别为：“孝子郭钜煞儿养母”、“孝子郭巨”（图四；图版17）。卢芹斋（C. T. Loo）旧藏的一组石棺床屏风其一为掘地得金，榜题为“孝子郭巨”，其二为供养母亲，榜题为“孝子郭巨天赐皇金”，文字似有错乱（图五）。[21]安阳固岸东魏武定六年谢氏冯僧晖墓出土石棺床屏风的两幅榜题分别为：“郭拒夫妻埋儿天赐黄金与之”、“孝子郭拒母（？）祠孙儿时”[22]，其画面与深圳展出北朝石棺床屏风较为接近。

纳尔逊·阿特金斯美术馆藏北魏石棺床屏风（长广敏雄简称之为“KB本”）上的郭巨画像只是一个单独的画面（图六）[23]，选取了故事最富戏剧性的掘地获金釜一节，与深圳博物馆藏石棺床和固岸东魏谢氏冯僧晖墓石棺床屏风第一幅相近。在单幅式画像中，2004年纽约展出的北朝彩绘贴金石棺床上的一例略有不同，其中郭巨肩荷耒，似背负一釜；郭巨子为郭妻牵引行走，而不是像其他例子那样在其怀抱中；画面右下角还有一冒着金光的釜；榜题曰“孝子郭钜煞儿养母天金一釜”（图七）。[24]这个画面把不同时间点上发生的故事集中在一起，可

图四　深圳展出北朝石棺床屏风郭巨画像

[20] 滕磊：《一件海外回流石棺床之我见》，《故宫博物院院刊》2009年第4期，第22~32页。

[21] 长广敏雄：《六朝時代美術の研究》，图版39。感谢林圣智先生惠赠这组石棺床画像的图片。

[22] 有关介绍见河南省文物考古研究所《河南安阳固岸墓地考古发掘收获》，但该文未发表郭巨故事画像的图片。

[23] 长广敏雄：《六朝時代美術の研究》，图版45。

[24] Annette L. Juliano and Judith A. Lerner, Stone Mortuary Furnishings of Northern China, *Ritual Objects and Early Buddhist Art*, Gisele Croes, Brussels, 2004, pp. 15–23, plates from page 24 to page 57. 有线索证明，这套石棺床是近年从西安地区流出的，可能属于北周的遗物。

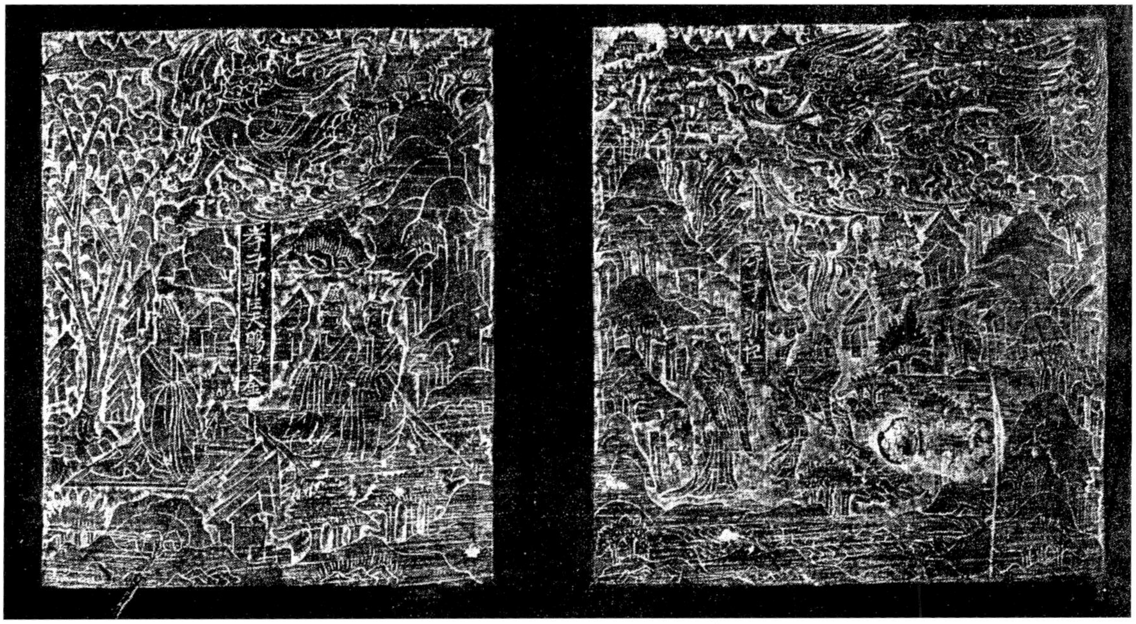

图五　卢芹斋旧藏北魏石棺床屏风郭巨画像（林圣智先生提供）

图六　纳尔逊美术馆藏北魏石棺床屏风郭巨画像
（郑岩绘图）

图七　2004年纽约展出北朝石棺床屏风郭巨画像
（郑岩绘图）

看作三幅式结构之第一、二部分的整合。美国明尼阿波利斯美术馆（The Minneapolis Institute of Arts）藏早年洛阳出土的北魏正光五年赵郡贞景王元谧石棺左侧的郭巨画像也是单幅式，但画面选择了最后的结局，而不是高潮，有榜题曰“孝子郭巨赐金一釜”（图八）。[25]此外，在河南邓县学庄（图九）、湖北襄阳贾家冲（图一〇）和襄樊麒麟村三座南朝墓出土的画像砖中也有单幅式的郭巨故事，皆表现了掘地获金釜的情节，由此或可窥见南北文化交流之一斑。

图八　明尼阿波利斯美术馆藏北魏元谧石棺郭巨画像（郑岩绘图）

这几种画像的形式繁简不同，但不管是“进化论”还是“退化论”，都不足以概括它们之间的关系，从比较丰富的北魏洛阳时代的材料可以看出，各种形式是并行不悖的，并不因为一种新的形式出现，旧的形式就退出历史舞台。深圳展出的一件北朝石棺床基座的横栏上，甚至再度出现了雷祖庙漆木棺所见的以三角纹分区的形式，只是其中的火焰改变为山峰，而山峰的刻画又综合了北魏洛阳的样式（图一一；图版 13）。

图九　河南邓县学庄南朝墓郭巨画像砖（郑岩绘图）

图一〇　湖北襄阳贾家冲南朝墓郭巨画像砖（采自《江汉考古》1986 年第 1 期，第 21 页）

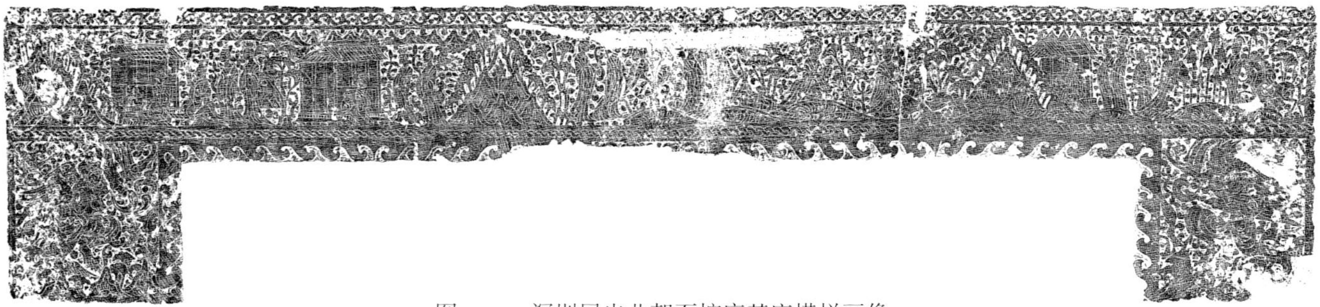

图一一　深圳展出北朝石棺床基座横栏画像

[25] 黄明兰：《洛阳北魏世俗石刻线画集》，第 38 页，图 43。

二

《后汉书》卷十下《顺烈梁皇后传》：“（顺烈梁皇后）少善女工，好史书，九岁能诵《论语》，治《韩诗》，大义略举。常以列女图画置于左右，以自监戒。”[26]皇后幼年的儒家启蒙教育，图史并用，可谓尽善尽美。其中“列女图画”盖指刘向编订的《列女传》的插图，此类图画在汉代民间流传较广，陕西绥德辛店呜咽泉东汉画像石墓中有题记云：“览樊姬观列女崇礼让遵大雅贵组绶富支子”。[27]但是，观看列女图的过程和效果真的如此高蹈清尚吗？《后汉书·宋弘传》曰：

弘当谯见，御坐新屏风，图画列女，帝数顾视之。弘正容言曰：“未见好德如好色者。”[28]

列女图原初的意义是“德”，但吸引汉光武帝的却是“色”。这是画工的责任，还是观者的责任呢？北朝葬具孝子图包含的问题可能更为复杂。工匠们所面临的任务不仅是忠实地表现原有的故事，他们还必须同时考虑到葬具及其画像的功用。这些葬具是各种利益和力量的交汇点，其图像可能受到不同人的左右。在这样的背景下，无论制作还是使用，图像形式和意义的转变都在所难免。

除了叙事方式的不同，图像与原有故事之间的差异更值得注意。例如，在纳尔逊石棺床屏风掘地得金一幅中，郭巨妻身后多了一个人物（见图六）；纽约展出的一例，郭巨子的年龄较大（见图七）；卢芹斋旧藏的石棺床屏风第二幅出现了一对男女和一位男子对坐（见图五）；元谧棺画像中一对男女和一个小童并肩坐于榻上，对面一男子合掌而拜（见图八）。在后两个例子中，被供奉的人物除了郭母，还有郭巨的父亲吗？或者工匠误将郭巨夫妇放置在了榻上？如果合掌叩拜者是郭巨的话，那么他的妻子又去了何方？在卢芹斋旧藏的屏风中为何不见小童？这些画面的差异，有的或许是由于工匠所依据的文本（包括口传的故事）不同，有的可能源于工匠的失误，有的则可能有着更为复杂的背景。

元谧棺两侧各刻有六幅孝子故事，这些故事的情节并不雷同，但画像中的每个部分均为山林间坐在大树下人物，为了追求这种同一性，工匠不惜回避故事的高潮情节，只有夹杂在其中的一些道具（如郭巨故事中的金釜）和榜题仍与故事原有情节保持着有限度的关联（图一二）。元谧棺画像对于原有故事的“偏离”不是偶然的，1977年洛阳出土的北魏石棺床屏风画像[29]进一步发展了这种倾向。有研究者认为其中一幅为郭巨故事（图一三）[30]，的确，我们可以注意到这幅画像与元谧棺画像的相似之处，如人物都坐于树下，榻上夫妇并坐，榻和大树之间还有一小童。但是，画像中人物的身份更加模糊，“供奉与被供奉”的二元对立关系不复存在，小童不在榻上，标志性的金釜也不翼而飞。更为重要的一个变化是，画面中没有题记，作者不再借助文字来建立图像与故事内容的链接，只有空白的榜框作为一种失去功能的形式遗留下来。这套石棺床其余多扇屏风上的画面主题更为模糊，尽管有研究者将其解释为丁兰、原縠、老莱子、眉间赤等故事[31]，但这些画面大同小异，大多缺少与故事情节、人物身份相关的标志，也没有题记，我们看到的只是在大树下、山石间或立或坐的人物（图一四）。

更为复杂的是深圳展出北朝石棺床基座横栏一图（见图一一、图版13）。上文谈到，该图的三角形的山峰来源于固原雷祖庙漆木棺的火焰纹，但是，

[26]《后汉书》，第438页，中华书局，1965年。

[27] 吴兰、志安、春宁：《绥德辛店发现的两座画像石墓》，《考古与文物》1993年第1期，第17~22页。题记释读据张俐《论陕北东汉铭文刻石》，朱青生主编《中国汉画研究》第二卷，第215~216页，广西师范大学出版社，2006年。

[28]《后汉书》，第904页。

[29] 黄明兰：《洛阳北魏世俗石刻线画集》，第73~76页，图81~84；周到主编：《中国画像石全集》第8卷，第55~78页，图74~78。

[30] 周到主编：《中国画像石全集》第8卷，“图版说明”第20页，图74解说词。

[31] 周到主编：《中国画像石全集》第8卷，“图版说明”第21页，图75~78解说词。这套画像中有一幅未收入该书，但见于黄明兰《洛阳北魏世俗石刻线画集》第74页图82右端，该图中有一蛇，赵超据此考为伯奇故事，其说应可成立（见氏著《关于伯奇的古代孝子图画》，《考古与文物》2004年第3期，第68~72页）。

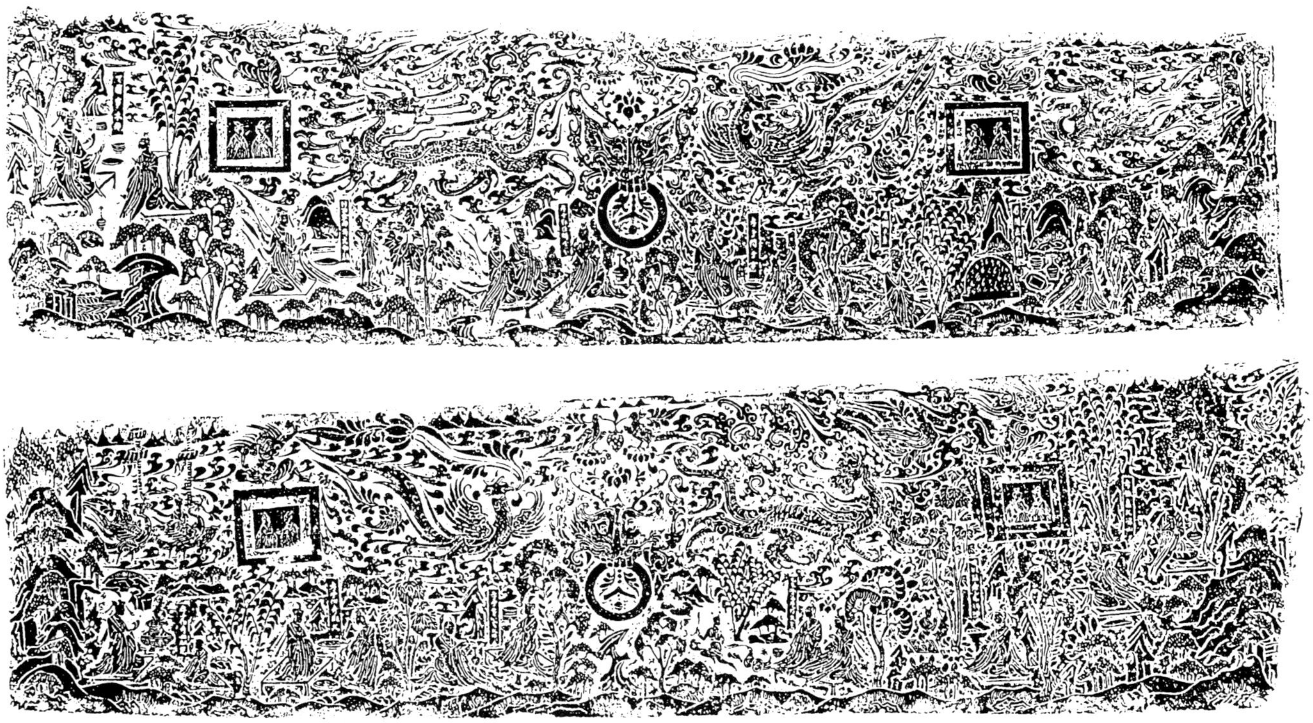

图一二　明尼阿波利斯美术馆藏北魏元谧石棺画像
（采自《瓜茄》第5号，大阪瓜茄研究所，1939年，插页图）

图一三　河南洛阳出土北魏石棺床屏风郭巨画像
（拓片，采自周到主编《中国画像石全集》第8卷，第55页，图74；线图，郑岩绘图）

一个重要的改变是，深圳展出北朝石棺床基座横栏一图并没有保留雷祖庙棺严谨的叙事程序，相反却变得十分混乱，故事的高潮出现于D区；B、E两区的画面大同小异，似乎重复表现了故事大团圆的结局[32]；A区的房屋与B、E区所见近似，但房屋内外的人数却与故事不符；E区的郭巨夫妇（？）身后多了一位手持盖的侍者；C、F区的人物、鞍马完全与故事无关（图一五）。

综合来看，这些葬具上的画像可以分为两个层次，其一是画像的局部，其二是整套画像的集合。第一层次表现故事的情节和人物的个性，第二层次强调总体视觉效果和共同的意义。这两个层次在不同作品中的表现有所差别，以固原雷祖庙漆木棺画像为例，在第一个层面上，郭巨故事完整有序，观者可以依次观看故事的各个单元，就像阅读文字记述的故事一样。着眼于第二个层次来看，这些画像位于棺

图一四　河南洛阳出土北魏石棺床屏风人物画像（采自周到主编《中国画像石全集》第8卷，第56~59页，图75~78）

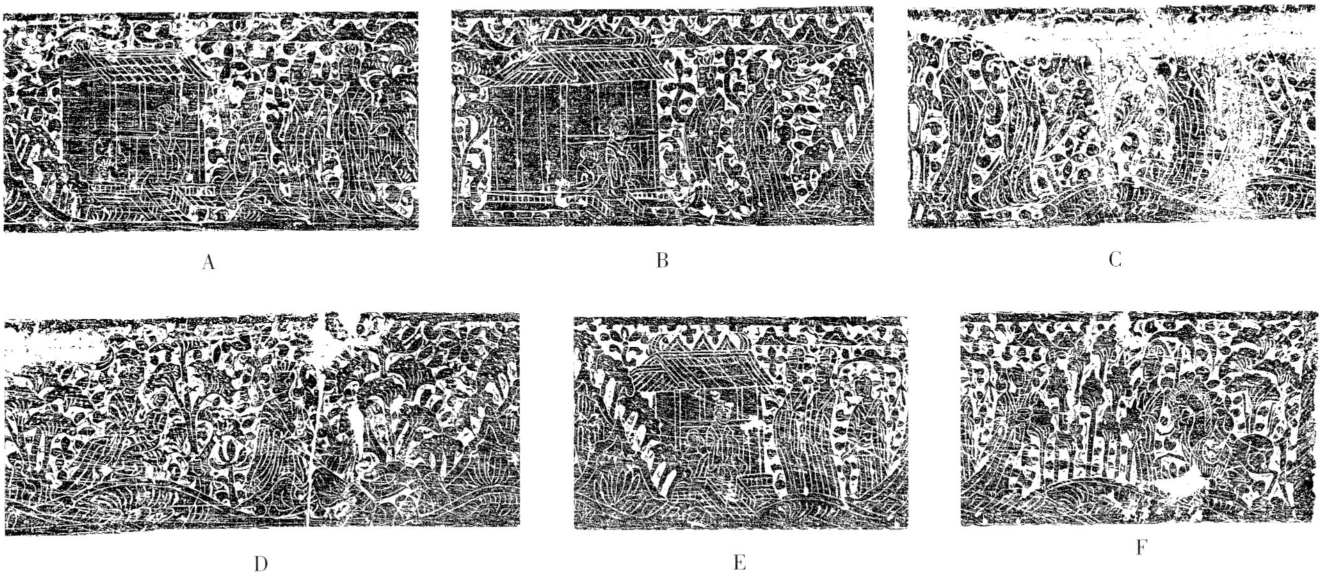

图一五　深圳展出北朝石棺床基座横栏画像局部

［32］这些带有房屋的部分或者将丁兰、老莱子等故事混入，但具体的主题难以考证。

侧面的上部近边缘处，各单元之间杂有三角形火焰纹，中心部分为龟甲纹和圆形交织的纹样所占据。这些杂侧于各种几何纹样中的故事图画更像是一个装饰系统的附件，而不是独立的绘画，或者说，故事本身所表达的意义在整个漆棺上并不突出。观者如果没有足够的耐心按部就班地观看，那么，这些孝子故事就只能是“装饰性”地存在。第一个层次的叙事性在纳尔逊孝子棺的表现最为成功，其故事情节完整准确，个性鲜明，内容与形式有着完美的结合。[33]但这并不影响它同时在第二个层次上显示出一些共性，如整套石棺每侧三个故事的布局、均匀排列的榜题，都突出了形式上的整体感，山石、树木在分割空间的同时，也使得每个故事历时性展开的各单元具有了视觉上的共时性，如果观者原本不熟悉故事的内容，恐怕也难以从中找到头绪（图一六）。[34]元谧石棺画像在第一个层次上更为弱化，每个故事的个性特征模糊，迅速地转向第二个层次上的同一性（见图一二）。在深圳展出北朝石棺床基座横栏上，第一个层次上的时间概念变得十分凌乱，而强化了由总体形象所营造的一种视觉氛围，原有的故事只是若有若无地浮现出来（见图一一、图版 13）。

在北魏洛阳时代，那些处于同一时期、同一地域、同一社会阶层、选取了同样艺术母题的画像，显现出各不相同的指向，而上述两个层面的变通、协调、转换，实际上也包含了工匠们煞费苦心的筹算与经营。要对这些现象做出解释，不能不将葬具及其画像的外围的各种因素考虑进来。

图一六　纳尔逊孝子棺画像

（采自 William Watson, *The Arts of China to AD 900*, New Haven and London: Yale University Press, 1995, p.156, fig.252）

[33] 我曾在他处分析过纳尔逊孝子棺王琳画像形式与情节之间的关系，见《正面的马，背面的马》，《文物天地》2002 年第 2 期，第 58~59 页。

[34] 例如，当纳尔逊孝子棺上的郭巨故事大致按照自左而右的顺序展开时，相邻的孝孙原榖故事却是从右至左展开。

三

孝，最初指的是尊祖敬宗，后演变为对近亲的敬重与奉养。具体到丧葬环境中，孝子图必须满足和平衡死去的父亲和（或）母亲与其子女两方面的利益。

首先讨论孝子图与死者子女的关系。我们暂时告别郭巨，借助蔡顺画像对此加以观察。蔡顺在火灾中以身体保护亡母之棺的事迹见于《后汉书·周磐传》：

> 母年九十，以寿终。未及得葬，里中灾，火将逼其舍，顺抱伏棺柩，号哭叫天，火遂越烧它室，顺独得免。[35]

蔡顺画像最为精彩的一例见于纳尔逊孝子棺，该棺右侧中部刻画了蔡顺护棺的情景（图一七）[36]。我在这里不再讨论画像的叙事方式问题，换一个角度看，这幅画像还透露出葬具制作完毕而“未及得葬”期间存放的情况，以及孝子和葬具的关系。故事是汉代的，但画像可能同时反映了北朝的状况。

葬具是从墓室中出土的，然而除了结合墓室的环境来理解其形制及画像，还要考虑到在葬具埋入墓室之前制作、赠送、购买和丧礼等环节，考虑到在这些环节中葬具与各种人物之间的联系。由于文献中缺少相关记载，因此蔡顺画像所透露出的这类信息就特别值得注意。在此基础上，我提出一个假

图一七　纳尔逊孝子棺蔡顺画像

（拓片反相，采自黄明兰：《洛阳北魏世俗石刻线画集》，第4页，图6）

[35]《后汉书》，第1312页。

[36] 黄明兰：《洛阳北魏世俗石刻线画集》，第1~10页。

设：在死者安葬之前，人们有机会看到葬具以及上面的画像，有机会在视觉和意义上建立起画像与死者后人——那些新孝子——之间的联系。

关于北朝葬具制作的情况，我们了解的十分有限。《洛阳伽蓝记》卷三记汉代人崔涵复活的故事：

> 洛阳太市北奉终里，里内之人多卖送死人之具及诸棺椁，涵谓曰："作柏木棺，勿以桑木为欀。"人问其故，涵曰："吾在地下，见人发鬼兵，有一鬼诉称是柏棺，应免。主兵吏曰：'尔虽柏棺，桑木为欀。'遂不免。"京师闻此，柏木踊贵。人疑卖棺者货涵，发此等之言也。[37]

由此可知北魏洛阳太市以北奉终里的居民"多卖送死人之具及诸棺椁"，这些棺椁多为木质。唐人段成式《酉阳杂俎》十三"尸穸篇"云："后魏俗竞厚葬，棺厚高大，多用柏木，两边作大铜环钮。"[38]对比元谧石棺的形制，可知北魏的石棺模仿了这些木棺的造型。也许那些木棺上也有着华美的画像，固原雷祖庙出土的漆木棺就是一个旁证，如雷祖庙漆木棺上"窥窗"的细节，就呈现于元谧石棺上[39]。

美国波士顿美术馆藏1931年洛阳故城北半坡出土北魏孝昌三年（527）横野将军甄官住簿宁想石室正面门侧有"孝子宁万寿"、"孝子弟宁双寿造"的题名[40]，文字刻划十分粗陋，与石室其他榜题中精心雕刻的文字风格差别明显，疑为宁想的两个儿子双寿、万寿购得葬具后加刻的题名。邹清泉推测宁想石室可能是从负责制作宫廷丧葬用品的"东园"订购的[41]。果真如此，则需要对于东园的性质重新加以评估。不管何种可能性成立，这套葬具仍属于商品。那么，这就意味着其上的画像可能在出售时被人们看到。

按照贺西林的意见，有些刻有画像的北朝葬具，如元谧石棺，属于由官方制作的"东园秘器"[42]。那么，这些代表着帝王恩泽的葬具，很有可能在葬礼的过程中有一段时间陈列出来，成为被众人观看的对象。另外，在中国古代，乃至今天许多地区的农村，预制寿材比预作寿藏是更为普遍的现象[43]。那些事先制作的葬具，有更长的时间、更多的机会被其他人看到。

在先秦和汉代的送葬行列中，棺可能以柩车、輀车等运载，其外部多有包装和装饰[44]，但山东青州傅家北齐武平四年（573）墓画像石还表现了葬礼行列中一具木结构的房屋形葬具完全展现在公众视野中的情景（图一八）[45]。由此推测，在葬礼的某

---

[37] 范祥雍：《洛阳伽蓝记校注》，第174~175页。

[38] 段成式：《酉阳杂俎》，第123页，中华书局，1981年。

[39] 郑岩：《说"窥窗"》，《设计艺术研究》2012年第1期，第29~32页。

[40] 黄明兰：《洛阳北魏世俗石刻线画集》，第95~96页；郭建邦：《北魏宁懋石室线刻画》，人民美术出版社，1987年。国内多种出版物在介绍该石室时，误认为该画像在祠堂正壁的内面，实际上应在正壁外侧。我多次到波士顿美术馆目验实物，该馆对该石室的拼合配置并无错误。此前的研究者多将与石室同出的墓志中死者的姓名读作"宁懋"，最近曹讯主张读为"宁想"，这样便可与其字"阿念"互训（见曹汛《北魏宁想石室新考订》，王贵祥主编：《中国建筑史论汇刊》第4辑，第77~125页，清华大学出版社，2011年）。林圣智及曹汛均认为石室为祠堂而非葬具，其理由恐嫌不足（见林圣智：《北魏宁懋石室的图像与功能》，《美术史研究集刊》第十八期，2005年，第1~74页）。

[41] 邹清泉：《北魏孝子画像研究》，第43~45页。

[42] 贺西林：《北朝画像石葬具的发现与研究》，第361~362页。贺西林主要的依据是《魏书·元谧传》的记载"（谧）正光四年（523）薨。给东园秘器、朝服一具、衣一袭，赗帛五百匹"（《魏书》，第544页）。

[43] 例如，摄影家焦波曾拍摄其在山东博山区天津湾村生活的父母在寿材前的合影（焦波《俺爹俺娘》，第102~104页，山东画报出版社，1998年）。

[44]《仪礼·既夕礼》："商祝饰柩"，郑玄注："饰柩为设墙柳也，巾奠乃墙，谓此也。墙有布帷，柳有布荒。"贾公彦疏云："云'饰柩为设墙柳也'者，即加帷荒是也。"（郑玄注，贾公彦疏，十三经注疏整理委员会整理：《仪礼注疏》，第847~848页，北京大学出版社，2000年）《礼记·丧大记》郑注："棺饰者，……荒，蒙也，在旁曰帷，在上曰荒，皆所以衣柳也。"孔颖达疏："'黻荒'者，荒，蒙也，谓柳车上覆，谓鳖甲车也。"（郑玄注，孔颖达疏，十三经注疏整理委员会整理：《礼记正义》第1496~1497页，北京大学出版社，2000年）汉代送葬的画像见于山东微山沟南墓石椁画像（王思礼、赖非、丁冲、万良：《山东微山县汉代画像石调查简报》，《考古》1989年第8期，第707页）和江苏沛县龙固镇三里庙村画像石（刘尊志：《徐州汉墓与汉代社会研究》，第284页，科学出版社，2011年）。

[45] 夏名采：《青州傅家北齐画像石补遗》，《文物》2001年第4期，第92~93页。对于这一画像性质的研究，见郑岩《魏晋南北朝壁画墓研究》，第241~246页，文物出版社，2002年；郑岩：《葬礼与图像——以两汉北朝材料为中心》，《美术研究》2013年第4期，第64~76页。

图一八　山东青州傅家北齐墓画像石

（郑岩绘图）

个环节，葬具的画像有可能被公众看到。[46]

考虑到上述制作、颁赐、送葬等情况，这些葬具就具有了双重的性质，即除了最终秘藏于墓室之中，还可能在安葬之前用以陈列和展示。葬具上的画像造型准确，线条优雅畅达，外表施以鲜艳的色彩和贴金（可惜较少保存下来），这些画面除了表现道德或宗教的意义，还愉悦我们的眼睛[47]。这些跨越了千百年的图画至今能够打动我们，相信6世纪的人也应该有着与我们相近的感受。也许只有在“被观看”的前提下，才能更好地解释这些画像风格之精妙、形式之多样。

葬具画像所预设的第一批观者可能并非死者的后人，这些画像不是童蒙读物的插图，对新孝子的教化应该发生在更早的时候，而不是在其父母的葬礼上。帝王将带有孝子图的葬具赐予逝者，包含了对于死者后人——那些新一代的孝子——的赞誉，因此新孝子们会急不可待地将这种荣耀展现给公众。即使是死者后人出资制造和购买的葬具，他们也希望参加葬礼的人们看到葬具上的画像。

的确，父母的去世，是那些意欲博取名声的新孝子们表演其孝行难得的时机。在南北朝正史“孝友”、“孝行”、“孝德”之类的列传中，传主的孝行常常体现于如何安葬和追悼逝去的父母，故“负土成坟”、“庐于墓侧”、“三年泣血”之类的套话比比皆是。如同郭巨故事一样，蔡顺的故事在六朝正史中也被一再被抄袭[48]，甚至多处用词雷同，如“母”、“居丧”、“为邻火所逼”、“号哭”等，都出现于新的孝子故事中。换言之，作者套用了描述既有孝子事迹的文字来记录新的故事。这种抄袭、移植欺世盗名，但另一方面也建立了古代典范与现世人物之间的关联，古孝子不仅是新孝子的道德榜样，而且成为塑造新孝子形象的“模具”，新孝子

［46］我此前曾谈到，该墓画像石可能受到粟特入华美术的影响（郑岩：《魏晋南北朝壁画墓研究》，第236~284页）。乐仲迪（Judith Lerner）指出，该画像中的犬应与粟特丧葬中的“犬视”（Sagdīd）有关（Judith Lerner, “Zoroastrian Funerary Beliefs and Practices Known from the Sino-Sogdian Tombs in China,” *The Silk Road*, Volume 9, [2011], pp. 18~25），进一步证明画像表现的是送葬的场面。值得注意的是，在纳尔逊孝子棺蔡顺画像的右下部也有一只犬，这一细节与蔡顺故事原有的情节并无直接关系，这是否说明北魏葬具画像的制作，也受到粟特美术的影响呢？《魏书·宣武灵皇后胡氏列传》记：“后幸嵩高山，夫人、九嫔、公主已下从者数百人，升于顶中。废诸淫祀，而胡天神不在其列。”（《魏书》，第338页）陈垣据此认为“胡天之祀，始于北魏”（陈垣：《火祆教入中国考》，《国学季刊》第1卷第1号［1923年］，第29~30页），但是如果说到这一时期与祆教信仰相关的习俗和图像对中原墓葬的影响，则未敢过分估量之。我们尚不能完全排除同时存在的犬也与丧葬有着特定的关联。如果这种可能性存在，那么，这或许意味着画像除了表现蔡顺的故事外，同时也与丧礼的场景有关。我于此暂备一说，更待后证。

［47］类似优雅的风格，并且同样是用了多种技术和材料的另一个相近的例子是南朝高等级大墓中的竹林七贤和荣启期彩绘模印拼镶砖画。南朝砖画密封在墓室中，似乎与审美的眼睛无关，但这种风格确也曾引导研究者推测这些墓葬中的绘画，原本是对于一些著名画家的画稿的复制。根据文献记载，竹林七贤是许多画家画过的题材。

［48］邹清泉首先注意到这个问题，见氏著《北魏孝子画像研究》第109~110页。这种例子极多，如《晋书·孝友·何琦》：“及丁母尤，居丧泣血，杖而后起。停柩在殡，为邻火所逼，烟焰已交，家乏僮使，计无从出，乃匍匐抚棺号哭。俄而风止火息，堂屋一间免烧，其精诚所感如此。”（《晋书》，中华书局，第2292页，1974年）《宋书·孝义列传·贾恩》：“元嘉三年（426），母亡，居丧过礼。未葬，为邻火所逼，恩及妻桓氏号哭奔救，邻近赴助，棺榇得免。恩及桓俱见烧死。”（《宋书》，第2243页）

也因此成为古孝子穿越时空的化身。在葬具上刻画孝子图，则又一次将孝的主题与墓葬结合在一起。这些葬具上的孝子图并不直接描绘新孝子的形象，而是继续表现那些古代的样板。在葬具和墓葬中描摹活人的形象，既不吉利，也缺乏恒久的价值；只有那些经受了岁月的考验古代孝子，才可以镌刻在坚硬石头上，彰显其恒久的价值。在这里，这些形象起到一种媒介的作用。

与从文本到文本的复制方式不同，图像的复制则通过更为物质性的手段，在具体的礼仪环境去实现。纳尔逊孝子棺两侧除了蔡顺故事，还刻画了其他的孝行故事，包括舜、郭巨、原榖、董永和王琳。如上文所述郭巨故事所见，这些画面多以两个或三个单元表现同一个故事，主人公在画面中多次出场。但蔡顺的故事却只有一个场景，虽然画面看上去大致可分为蔡宅和邻宅两部分，但实际上，这两个部分是共时性的关系——在邻居的房屋火焰正旺的时候，蔡顺俯卧到母亲的棺上。作者意在集中表现这个高潮情节，而不是故事的来龙去脉。换言之，画面没有凸显故事的起承转合，而是一个相对静态的场景，突出了蔡顺与棺的关系。这种“静态”还来源于房屋、棺的直线所形成强烈的“块面感”，这种视觉效果与其余部分山石、树木所形成的漫回流转的动感迥然不同，它使得这部分画像成为视觉的焦点。

上文在分析郭巨画像时谈到了葬具画像的“两个层次”，结合蔡顺画像独特的形式，并将观者的因素考虑进来，我们可以继续发展“层次”的概念，对当时的“观看”作推测性的复原：第一，观者被各个局部画面戏剧性的故事情节所吸引，思绪进入画面所营造的虚拟时空中，而忘记了石棺的存在；第二，观者后退一步，故事的细节逐渐模糊起来，画面的整体性变得更为重要，那些事迹不同的孝子们作为一个集合所具有的共同意义凸显出来；第三，在丧礼中，如果观者的视阈继续扩展，石棺作为一件“实物”的形象呈现出来，更为重要的是，观者可能还会看到新孝子就站立在棺的旁边（图一九）。

在最后一步，“新孝子和石棺的关系”与画像中“蔡顺和蔡母之棺的关系”相平行，新孝子对应着蔡顺，真实的棺对应着画像中的棺，画中的场景在画外重现。在新孝子表演着古孝子故事的同时，古孝子图也成为新孝子映射在石棺上的影子。不管死者的后人是否真的富有孝心，至少在仪式和图像的综合作用下，他已经被装扮成一位孝子。

也许蔡顺画像只是个特例，实际上，多数孝子图与新孝子的关联并不需要如此机械和复杂，孝子

图一九　孝子与孝子棺（郑岩绘图）

图所包含意义可以被轻易地转移到新孝子身上。石棺画像题榜上古孝子的姓名彰彰在目，无法剥夺其事迹的归属权，然而，新孝子俨然可以与这些古代样板相提并论，当人们称赞新孝子的德行时，用在古孝子身上的赞辞便可随时发挥作用，就像史书中将蔡顺的事迹套在新孝子身上一样。

当制作者和观者的兴趣更多地转向孝子图作为一个集合所具备的共同意义时，故事本身就不再重要。复杂的是，如果原有的人物身份、事件、年代、场合等被淡化，那么，一旦有其他的力量介入，孝子故事就不再具备原有的控制力，图像的意义就会发生偏移。

四

另一种力量来自死者。

孝子们在丧礼中的孝行是一次性的表演，“庐墓三年”、“三年无改于父之道”，以及定期的祭祀，虽然可以使他们的孝行在一定程度上得以延续，但那些葬具终究要与死者一起进入另一个世界。也许新孝子的德行可以通过古孝子的画像获得永恒的价值，从而永远陪伴在死者的左右，缓解了死者在另一个世界的孤独。[49]但是，在汉代人看来，生者有室宅，死者有棺椁，二者是互无干涉的。那么，埋入墓葬以后，葬具上的孝子图还会起到什么作用？它们与死者的利益有何关系呢？

我们上文谈到郭巨故事的“变形”，实际上，这种现象并不罕见。

町田章注意到江苏丹阳吴家村南朝墓竹林七贤与荣启期砖画的人物都老人化，他指出：“这不外乎是把作为实在的隐士的竹林七贤，改变为理想境界的隐士和方士。”“壁画的意义在很大程度上转向对神仙的礼赞。”针对金家村和吴家村墓题记中出现的混乱，他谈道：“对于每个人物的人名也未予以重视，这不正说明了把全体作为理想的隐士的看法是能够成立的吗？”[50]赵超曾研究南北朝时期竹林七贤的形象被神仙化的问题，认为“‘竹林七贤’由于其秉承老庄，宣扬玄学，加上世人的渲染，道教的流行，使得他们已经有所神化，成为具有道教意义的宗教偶像”[51]。我也讨论过南北朝墓葬中高士题材意义的转化，指出这些在南北朝社会受人尊崇的文化样板，在墓葬中被看做了墓主升仙途中的同道者或伙伴，而丧失其原有的意义。[52]元谧石棺画像所见人物坐在树下的图式并不是孝子们特有的，南北朝墓葬中的高士画像也多是这种树下的坐像（图二〇）。[53]尽管可以在南京西善桥墓的砖画中看到高士个人之间微妙的差别，但作为集合式的肖像（collective portrait）[54]，他们共同的特征十分明显。其求仙意义的表达，是通过在不断复制的过程中弱化每位高士的个性特征来实现的。在山东临朐海浮山北齐天保二年（551）崔芬墓壁画中所见的高士图，已经无法分辨每个人的身份，更无法讲述其独特的故事，我们看到的只是一些坐在树下大同小异的人物（图二一）。[55]这种趋向和元谧石棺画像所见非常相似。

穿插在深圳石棺床基座横栏郭巨画像间的一些细节也值得注意，如C区所见的人物（见图一五），在王子云发表的一套石棺床屏风[56]（图

---

[49] 如林圣智指出，孝子图可以作为生者与死者之间的连接，并代替生者在墓葬中侍奉墓主。见林圣智：《北朝时代における葬具の图像と机能—石棺床围屏の墓主肖像と孝子传图を例として—》。

[50] 町田章著，劳继译：《南齐帝陵考》，《东南文化》第2辑，第51页，江苏古籍出版社，1987年。

[51] 赵超：《从南京出土的南朝竹林七贤壁画谈开去》，《中国典籍与文化》2000年第3期，第4~10页。

[52] 郑岩：《魏晋南北朝壁画墓研究》，第209~235页，文物出版社，2002年。

[53] 这种形式在康业墓中，还用以表现墓主的形象。见郑岩《逝者的“面具”——论北周康业墓石棺床画像》（修订稿），收入《从考古学到美术史——郑岩自选集》，第124~130页，上海人民出版社，2012年。

[54] Audrey Spiro, *Contemplating the Ancients*, Berkeley: University of California Press, 1990, p.98.

[55] 临朐县博物馆：《北齐崔芬壁画墓》，文物出版社，2002年。

[56] 王子云：《中国古代石刻画选集》，图5.7、5.9。这套石棺床的其他相关的图版又见：黄明兰《洛阳北魏世俗石刻线画集》，第79~90页，图87~98；周到主编《中国画像石全集》第8卷，第67~68页，图86~87，该书图版说明称“原石流失美国”。

图二〇　江苏南京西善桥宫山南朝墓竹林七贤与荣启期模印拼镶砖壁画
（采自姚迁、古兵：《六朝艺术》，文物出版社，1981 年，图 162、163）

图二一　山东临朐海浮山北齐崔芬墓西壁壁画（郑岩绘图）

二二）、分藏于日本天理参考馆和旧金山亚洲艺术博物馆的一套石棺床屏风[57]中都可以见到相近的例子，长广敏雄将后者称为“林间逍遥图”[58]，我怀疑是一些出入于山林间的高士或神仙。李小旋注意到，邓县学庄南朝墓画像砖中的郭巨妻高髻峨峨，身穿华服，竟与纳尔逊孝子棺上董永画像中的女仙无异。她将这一现象解释为对于汉代以来既有人物画模本的“传移”。[59]除此之外，脱离故事原有人物身份的变形现象，也应当有着意义层面的背景。孝子图中的这些变化，可能意在将故事中的人物转化为与神仙无异的角色，陪伴在死者左右，从而使得葬具和墓葬诗化为死者去往仙境的通道。[60]

在江苏丹阳鹤仙坳墓[61]、建山金家村墓[62]、胡桥吴家村墓[63]等大型南朝墓，墓室后部有竹林七贤与荣启期画像，前部有大幅的仙人引导的青龙、白虎（图二三），砖侧阴刻“大龙”、“大虎”等文字。南朝大墓所见的龙虎，在元谧棺画像中也可看到。后者的变化，不过是将竹林七贤与荣启期更换为各种孝子的形象，但二者树下人物的图式，以及与大龙大虎的组合，都十分相近，这些画面所衍生的意义也没有根本性的差别。

在洛阳出土的多套装饰龙虎的北魏石棺增加了前后引导的羽人，与南朝墓所见更为类似。例如，1977年洛阳北郊上窑浐河东砖瓦厂出土的一具石棺，

图二二　河南洛阳出土北魏石棺床屏风人物画像（采自王子云：《中国古代石刻画选集》，图5.7、5.9）

[57] 长广敏雄：《六朝時代美術の研究》，图版29~34，第148页，图41。
[58] 长广敏雄：《六朝時代美術の研究》，第148页。
[59] 李小旋：《试论中国早期绘画中人物形象的再利用——以邓县南朝画像砖墓之郭巨故事图为例》，《中国美术研究》16辑，第25~33页，东南大学出版社，2015年。
[60] 邓菲研究了宋金墓葬中孝子图与升仙的关系（邓菲：《关于宋金墓葬中孝行图的思考》）。这些变化与北朝葬具石棺床孝子图之间的关系还值得进一步思考。
[61] 南京博物院：《江苏丹阳胡桥南朝大墓及砖刻壁画》，《文物》1974年第2期，第44~56页。
[62] 南京博物院：《江苏丹阳胡桥、建山两座南朝墓葬》，《文物》1980年第2期，第1~17页。
[63] 南京博物院：《江苏丹阳胡桥、建山两座南朝墓葬》，《文物》1980年第2期，第1~17页。

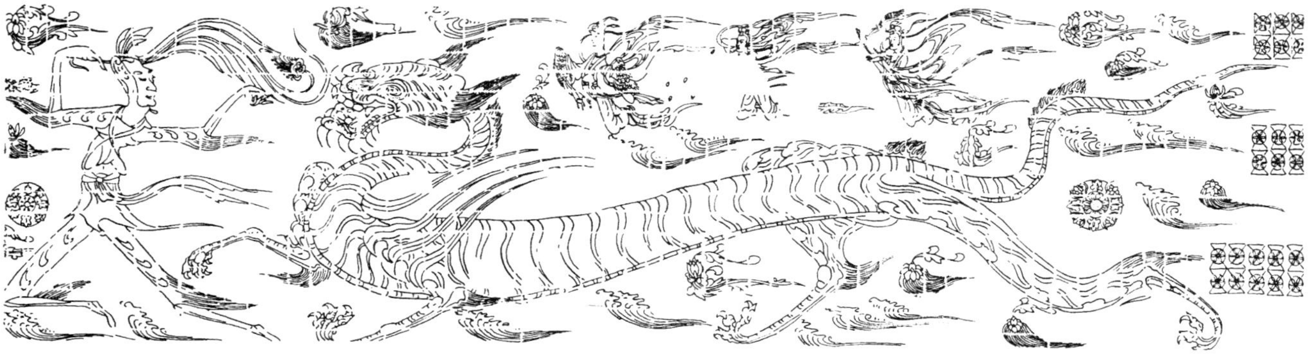

图二三　江苏丹阳金家村南朝墓白虎模印拼镶砖壁画（郑岩绘图）

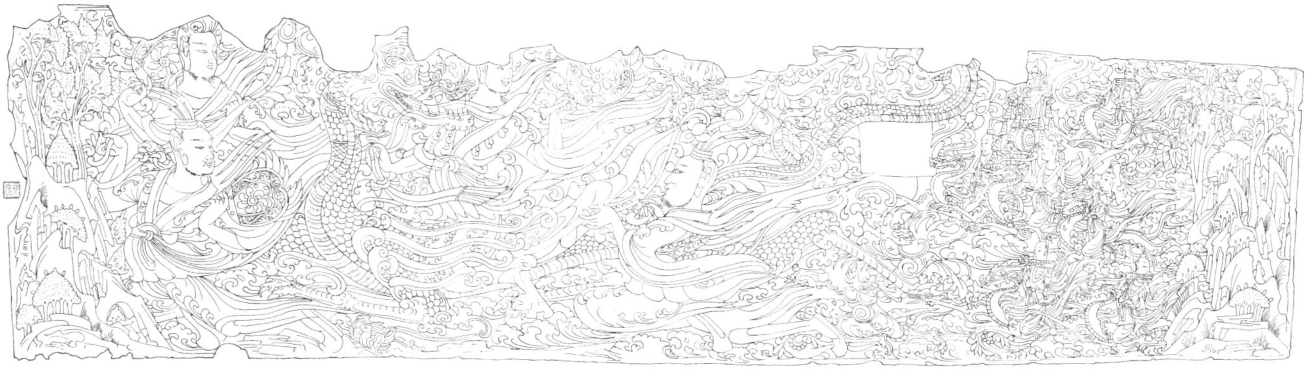

图二四　河南洛阳上窑出土北魏石棺左侧男墓主升仙画像（郑岩绘图）

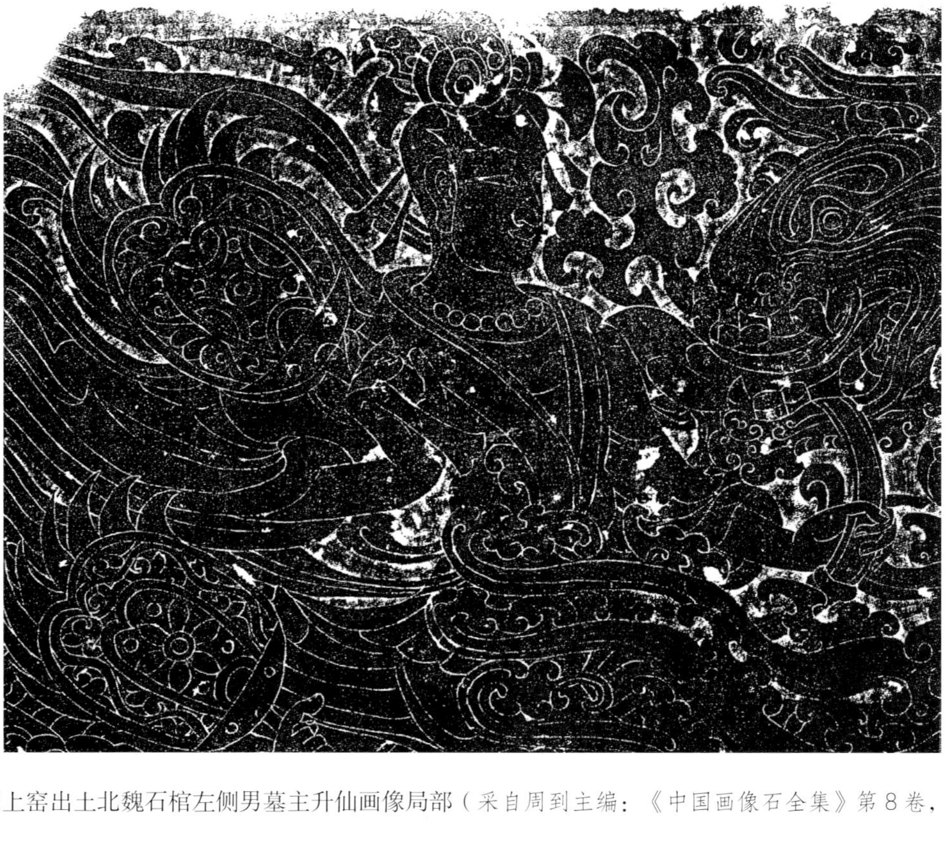

图二五　河南洛阳上窑出土北魏石棺左侧男墓主升仙画像局部（采自周到主编：《中国画像石全集》第8卷，第45页，图60）

刻画了墓主骑龙骑虎，在仙人、乐伎、怪兽的呼拥下升仙的场景（图二四、二五）。[64]这套画像表面上与孝子题材不同，但却可以通过元谧棺所见的龙虎、怪兽等共有的图像衔接起来，而孝子图本身的变形，则是更为巧妙的一种衔接方式。而这类驮载有神人的龙虎、怪兽在北齐崔芬墓壁画中也可以见到，只是与之相配的是屏风上的高士而已（见图二一）。

龙虎是求仙者的坐骑，羽人是求仙者的引导、护卫者，身份转换后的高士、孝子是求仙者同道，而求仙者则是死者本人。孝子图最初主要指向死者后人的荣耀，而转换后的画面又与死者的利益结合在一起。在1977年洛阳出土的石棺床和深圳展出北朝石棺床屏风中，还可以看到孝子图与墓主的偶像并存。即使没有出现墓主的画像，这些葬具还是要和死者的遗体一同被掩埋在墓葬之中。

制作北朝葬具画像的工匠可以在一项作品中强调与死者后人声誉相关的孝，也可以在另一项作品上突出与死者利益相关的升仙，更可以在同一项作品中通过其巧妙的手法，取得“一语双关”的效果。这样，无论是死者的利益，还是其后人的荣耀，便都可以在这些葬具上呈现出来，又不至于造成这些图像的对立与分裂。

从思想史的角度来看，这里的孝道或神仙观念并没有多少超越前代的实质性发展。无论孝子，还是升仙，就其内容而言，均是一些陈词滥调。孝子图固然是汉代以来就流行的题材，而升仙题材在内容上也缺少任何新鲜的发明。只要对比一下汉代的情况，就可以感受到南北朝升仙题材在思想方面的是何等苍白。虽然文献中并没有明确留下汉代关于死后成仙的系统的理论，但是在墓葬和祠堂中，却可以看到汉代人正通过各种艺术形式来建构一套与神仙信仰有关的图像体系。也许这些图像最初并非出现于墓葬或祠堂中，但它们的确对丧葬产生了深刻的影响。初步看来，这个图像体系大致包括三个方面：其一是以西王母为核心，以各种仙人为辅的神格系统；其二是关于仙境的想象与描述，包括仙岛、昆仑山、天门、楼阁等母题；其三是去往仙境的途径，包括天马、神鹿、玉女、六博以及部分车马行列。这个系统可能只是流行在某些地区或社会中下层，也并未为所有的人接受，更没有最后完成和定型，但是这些尝试性的图像却生动鲜活，富有想象力和创造性。

与之相比，北朝葬具上所见的升仙画像却显得单薄、空洞，无非是四神、引导的羽人、各种怪兽和乘龙骑风的乐工等等，关于仙境的具体描述以及有关的神格，均十分少见，更不见创造性的新母题。至于有的学者将这些图像看作是道教美术，更是难以切中肯綮。实际上，这些图像缺乏制度化宗教中所具备的系统的理论和相关仪式，我们只能从中看到传统思想的延续。关于死亡更为系统、新颖的理论和思想，可能要到那些石窟和佛教造像上去寻找。洛阳城内外寺塔林立，伊阙、巩县的石窟正在大规模地开凿，越来越多的人祈求死者的灵魂能够进入佛教经典细致描述、大量图像精心构筑出天堂，而对于死者肉身的安葬，只是依据传统的礼仪照章办事而已。除了一些装饰性的莲花图案，佛教思想、教义和相关利益，并没有大量融入这些葬具画像中。至于所谓的祆教信仰，则只是有限地出现于这一时期进入中原的粟特等外来移民的墓葬中。如果说南北朝的工匠对于建构升仙图像系统还有一些贡献的话，那么就是模糊了与高士和孝子题材绘画的边界，甚至在某种意义上将这些人物故事题材吸收到了以神仙信仰为核心的图像系统中。

与内容相比，更重要的是图像形式上的变化。在这些围绕着死亡展开的艺术创作实践中，身份卑微的工匠们通过对于形式的微妙调整，平衡着相关的各种利益，将沉闷乏味的主题表现得丰富多彩，各有千秋。至于构图中对于空间关系的探索，对于树木、山石这些新物象的描摹，疏密有致雍容条畅的线法，以及彩绘与贴金，更是在内容之外对于艺术语言的积极追求。可以说，这个时代特有的“艺术自觉”，不仅呈现于那些师承有序的大师身上，也不仅呈现于形形色色的绘画样式和理论中，而且，也一斧一凿，镌刻在这些深埋于黄泉的青石之上。

[64]洛阳博物馆：《洛阳北魏画像石棺》，《考古》1980年第3期，第229~241页。

The Shapes and Meanings of Filial Piety Images on Northern Dynasties Burial Furnishings

Zheng Yan
(Professor, China Central Academy of Fine Arts)

The Shenzhen Museum's "The Eternal Northern Dynasties" stone-engraving art exhibit displays a group of exquisite and varied Northern Dynasties (386-581) burial goods, such as stone coffins, beds and even a complete stone screen. These objects have great worth both as cultural relics and artifacts for the study of historical archaeology. On this stone screen in recessed areas, through the carving of fine lines, many images of human figures have been engraved in shallow relief. These images both reflect scenes from the tomb lord's life and depict filial piety tales. These pictures are representative of stone-engraved art objects found in Northern Dynasties' burials, especially the images of filial piety tales, which deserve much greater research.

In ancient China, where Confucianism was the main ideological current, paintings and sculptures of filial sons and filial conduct were especially numerous. In religious or vulgar art, this type of content was even more common. For example, beginning with the Yuan Dynasty and afterwards, full sets of filial piety images, such as the *Illustrations of the Twenty-four Filial Exemplars*, were copied in voluminous numbers and broadly disseminated. Archaeological discoveries have revealed the history of the transmission of this type of artistic motifs in burials; among these materials, the most plentiful are from the Han Dynasty, Song, Liao, Jin, and Yuan periods.[1] In addition, the many images of filial children on Northern Dynasties burial equipment have also commanded attention. The burial furnishings of the Northern Dynasties are mostly made from stone. They primarily consist of coffins and couches upon which coffins are placed. The coffins are divided into two types: those shaped like a palace or temple hall and those shaped like a casket. Coffin beds have screens with three or more panels. The shallowly engraved pictorial images on the funerary equipment were painted in multiple colors and had applied gold leaf; the images often consisted of the tomb lord, a saddled horse and ox cart setting out on a procession with an honor guard, filial piety tales, or immortals. Perhaps this is the type of funerary equipment alluded to in the *History of the Wei*'s biography of Mu Guan that states, "His whole body was concealed in a coffin adorned with gold-filled intaglio"[2]. Since the beginning of the twentieth century, much of

---

1 In regard to the origins and development of the "Twenty-four Filial Exemplars" as well as the *Illustrations of the Twenty-four Filial Exemplars*, see Zhao Chao , "'Ershisi xiao' zai heshi xingcheng", *Zhongguo dianji yu wenhua* 1 (1998)1: 50-55, and 2: 40-45. As for the fruits of research on filial piety images in burials they are voluminous. In terms of the Han Dynasty, the two most representative sites are the Wu Liang Shrine in Shandong's Jiaxiang County and the Han tomb at Helinge'er in Inner Mongolia. Relevant studies include Wu Hung, *The Wu Liang Shrine: The Ideology of Early Chinese Pictorial Art* (Stanford: Stanford University Press, 1989); Chen Yongzhi and Kuroda Akira, eds., *Helinge'er Hanmu xiaozi zhuantu jilu* (Beijing: Wenwu chubanshe, 2009). As to research on images of filial piety stories in the burials of the Liao, Song, Jin, and Yuan, see Deng Fei, "Guanyu Song Jin muzang zhong xiaoxingtu de sikao", *Zhongyuan wenwu* 4 (2009): 75-81; Wan Yan, "Song Liao Jin Yuan muzang zhong nu xiaozi tuxiang de jiedu", *Yishu tansuo* 5 (2009): 17-19.

2 *Wei shu* (Beijing: Zhonghua shuju, 1974), 664.

this funerary equipment has scattered abroad. After expending considerable effort in recent years, a number of these items have been repatriated to China.[3] Based on the previous research of others,[4] this essay will integrate newly publicized materials in an effort to enrich our knowledge of images of filial piety stories on Northern Dynasties funerary equipment.

Stone funerary paraphernalia that have filial piety stories largely date to the period in which Luoyang was the capital of the Northern Wei (493-534). In 2007, in the place called Gu'an in Henan's Anyang city, archaeologists recovered a stone coffin bed from the tomb of Feng Senghui that dates to the sixth year of the Eastern Wei's (534-550) Wuding reign period (548).[5] This is a comparatively late example. In addition, archaeologists have obtained a lacquered, multi-colored coffin that has images of filial piety tales outlined in gold from a Northern Wei tomb at the Leizumiao site in Guyuan, Ningxia.[6] It was created sometime between the years 484 and 486.[7] From the same period, there are pictorial bricks from Southern Dynasties tombs that also have illustrated filial piety tales.[8] These images can be compared and contrasted with the ones on the Northern Dynasties funerary equipment. These images of filial piety tales became popular within the larger context of shifting public morals. During the Northern and Southern Dynasties period, regimes frequently changed, causing the Qing scholar Zhao Yi (1727-1814) to cry out, "None of the loyal retainers of the Six Dynasties died for the moral integrity!"[9] A modern historian, Meng Siming, has indicated that, since Wei-Jin (220-420) times, the family was more significant than the state; being filial to your parents was even more important than being loyal to your ruler. Furthermore, the

---

3 For a number of comparatively concentrated reports on materials, see Guo Yutang, *Luoyang chutu shike shidi ji* (Luoyang: Dahua shubao gongyingshe, 1941); Wang Ziyun, *Zhongguo gudai shikehua xuanji* (Beijing: Zhongguo gudian yishu chubanshe, 1957); Huang Minglan, *Luoyang Bei-Wei shisu shike xianhua ji* (Beijing: Renmin meishu chubanshe, 1987); Wang Shucun, *ed.*, *Zhongguo meishu quanji – huihua pian – shike xianhua* (Shanghai: Shanghai renmin meishu chubanshe, 1988); and Zhou Dao, *ed.*, *Zhongguo huaxiangshi quanji: Volume 8* (Ji'nan & Zhengzhou: Shandong meishu chubanshe & Henan meishu chubanshe, 2000). For a general assessment, see He Xilin, "Beichao huaxiangshi zangju de faxian yu yanjiu", in *Between Han and Tang: Visual and Material Culture in a Transformative Period*, Wu Hung *ed.*, 341-367, (Beijing: Cultural Relics Publishing House, 2003). In recent years, numerous excavated tombs of people from the Western Regions who moved to China from the Northern Qi and Northern Zhou, through the Sui Dynasties, contain funerary equipment that are similarly shaped. However their pictorial content differs greatly from the traditions established since the Northern Wei to the extent that one does not see filial piety stories; as a result, they are beyond the scope of this essay.

4 For the most significant research on filial piety stories on Northern Dynasties' funerary equipment, see Nagahiro Toshio, *Rikuchō jidai bijutsu no kenkyū* (Tokyo: Bijutsu shuppansha, 1969); Eugene Wang, "Coffins and Confucianism – The Northern Wei Sarcophagus in the Minneapolis Institute of Arts", *Orientations* 30, no.6 (1999): 56-64; Eugene Wang, "Refiguring: The Visual Rhetoric of the Sixth – Centuru Northern Wei 'Filial Piety' Engravings", in *Gu Kaizhi and the Admonitions Scroll*, Shane McCausland ed,. 108-121 (London: The British Museum Press & Percival David Foundation of Chinses Art, 2003); Sheng-Chih Lin, "Hokuchō jidai ni okeru sōgu no zuzō to kinō – sekikan shōkakobyō no bonushi shōzō to kôshidenzu o rei toshite", *Bijutsushi* 52, no.2 (2003): 207-226; Zhao Chao, "Guanyu Bo Qi de gudai xiaozi tuhua", *Kaogu yu wenwu* 3 (2004): 68-72; and Zou Qingquan, *Bei-Wei xiaozi huaxiang yanjiu: Xiaojing yu Bei-Wei xiaozi huaxiang tuxiang shenfen de zhuanhuan* (Beijing: Wenhua yishu chubanshe, 2007).

5 Henansheng wenwu kaogu yanjiusuo, "Henan Anyang Gu'an mudi kaogu fajue shouhuo", *Huaxia kaogu* 3 (2009): 19-23, color plates 15-20.

6 Ningxia Guyuan bowuguan, *Guyuan Bei-Wei mu qiguan hua* (Yinchuan: Ningxia renmin chubanshe, 1988). Before this discovery, researchers believed that the fifth register on the eastern face of the Qimu gate tower on the southern slope of Mt. Taishi, in Dengfeng, Henan province, "seems to be the story of Guo Ju burying his son" (Lv Pin, *Zhongyue Han sanque* [Beijing: Wenwu chubanshe, 1990], 37, 69, 134; an image of the pictorial stone is on p.124. The evidence for this, though, is insufficient. This pictorial stone has an engraving of a person sitting under a tree, while another is holding a long implement and appears to be farming. Both figures are facing and looking at each other. Nevertheless, the pictorial stone lacks Guo Ju's wife, his son, the pot of gold, and other necessary visual markers. If it is an illustration of a filial piety story, then it can be explained as that of Dong Yong or Zhao Gou.

7 Sun Ji, "Guyuan Bei-Wei qiguanhua yanjiu", in his *Zhongguo Shenghuo: Zhongguo gu wenwu yu dongxi wenhua jiaoliu zhong de ruogan wenti* (Shenyang: Liaoning jiaoyu chubanshe, 1996), 122-138.

8 Henansheng wenhuaju wenwugongzuodui, Dengxian caise huaxiangzhuan mu (Beijing: Wenwu chubanshe, 1958); Xiangfanshi wenwu guanlichu, "Xiangyang Jia Jiachong huaxiangzhuan mu", *Jianghan kaogu* 1 (1986): 16-33; Yang Yi, "Xiangchengqu Qilincun Nanchao huaxiangzhuan shangxi", *Xiangfan ribao* 2/13 (2009), B3.

9 Zhao Yi, *Gaiyu congkao*(Shanghai: Commercial Press, 1957), juan 17, 322-324.

"Abnormality that is filial piety" was meant to protect and strengthen the status of the famous lineages.[10] Tang Changru has also mentioned that, putting aside the political and economic interests of influential lineages, the Sima family's seizure of political power from the Wei regime in no way meets the traditional Confucian criterion for the value of "loyalty;" indeed, this act advanced the development of the idea that parents come before the ruler, that filial piety has precedence over loyalty.[11] Recently, one scholar has begun to discuss the Northern Wei palace system as the context of the Northern Wei filial piety tales' images' popularity.[12]

Filial behavior related to funerals and burials, as well as surviving material goods, such as burial equipment, murals, and grave goods, are all embodiments of the concept of filial piety and moral norms in general; conversely, they actively give shape to this type of ideology. The purpose of the study of art history is to provide a historical understanding of the symbolic meanings of these images; it is not to furnish writings on social or intellectual history with helpful illustrations. If we only linger on the general social background, there is no way that we can concretely explain the special choices made in regard to the subject matter and forms, and so on, of the images on the funerary equipment. We should devote ourselves to seeking a method that concretely relates the phenomenon with its meaning, which requires us to explicate the image's depiction – we should not merely base our conclusions on the judgments of previous research. The questions we should be thinking about include the following: in that era's special funerary environment, what was the intention behind creating these types of images? How did these images embody that meaning? Are the images of filial piety stories strictly kept within the scope of Confucian thought? Although these types of questions are related to social and intellectual history, their focus is still on the pictures themselves; as a result, the elementary concepts that they touch upon are the images' subject matter, form, and meaning. Based on this understanding, my essay uses as illustrations of two filial piety stories, that of Guo Ju and Cai Shun, to make exploratory discussions that will include observations of the pictures' internal visual elements and touch upon their external ritual environment, as well as each type of interests that motivated their depiction.

I

Presently we have already discovered comparatively many pictorial representations of the Guo Ju story on Northern Dynasties' funerary equipment that can aid us in analyzing and comparing the method with which they were depicted. We have fairly complete records of the Guo Ju story during the Western Han:

Liu Xiang's *Illustrations of Filial Children* states, "Guo Ju was a man from Wen in Henei. His family was exceedingly rich. When his father died, he divided his father's wealth of twenty million cash into two portions and gave them to his two younger brothers. He had already decided to reverently care for his mother without the help of his brothers, but he was lodging at their home. In the neighborhood, he was temporarily residing in there was an unlucky household (visited by a sha demon) in which no one was occupying. The owner gave it to Guo Ju. He and his family lived there without any catastrophes occurring. His wife gave birth to a son. However, Guo Ju thought that if they raised it, then it would hinder their effort to nourish his mother; thus, he ordered his wife to hold the child while he dug a hole, so that they could bury him in the earth. However, within the ground he found a pot filled with gold. On it was an iron plate that read: 'This is to be bestowed to the filial son Guo Ju.' Guo Ju gave it to the owner of the home, but he did not dare take it. He thereupon asked the local magistrate about the matter. The official, in accordance

10 Meng Siming, *Wei-Jin Nanbeichao de shehui* (Shanghai: Shanghai renmin chubanshe, 2007), 128-131.

11 Tang Changru, "Zhongxiao xianhou lun" in his *Wei-Jin Nanbeichao shi luncong xubian* & *Wei-Jin Nanbeichao shilun shiyi* (Beijing: Zhonghua shuju, 2011), 235-250.

12 Zou Qingquan, *Bei-Wei xiaozi huaxiang yanjiu*, 76-116.

with the statement on the plate, gave it to Guo. Guo was thereby able to support both his mother and his child."[13]

This story really does not suit the tastes of modern people,[14] but during the Wei-Jin and Northern and Southern Dynasties periods it was especially popular. For example, in the *History of the [Liu-] Song*, Guo Ju's actions are attributed to another person, "Guo Shidao... his household was poor and without any property, to the extent that he had to hire out his labor to support his step-mother. His wife had a son. Discussing the matter with her, he said: 'We exert ourselves to nurture both, but our ability to do so isn't enough. If we nurture this child the cost (in regard to nurturing my step-mother) will be steep.' Thereupon he tearfully buried his son."[15] In a village named the "Filial Hamlet Station" (Xiaolipu) in Shandong's Changqing County, there is a Mt. Filial Hall (Xiaotangshan) that has a stone offering shrine from the early Eastern Han. At the latest, during the Northern Dynasties, it was mistakenly remembered as Guo Ju's offering hall.[16] From these facts, we can see that, during that era, the Guo Ju tale had considerable influence.

Up to this point in time, the earliest image of the Guo Ju story is on the lacquered, gold-outlined, multi-colored coffin from the Northern Wei tomb unearthed at the Leizumiao site in Guyuan.[17] On the lacquered coffin's already fragmented and damaged left side, within the upper long horizontal area, separated into frames by triangular flames, there are a number of painted filial piety stories. Among them, at least three frames are devoted to the Guo Ju story (Fig. 1). The tale seems to go from the left to the right. The still extant first scene displays Guo Ju digging into the earth and obtaining gold. The inscription within the cartouche on the side reads something like, "XX relies on virtue to discard [his son?]; those who are selfish cannot be given [this gold]." The second scene depicts Guo Ju and his wife standing shoulder to shoulder. Both sides of this scene have side cartouches; their inscriptions read, "A pot of gold found underground is bestowed by Heaven," "Fearing that there might not be enough food to respect X his mother." The third scene has two people sitting in a room; this should be Guo Ju's mother and son. The inscription in the side cartouche reads, "The filial son Guo Ju reverently caring for his mother." The majority of Han Dynasty images only use one frame to depict a story. Not only does that frame capture the climax of the tale, it also strenuously assembles together different parts of the plot.[18] The use of multiple and continuous scenes to narrate the same tale perhaps reflects the influence of stories depicted in Buddhist art. In this new form, the tale is narrated through following the line of scenes, rather than through written characters. This requires that the viewer's gaze proceeds along the images in a special sequence and in a set order, just as clock hand passes over the numbers on the face of the clock; thereby, making it that shapeless time "can be seen."

The Nelson-Atkins Museum of Art in America has

---

13 Li Fang *et al.*, *Taiping yulan* (Beijing: Zhonghua shuju, 1960), 411, 1898-1899. According to Zou Qingquan's analysis, the story of Guo Ju also appears in Song Gong's *Xiaozi zhuan* (*Taiping yulan*, *juan* 811 & *Chuxue ji*, *juan* 17); an anonymous *Xiaozi zhuan* (*Fayuan zhulin*, *juan* 49); it can also be found in a Dunhuang version of the *Xiaozi zhuan*, as well as the *Yōmei bunko* and *Funahashi Xiaozi zhuan* manuscripts that have survived in Japan. See Zou Qingquan, *Bei-Wei xiaozi huaxiang yanjiu*, 124-125. This tale can also be found in Gan Bao's (fl. 317-350) *Soushen ji* (Gan Bao, *Soushen ji*, Wang Shaoying ed. [Beijing: Zhonghua shuju, 1979], 136).

14 For example, Lu Xun severely criticized the Guo Ju story. See his "Ershisixiao tu" in *Zhaohua xishi*, which is reproduced in *Lu Xun quanji* (Beijing: Renmin wenxue chubanshe, 2005), 2, 258-264.

15 Shen Yue, *Song shu* (Beijing: Zhonghua shuju, 1974), 2243.

16 Jiang Yingju believes, it was around 570 in Hu Changren's "Eulogy to the Prince of Longdong's Feelings of Filiality", that the Xiaotangshan offering hall became reconceived as the Guo Ju offering shrine. See his "Xiaotangshan shici guanjian", in *Handai huaxiangshi yanjiu* (Beijing: Wenwu chubanshe, 1987), 206. Because of the line from this eulogy that reads, "I interviewed the elders", Sheng-Chih Lin believes that Hu Changren merely recorded a legend that was already widespread among the people in that village. See his "Bei-Wei Ning Mao shishi de tuxiang yu gongneng", *Meishushi yanjiu jikan* 18 (2005), 48-49.

17 Ningxia Guyuan Bowuguan, *Guyuan Bei-Wei mu qiguan hua*, the third pull-out line drawing.

18 Liu Dunyuan, *Meishu kaogu yu gudai wenming* (Beijing: Renmin meishu chubanshe, 2007), 49; I-tien Hsing, "Getao, bangti, wenxian, yu huaxiang jieshi (Revised edition) in his *Hua wei xinsheng: huaxiangshi, huangxiangzhuan yu bihua* (Beijing: Zhonghua shuju, 2011), 106-110.

a Northern Wei stone coffin (hereafter known as the Nelson filial piety coffin) that was taken from Luoyang in the early years of the twentieth century. The middle of its left side has the Guo Ju story in three scenes. However, the scenes are not in a straight hard line: the image of Guo Ju digging and finding the pot of gold is on the left-hand side of the pictorial representation, while just above is the scene of Guo Ju and his wife returning home carrying the pot of gold, the latter having occurred later in time. The direction that husband and wife are walking leads into the third scene that is on the right-hand side of the story's representation. There we see Guo Ju and his wife respectfully serving Guo Ju's mother who is with their child. Mountainous stones and trees, pictured between frames, create segments as well as continuity. The concept of "a border" becomes comparatively hazy (Fig. 2). The inscription in its accompanying cartouche reads, "[Filial] child Guo Ju." This is not an explanation for a certain part of the plot or the identity of one of the tale's characters, but rather an inscription for the entire story. The sophisticated structure of this image with its three dimensional portrayal leaves quite an impression.

The Kubozo Art Museum in Isumi City, Osaka, Japan, possesses a Northern Wei stone coffin bed, dated to 524, that was unearthed from the tomb of Kuang Seng'an. The right side screen of the stone bed also uses three scenes to represent the story of Guo Ju (Fig. 3).[19] It has cartouches, but no inscriptions. The contents of each scene match those found on the Nelson filial piety coffin with only small differences in details. For example, in the second "Going home" scene, Guo Ju shoulders the pot of gold and is not sharing the burden with his wife. The last scene in which Guo Ju's mother sits upright within a house is identical to the same scene depicted on the Leizumiao lacquered coffin.

In the few other screens attached to stone coffin beds that depict the Guo Ju story, most do so in two scenes. The first scene shows the moment that Guo Ju digs up the gold, while Guo Ju's wife holds their child and stands to one side. The second scene has Guo Ju's mother sitting on a bed playing with her grandson, while Guo Ju and his wife stand within the hall. These depictions omit the linking scene of the couple shouldering the gold home. For example, on the screen of a stone coffin bed that came to the Capital Museum in 2004, the first scene has a cartouche inscription that reads, "The filial son Guo Ju buries his son; Heaven bestows upon him a pot of gold." The second cartouche inscription reads, "The residence of the filial son Guo Ju who buried his son," which is carved into the building within the image.[20] The screen of a stone coffin bed, recently received by the Shenzhen Museum, has this tale depicted in two scenes. Their cartouche descriptions read as follows: "The filial son Guo Ju kills his son to nurture his mother," and "The filial son Guo Ju (Fig. 4, Pl. 17)." As for the stone coffin bed screen formerly held by the C. T. Loo, its first scene is that of Guo Ju digging up the gold with a cartouche inscription that reads, "The filial son Guo Ju." The second scene depicts him reverently caring for his mother; its inscription reads, "The filial son Guo Ju; Heaven bestows gold [to him]." The words seem to be in some disorder (Fig. 5).[21] The two scenes on the screen of the stone coffin bed excavated from the Eastern Wei tomb in Gu'an, Anyang read: "Guo Ju and his wife bury their son; Heaven bestows gold upon them," and "The moment when the mother of the filial son was X and the grandson were venerated."[22] This scene is comparatively close to the one found on the screen of the Shenzhen Museum's stone coffin bed.

The Nelson-Atkins Museum of Art has the screen of a stone coffin bed (Nagahiro simply calls this artifact the

19 *Kubozō Kinen bijutsukan*(n.d.), Figure 13.

20 Teng Lei, "Yijian haiwai huiliu shiguanchuang zhi wo jian", *Gugong bowuyuan yuankan* 4 (2009): 22-32.

21 Nagahiro, *Rikuchō jidai bijutsu no kenkyū*, Image 39. I would like to gratefully thank Mr. Sheng-Chih Lin for giving me photographs of this stone coffin bed.

22 For an introduction to this artifact, see Henansheng wenwu kaogu yanjiusuo, "Henan Anyang Gu'an mudi kaogu fajue shouhuo." However, this article does not include any phtotographs of the images with the story of Guo Ju.

"KB Version") that illustrates the Guo Ju story with only one scene (Fig. 6).[23] The designer selected the scene of the Guo Ju tale that is theatrically the richest: that of him digging the earth and discovering the pot of gold. This image is similar to the first scene illustrated on the screens of the stone coffin beds in both the Shenzhen Museum and the Gu'an Eastern Wei tomb. Among single image depictions, the portrayal on the Northern Dynasties stone coffin bed, multi-colored and outlined in gold, on displayed in New York (in 2004), is somewhat different: Guo Ju carries his plow on his shoulder and a pot on his back. Guo Ju's wife leads their son by the hand; this is unlike the other depictions where she holds him in her embrace. In the right bottom corner of the image there is a pot emitting gold light. Its cartouche inscription reads, "The filial son Guo Ju kills his son to nurture his mother; Heaven [bestows] a pot of gold (Fig. 7).[24] This image combines different moments within the story: out of the typical three scene depiction of the tale, it synthesizes the first and second scenes. A Northern Wei stone coffin, dated to 524, which belonged to Yuan Mi, the Zhenjing Prince of Zhaojun Prefecture, was removed in the early Twentieth century from a tomb in Luoyang. It is presently held by the Minneapolis Institute of Arts. On its left side, the story of Guo Ju is depicted in a single scene; however, the designer chose to illustrate the last scene, rather than the story's climax. Its inscription cartouche reads, "The filial son Guo Ju is bestowed a pot of gold" (Fig. 8).[25] In addition, pictorial bricks from three Southern Dynasties tombs, such as that from Xuezhuang in Deng County, Henan (Fig. 9), that of Jiajiachong of Xiangfan in Hubei (Fig. 10), and that from Qilincun, Xiangfan, also have the Guo Ju tale depicted in one scene. All three portray the moment when Guo Ju finds the pot of gold. From this we can perhaps glimpse one aspect of cultural transmission between the north and south.

The degree of complexity or simplicity of the image shapes is not the same. Nevertheless, no matter whether we use a theory of "evolution" or "devolution," neither sufficiently captures the relationships between them. By no means can one state that an older form exited from the historical stage just because a new form emerged. From looking at the comparatively rich Northern Wei material from Luoyang, we can see that each form could be current without contradiction. For instance, on the horizontal railing of the stone coffin bed housed in the Shenzhen Museum, the triangular lines used to mark off spaces, witnessed on the lacquered wood coffin of Leizumiao, once again reappear. Except that in this instance, they are mountain peaks rather than flames, and the portrayal of the mountain peaks blends in with the style of Northern Wei Luoyang (Fig. 11, Pl. 13).

II

According to the *History of the Later Han's* "Biography of the Compliant and Heroic Empress Liang", "When young she excelled at the feminine arts and was fond of history books. At nine years of age, she could understand the *Analects* and delve deeply into Mr. Han's version of the *Book of Poetry*: she could highlight all of the greater principles. She often had images of the outstanding women placed around her to admonish herself."[26] In her youth, the empress had a Confucian elementary education that employed both history and paintings; this type of education can be said to be thorough and perfect. Among the people, this type of idea and practice were commonplace. The inscription on a pictorial stone from an Eastern Han tomb in Shaanxi's Wuyequan of Suide county, "[He or She] read about Fan Ji; observed that outstanding women venerated the rites and yielding;

23 Nagahiro, *Rikuchō jidai bijutsu no kenkyū*, Image 45.

24 Annette L. Juliano and Judith A. Lerner, "Stone Mortuary Furnishings of Northern China", in *Ritual Objects and Early Buddhist Art*, edited by Juliano, Lerner, Jean-Marie Simonet, and Marielle Tardy, 15-23, and the plates from pp.24-57 (Brussels: Gisele Croes, 2004). There are cluses to prove that this stone coffin bed was spirited out of the Xi'an area in recent years. It is probably an artifact that belongs to the Northern Zhou.

25 Huang Minglan, *Luoyang Bei-Wei Shisu shike xianhua ji* (Beijing: Renmin meishu chubanshe, 1987), 38 & Figure 43.

26 Fan Ye, *Hou Han shu* (Beijing: Zhonghua shuju, 1965), 438.

complied with the 'Great Hymns' of the *Book of Poetry*; esteemed using government posts and noble positions to enrich one's sons who were not the heir."[27] The question might be asked: Was looking at images of outstanding women always that lofty and high-minded? The "Biography of Song Hong" in the *History of the Later Han* tells us otherwise. It states, "Hong had an audience with the emperor while he was at rest. The emperor was seated [on a couch] with a new screen that had outstanding women painted on it. The emperor several times turned his head to look at it. Hong made his demeanor proper and said, 'I have never met any man who is as fond of virtue as he is of pleasant looks.'"[28] The images of the outstanding women originally were meant to showcase "virtue;" however, what attracted Emperor Guangwu (r. 25-57) was their "pleasant looks." Is this the artisan's fault who painted it, or is it that of the person who looks at the object? Questions related to the Northern Dynasties' images of filial sons are perhaps even more complicated. The artisans not only had to faithfully depicting the original story, but they also had to consider the function of the burial furnishings and their images. These burial furnishings were the place where the interests and strengths of several groups intersected. The images could thereby be influenced by several different people. With this type of background, no matter whether one creates or employs the images, that their forms and meanings undergo change is unavoidable.

Besides differing narrative methods, one needs to consider that the images and their original stories might have disparities. For instance, on the screen of the Nelson stone coffin couch, in the scene where the gold is being dug up, behind Guo Ju's wife is another person (See fig. 6); the stone coffin bed displayed in New York has Guo Ju's son being comparatively older in age than other representations (See fig. 7); the second scene of the stone coffin bed, formerly held by the C. T. Loo, has a man and woman and another man sitting down facing them (See fig. 5). The scene of Yuan Mi's stone coffin bed has a man and woman and a boy sitting side by side, another man facing them praying (See fig. 8). In these last two examples, did the figures being reverently cared for, besides Guo Ju's mother, include Guo Ju's father? Or did the artisan mistakenly put Guo Ju and his wife on the dais? If the person who is placing his palms together and paying obedience is Guo Ju, where did his wife go? On the screen of the C. T. Loo stone coffin bed, where is the image of the child? In regard to these differences in the scenes, some might be due to the fact that the artisan based his work on a different text (this includes orally transmitted stories); some were perhaps errors committed by the artisan; some perhaps had an even more complex background.

The two sides of the Yuan Mi coffin have six filial piety stories. The plots of these tales are not identical; nevertheless, the fact that each image has people sitting under a tree located in a mountainous forest demonstrates that they all draw from the same nature. The artisan who made this artifact did not care about omitting the tales' climaxes: only some intermingled props (such as Guo Ju's pot of gold) and the accompanying inscriptions preserve a limited connection to the original plot (Fig. 12). "The divergence" of the Yuan Mi illustrated coffin from the original story is no accident. An image on a screen of a Northern Wei stone coffin bed, excavated in Luoyang in 1977,[29] goes forward in this same direction. A researcher believes that one of its images is that of the Guo Ju story (Fig. 13).[30] Indeed, we can see that this image has similarities to the ones found on the Yuan Mi stone coffin, such as figures sitting under a tree: both man and woman are sitting on the dais, and between the dais and tree there is a small child. However, the identity of the depicted figures is

27 Wu Lan, Zhi An, and Chun Ning, "Suide Xingdian faxian de liangzuo huaxiangshi mu", *Kaogu yu wenwu* 2 (2006), 17-22. In regard to deciphering this inscription, see Zhang Li, "Lun Shaanbei Dong Han mingwen keshi", *Zhongguo Han hua yanjiu* 2 (2006), 215-216.

28 *Hou Han shu*, 904. Hong's statement is a quotation from the *Analects*.

29 Huang, *Luoyang Bei-Wei shisu shike xianhua ji*, 73-76, images 81-84; Zhou Dao, ed. *Zhongguo huaxiangshi quanji: Volume 8*, 55-78, and images 74-78.

30 Zhou Dao, ed. *Zhongguo huaxiangshi quanji: Volume 8*, "Explanations of Images" p.20, and Image 74and its explanatory comments.

even more unclear. The binary function of "The one who reverently serves and he who is reverently served" no longer exists, and there is no small child on the dais. The symbolic pot of gold has altogether disappeared. An even more significant change is that the image does not have an inscription. The author no longer uses words to connect the tale's image with its contents. An empty cartouche stands as an useless form. Many of the images' subjects remaining on the stone coffin couch's screen leafs are more vague. Even so, some researchers have identified them as the filial piety tales of Ding Lan, Yuan Gu, Laolaizi, Meijianchi, and so on.[31] Nonetheless, these images are largely the same with a few varying details. Most lack visual clues that indicate a relationship with a particular story's plot or principal characters; what is more, they lack inscriptions. All we see are figures that are standing or sitting under a large tree or among mountainous rocks (Fig. 14).

One of the horizontal railings on the base of the Shenzhen Museum's stone coffin couch is even more complex (See fig. 11 and pl. 13). As already mentioned, this picture's triangular shaped mountain peaks are derived from the flame patterns found on the lacquered coffin from Leizumiao at Guyuan. An important alteration, however, is that the Shenzhen depiction of the tale has no traces of the strict, narrative progression found on the Leizumiao coffin. On the contrary, it has become exceedingly chaotic: the story's climax comes out in the D Area; but image on the two areas of B and E are mostly identical with just minor variations. It is as if, the concluding scene of everyone being able to come together is repeated in both scenes.[32] The house in Scene A looks similar to those of B and E scenes; nevertheless, the number of people in and outside of the house does not match the story. In Scene E in back of the couple (Is it Guo Ju and his wife?), there is yet another person, an attendant who is holding a canopy. Among the figures in the C and F scenes, the man who is holding the horse has nothing to do with the tale (Fig. 15).

Looking at it comprehensively, the images on these burial furnishings can viewed on two levels. The first level is to look at just the individual scenes of the overall image of the story; the second level is to look at the assemblage of all the scenes as a whole. The first level depicts the story's plot and the personality of its characters. The second level emphasizes the common meaning and the visual effects of the entire image. In different pieces, these two levels manifest discrepancies. The images on the lacquered coffin from Leizumiao provide an example. On the first level, the Guo Ju story is completely in sequence. The viewer can rely on the sequence to observe each scene of the tale, just as if reading a written story. On the other hand, these images are situated along the upper edge of one side of the coffin; between each scene there is a triangular flame. Round figures interwoven with armor plate patterns occupy the center portion. These illustrated tales, placed miscellaneously alongside of every type of geometrical pattern, resemble one unit within a larger decorative system; they are not independent images. That is to say, within the entire context of the lacquered coffin, the stories' meanings certainly do not stand out. If the viewer does not have enough patience to look at each part, then the filial piety stories merely exist as decorations. The narrativity of the first level of the Nelson filial piety story coffin is the most successful. These story plots are the most accurately and completely rendered, the characteristics of the tales are the clearest, and the content and forms are perfectly blended.[33] However, this does not influence the overall

31 Ibid, "Explanations of Images" p.21 and images 75-78 and their explanatory comments. Among the images on the screen of this stone coffin couch, there is one that is not included in this book. But you can see it is Huang, *Luoyang Bei-Wei Shisu shike xianhua ji*, p.74 and the right end of image 82. This image has a snake. Based on this, Zhao Chao has identified this scene as belonging to the tale of Bo Qi. His theory is plausible. See his "Guanyu Bo Qi de gudai xiaozi tuhua",*Kaogu yu wenwu* 3 (2004), 68-72.

32 These scenes with houses could perhaps sneak into the stories of Ding Lan or Laolaizi; however, it is difficult to determine what the concrete themes of these scenes are.

33 In the past in another place I have analyzed the relationship between the form and plot in the illustration of the Wang Lin story on the Nelson filial piety tale coffin. See my "Zhengmian de ma, beimian de ma", *Wenwu tiandi* 2 (2002): 58-59.

character displayed on the second level: each side of the coffin displays three stories, all of which have evenly placed inscriptions that give prominence to a feeling of wholeness. Mountainous rocks and trees, while separating spaces, also cause the development of each scene's temporality to have a visual openness: if a viewer is not at all familiar with the tale's content, then perhaps he or she might seek the story's main thread from the middle (Fig. 16).[34] On the first level, the images of Yuan Mi stone coffin are even weaker. The special characteristics of each story are indistinct, so that one's attention quickly turns towards the unity of the second level (See fig. 12). On the horizontal railing of the Shenzhen museum's stone coffin bed, the first level's sense of time is utterly chaotic and this strengthens a certain visual atmosphere created by the entire shape of the pictorial program: the original tales only faintly appear before one's eyes (See fig. 11 and pl. 13).

Even though nearly all of these images from Northern Wei Luoyang come from the same era, region, social level, and select the same type of motif, each goes in a separate direction. The flexibility, negotiation, conversion of the two levels described above must truly include the calculations and operations of the artisans to reduce expenses and labor. If we are to explain these phenomena, then we must consider each factor surrounding the burial furnishings and their images.

III

At its beginning, filial piety (*xiao*) meant worshipping and venerating the ancestors; later, it evolved into respecting and caring for close relatives. More concretely, in the funerary context, illustrations of filial children must satisfy and strike a balance between the dead parent(s) and the interests of their sons and daughters.

First, I will write about the relationship between the illustrations of filial piety stories and the sons and daughters of the deceased. This means leaving the story of Guo Ju to focus on Cai Shun. The tale about Cai Shun using his body to protect his dead mother's coffin from a fire can be found in the "Biography of Zhou Pan" in the *History of the Later Han*.

When his mother was 90, her years finally came to an end. Before she was buried a fire broke out in the village. The fire was soon pressing down on their home. Shun embraced and cowered over the coffin and bier; he wailed and cried to Heaven. The fire thereupon leapt over his house and burned others. Shun's home was the only one to escape the fire.[35]

The finest portrayal of the Cai Shun story is found on the Nelson filial piety coffin. In the middle of this coffin's right side, there is carved the scene of Cai Shun protecting the coffin (Fig. 17).[36] Rather than focusing on the narrative aspects of the tableau, my analysis will center on how this image interprets the interval of time when the burial furnishings were ready, but not yet buried, and on the relationship between the burial furnishings and filial children. Even though the tale is from the Han Dynasty, the image probably reflects the circumstances of the Northern Dynasties.

Burial furnishings are excavated from the tomb chamber. To understand their shapes and images, in addition to knowing how a furnishing was integrated within the tomb chamber environment, one must also consider, the time prior to entombment, the links between their manufacture, funerary gifts, and the funeral rituals. One must also consider the links between the burial furnishings and each of the major figures involved. Since the historical record is missing relevant documents, the information that the portrayal of the Cai Shun tale discloses is especially worthy of notice. Based on these grounds, I can hypothesize that, before the deceased was laid to rest, people had an opportunity to see the burial furnishings as well as their images; they had the change to both visually and symbolically

34 For example, although on the Nelson filial piety story coffin the story of Guo Ju generally unfolds from left to right, the adjacent tale of the filial grandson Yuan Gu unfolds from the right to the left.

35 *Hou Han shu*, 1312.

36 Huang, *Luoyang Bei-Wei shisu shike xianhua ji*, 1-10.

connect the pictures with the deceased's descendants – those new filial children.

In regard to the manufacture of the burial furnishings, our understanding is extremely limited. The third chapter of the *Luoyang qielan ji* records the story of a Han Dynasty man named Cui Han who died and came back to life. One part of the tale reads as follows:

To the north of the main market of Luoyang was the Fengzhong Ward, most of the residents of which sold funeral articles and inner and outer coffins. To them [Cui] Han said: "In making cypress-wood coffins, do not use mulberry wood for liners." When asked why, [Cui] Han replied: "When underground, I notice one [of the ghosts] levying ghost-soldiers. One ghost protested, 'Mine is a cypress-wood coffin, so I should be exempted.' The officer then said: 'Although yours is a cypress-wood coffin, the liner is made of mulberry wood.' So he was not exempted in the end. When people in the capital heard about this, the price of cypress wood soared. It was suspected that coffin sellers bribed [Cui] Han to invent this kind of story.[37]

From this we know the following about the people in the Fengzhong Ward, which was north of the main market: "Most of the residents sold funeral articles and inner and outer coffins." These inner and outer coffins were mostly made of wood. In chapter 13, "Tomb of the Corpse," of his *Youyang zazu*, the Tang Dynasty scholar Duan Chengshi (c. 800-863) says, "In the Northern Wei, the vulgar competed in hosting lavish burials: coffins were thick and tall. Most were made of cypress wood and had large bronze handles on either side."[38] Upon comparing this description with the shape of Yuan Mi's stone coffin, we realize that Northern Wei stone coffins imitated the shape and features of these wooden ones. Perhaps those wooden coffins were also decorated with exquisite images. The lacquered coffin unearthed at the Leizumiao site in Guyuan is circumstantial evidence that this was the case. For instance, the detail of the "Windows for peeking out" also appears on the Yuan Mi stone coffin.[39]

In 1931, Boston Museum of Fine Arts acquired a Northern Wei stone offering house that was created in 527 and dedicated to the memory of the Hengye General Ning Xiang. It was unearthed in Banpo, a village north of Luoyang. On the side of the offering house's front door, there are inscriptions that read, "The filial son Ning Wanshou," and "Built by the filial son Ning Shuangshou." The utterly crude and simple carved characters are in stark contrast to the style of the eloquently carved characters of the cartouche inscriptions found in the stone offering hall.[40] It makes one suspect that these crude inscriptions were carved after Ning Xiang's two sons, Ning Shuangshou and Ning Wanshou bought the tomb furnishings. Zou Qingquan speculates that Ning Xiang's offering house perhaps was ordered from the Eastern Garden (Dongyuan) office, which was responsible for providing the palace with funerary goods.[41] If this is truly the case, then we need to reassess the nature of the Eastern Garden office. Regardless, these funerary goods were still commercial items. Thus, it is possible that when these items were being sold that people would see the images on them.

37 Fan Xiangyong, *Luoyang qielan ji jiaozhu* (Shanghai: Shanghai guji chubanshe, 1958), 174-175. The translator of this article have slightly modified the translation of Wang Yi-t'ung, tr. *A Record of Buddhist Monasteries in Lo-yang* (Princeton: Princeton University Press, 1984), 155-156.

38 Duan Chengshi, *Youyang zazu* (Beijing: Zhonghua shuju, 1981), 123.

39 Zheng Yan, "Shuo 'kuichuang'", *Shiji yishu yanjiu* 1 (2012): 29-32.

40 Huang, *Luoyang Bei-Wei shisu shike xianhua ji*, 95-96. Guo Jianbang, *Bei-Wei Ning Mao shishi xianke hua* (Beijing: Renmin meishu chubanshe, 1987). Many Chinese publications in introducing this stone offering house mistakenly think that the filial piety images are on the main wall inside the shrine. In truth, they are on the main wall of the shrine's exterior. I have been to the Boston Museum of Fine Arts many times to examine the object with my own eyes. The museum has put this shrine together in the correct manner. In the past, many researchers have read the name on the tomb epitaph inscription that was discovered with the offering hall as "Ning Mao." Most recently, Cao Xun has advocated reading it as "Ning Xiang." By doing so, it matches his style name "A'nian." See Cao Xun, "Bei-Wei Ning Xiang shishi xin kaoding", in Wang Guixiang, ed. *Zhongguo jianzhu shilun huikan*, 4 (2011): 77-125. Sheng-Chih Lin and Cao Xun both think that the stone house is an offering shrine and is not a burial furnishing, but I am afraid their reasons are insufficient. See Lin, "Bei-Wei Ning Mao shishi de tuxiang yu gongneng", 1-74.

41 Zou, *Bei-Wei xiaozi huaxiang yanjiu*, 43-45.

According to He Xilin, there are a number of Northern Dynasties burial furnishings carved with images, such as Yuan Mi's stone coffin, that were produced by the government and were known as "Eastern Garden secret vessels".[42] Thus, these are funerary goods that represent the emperor's abundant favor. It was probably very likely that, in the process of conducting the funeral and burial, there was a stretch of time in which it was displayed and that numerous people saw it. Furthermore, in ancient China and still today in rural villages in many places, it is a much more common phenomenon to have prefabricated coffins than prefabricated tombs.[43] Those funerary goods that are prefabricated exist for an even longer time, which gives people even greater opportunities to view them.

In pre-Qin and Han Dynasty times, in the process of burying the deceased, the coffin was transported by a hearse, etc. The exteriors of these vehicles were decorated.[44] In Fu Jia's tomb in Shandong's Qingzhou, which dates to 573 during the Northern Qi period (550-577), there is a pictorial stone about a funeral: there is one scene in which a burial good that looks like a room, seemingly made of a wood, is set out for everyone to view (Fig. 18).[45] From this we can surmise that at some point during the process of the funeral, many people viewed the images on the burial furnishings.[46]

If we dwell on the circumstances behind the creation the goods, their bestowal, and the funeral, these burial

42 He, "Beichao huaxiangshi zangju de faxian yu yanjiu", 361-362. He Xilin primary evidence is the "Biography of Yuan Mi" in the *Wei shu*, which states, "In 523 Yuan Mi passed away. He was bestowed with secret vessels from the Eastern Garden, a set of court clothing, and a robe. [His family] was presented with five hundred bolts of silk (*Wei shu*, 554).

43 For example, at their home in Tianjinwan Village, in the the Boshan Area of Shandong, the photographer Jiao Bo photographed his parents in front of their prefabricated coffins. Jiao Bo, *Andie an'niang*(Jinan: Shandong huabao chubanshe, 1998), 102-104.

44 According to the *Yili*'s "Jixi li" chapter, "The Shang invoker decorated the coffin." According to Zheng Xuan's commentary, "An adorned coffin means a hearse covered by a drape. A cloth offering (*qiang*) is a drape for covering the coffin. A *qiang* is a cloth curtain; a *liu* is a hearse." The sub-commentary of Jia Gongyan states, "'An adorned coffin means that a drape (*qiangliu*) covers the hearse.' This means they have added a curtain to it." (See Zheng Xuan's commentary and Jia Gongyan's sub-commentary in *Yili zhushu* (Beijing: Beijing daxue chubanshe, 2000, 847-848). Zheng Xuan's commentary to the "Sang daji" chapter of the *Li ji* states, "A decorated coffin is called *huang* which means to cover. On the side it is called *wei*; on top it is called *huang*: all of these are pieces of cloth that cover the hearse." Kong Yingda's sub-commentary states, "A *fuhuang* is a *huang*, that is it is a covering. It is that which one covers a hearse with. It is also called a *aojia* vehicle." See *Li ji zhengyi* (Beijing: Beijing daxue chubanshe, 2000, 1496-97). Images of funerary rituals can be seen on the stone vault at the Han Dynasty tomb at Weishangounan in Shandong (Wang Sili, Lai Fei, Ding Chong, Wan Liang, "Shandong Weishanxian Handai huaxiangshi diaocha jianbao", *Kaogu* 8 [1989], 707) and the pictorial stones found in Longguzhen's Sanlimiaocun in Pei County, Jiangsu (Liu Zunzhi, "Xuzhou Han mu yu Handai shehui yanjiu" [Beijing: Kexue chubanshe, 2011], 284).

45 Xia Mingcai, "Qingzhou Fu Jia Bei-Qi huaxiangshi buyi", *Wenwu* 4 (2001), 92-93; in regard to research into the characteristics of this image, see Zheng Yan, *Wei-Jin Nanbeichao bihuamu yanjiu* (Beijing: Wenwu chubanshe, 2002), 241-246; Zheng Yan's "Tuxiang yu zangli – yi Liang-Han Beichao cailiao wei zhongxin", *Meishu yanjiu* (2013), 64-76.

46 I have already mentioned that this tomb's pictorial stone perhaps was stylistically influenced by Sogdian art (See Zheng, *Wei-Jin Nanbeichao bihuamu yanjiu*, 236-284). Judith Lerner has pointed out that the dog in this pictorial stone is related to the Sagdīd (watch dog) found in the tombs of Sogdians. See Judith Lerner, "Zoroastrian Funerary Beliefs and Practices Known from the Sino-Sogdian Tombs in China", *The Silk Road* 9 (2011), 18-25. This proves even more that this scene is that of a funeral. What is worth noticing is that the lower right section of the image of the Cai Shun tale on the Nelson filial piety stories coffin also has a dog. This detail has absolutely no relation to the Cai Shun narrative. Might this not indicate that the fabrication of images on Northern Wei funerary equipment received Sogdian artistic influence? The *Wei shu*'s biography of the Xuanwu Empress Ling, Lady Hu, records that, "Later, she and the emperor traveled to Mt. Songgao. The consorts, court ladies, princesses, and their attendants were several hundred in number. Upon ascending to the peak, they abolished all of the licentious cults, but the gods of Zoroastrianism were not among these prohibited cults (*Wei shu*, 338). Based on this Chen Yuan believed that "The worship of Zoroastrianism began during the Northern Wei" (See Chen Yuan, "Monijiao ru Zhongguo kao", *Guoxue jikan* 1, no.1 [1923], 29-30. Nevertheless, if we are speaking of customs and images related to Zoroastrianism and their influence on tombs in the Central Plains during this period, we do not dare to excessively overestimate their reach. There is an owl perched on top of the main beam of the room in which Cai Shun's mother's coffin rests. As a result, we cannot entirely rule out that at the same time the dog has a special relationship with the funeral. If this possibility exists, then this perhaps means that the image, in addition to depicting the Cai Shun tale, at the same time is related to the scene of the funeral. For the time being this is my theory; I will wait until later for more evidence.

furnishings have a dual nature: they were meant to be forever shut within the tomb and perhaps, they were also meant to be exhibited and displayed before the burial. The images on the funerary goods are precisely modeled: the carved lines are elegant and fluent and the exterior has tantalizing colors with images that are outlined with gold (it is a shame that little of it has been preserved). Besides expressing moral goodness and religious meaning, these images also delight our eyes.[47] Pictures that are more than a thousand years old can still move us. I believe that sixth century people likely had a reaction similar to our own. It is only under the assumption "that they were seen" that we can better explain the splendid style and shape of many of these forms.

We can presuppose that the first group of people to view the burial furnishings' images was perhaps by no means the descendants of the deceased. These images were not illustrations of children's reading materials: the process of turning the descendants into newly committed, filial children should have happened much earlier, rather than at the time of the funeral. The emperor bestowed funerary goods adorned with images of filial children to the deceased and his or her descendants; in other words, it was a way of recognizing this new generation of filial children. Consequently, the new filial children would want to immediately and without delay show this honor to others. Even the descendants of the deceased, who expended their wealth to contract and purchase the funerary equipment, would want people attending the funeral to see the images on the burial paraphernalia.

In truth, for those new filial children yearning for widespread fame, when their parents expired, it was a rare opportunity to display their filial conduct. In the dynastic histories of the Six Dynasties, chapters labeled "Filial and Friendly," "Filial Conduct," and "Filial and Virtuous" feature their biographical subjects manifesting filiality through the burial and mourning of their deceased parents. Thus, phrases like "to shoulder dirt to make a tumulus," "residing in a hut next to the tomb," and "crying blood for three years" can be found everywhere. Just like the Guo Ju story, in the dynastic histories of the Six Dynasties period (222-589), the tale of Cai Shun was repeatedly copied.[48] This occurred so often that new filial piety stories contain vocabulary, such as "mother," "residing in mourning," "a fire was soon pressing down on their home," and "to wail and cry," etc., that is identical to that employed in the Cai Shun narrative. In other words, the authors cribbed the written characters used to describe the acts of previous renowned filial children to record a new story. Through this form of plagiarism, a reputation was stolen; even so, a relationship between ancient exemplars and figures of the present was firmly established. Thus, ancient filial children not only served as moral exemplars, but they also became a "mold" for the

47 A similar example of something that had a comparable style and at the same time employed many different kinds of techniques and materials is the multi-colored and molded images on bricks of the Seven Sages of the Bamboo Grove and Rong Qiqi that were found in the large tombs of high status persons of the Southern Dynasties. Southern Dynasties pictorial bricks were sealed away in the burial chamber, so it would seem that they would have nothing to do with the aesthetic tastes of the eye. Nevertheless, in the past this type of style indeed led scholars to surmise that these paintings in the tombs were copies of paintings done by famous artists. According to literary records, the Seven Sages of the Bamboo Grove was a subject that many painters portrayed in their works.

48 Zou Qingquan was the first to notice this phenomenon. See his *Bei-Wei xiaozi huaxiang yanjiu*, 109-110. This type of example is extremely numerous. For example, according to the biography of He Qi in the "Filial and Friendly" chapter of the *Jin shu*, "When his mother died, he cried blood while residing in mourning and could only stand by use of a cane. When the coffin was still awaiting burial, flames were already raging [within the village]. Their household had no servants; [He Qi] calculated that there was no way to get the coffin out. He cowered and comforted the coffin all the while crying and wailing. Shortly afterwards, the wind stopped and the flames ceased. That room of the hall alone escaped destruction. His refined sincerity evoked this type of response [from Heaven]" (*Jin shu* [Beijing: Zhonghua shuju, 1974], 2292). The biography of Jia En from the "Filial and Righteous" chapter of the *Song shu* has the following account: "In 426 his mother died. He resided in mourning to an extent that surpassed what is called for in the [*Book of*] *Rites*. But before she was buried, a fire from the house next door pressed in upon her coffin. En and his wife, Lady Huan, while sobbing and wailing, made every effort to save the coffin. Their neighbors rushed over to help. The coffin and funerary vessels thereby escaped the fire. However, En and Lady Huan were both burned to death" (*Song shu*, 2243).

shaping of new filial children; the new filial children thereupon became incarnations of ancient filial children who transgressed time and space. The images of filial children that were carved on funerary equipment yet again united the subject of filial piety with the burial. The filial piety pictures on these burial goods by no means directly portrayed the acts of new filial children; instead, they continued to display the ancient prototypes. If one portrayed the feats of living people on funerary equipment and in the tomb, this would not only be inauspicious, but it would also be bereft of long-lasting value. Only those ancient filial children who had withstood the challenges of the passing of time displayed permanent worth and could be carved on the hard surface of stone. In this case, these forms had a mediating function.

The method of copying images is not the same as replication from one literary form to another; the duplication of images undergoes an even more physical method that is realized in an environment of concrete ritual. The two sides of the Nelson filial piety coffin, in addition to the tale of Cai Shun, have other filial piety narratives, including those of Shun, Guo Ju, Yuan Gu, Dong Yong, and Wang Lin. As we have already seen with the Guo Ju tale, most of these images use two or three scenes to narrate the story; the protagonist appears multiple times in these scenes. However, the story of Cai Shun is rendered in only one scene. Even though the image can generally be divided into two parts featuring Cai Shun's home and the neighbor's home. In reality, these two parts share the same moment in time: precisely when the neighbor's house is being consumed by fire, Cai Shun embraces his mother's coffin. The artist juxtaposed these images to display the tale's climax, not to show its sequence of events. In other words, the image does not thrust into prominence the turn of events; instead, in a relatively static setting, it calls attention to the relationship between Cai Shun and the coffin. This type of "static" effect is rooted in the room. The straight lines of the coffin form striking "square and rectangular graphics." This visual effect is markedly different than the unrestrained, wandering feeling created by mountainous rocks or trees. It causes this section of the image to become the visual focal point.

In analyzing the depiction of Guo Ju, we spoke of the burial furnishing as having "two levels." Bringing together the unique form of the Cai Shun image, while considering the viewer, we can continue to develop the concept of "levels." In regard to the Northern Wei "viewing," we can make a speculative reconstruction. First, a viewer might be attracted by the dramatic aspects of each of the scenes; his thoughts enter the artificial time and space created by the image and he forgets the existence of the coffin. Second, the viewer might step a pace backwards, causing the stories' details to gradually become indistinct. The entirety of the whole tableau thereby becomes even more significant. The shared meaning of the actions taken by the different filial children becomes prominent. Third, during the funeral, if a viewer's horizon continues to expand, the stone coffin thereupon becomes a "concrete object" and its form prominent. More importantly, the viewer might perhaps see the new filial child standing on the side of the coffin (Fig. 19).

Lastly, if we take a parallel view of "the relationship between new filial children and the stone coffin" and "the relationship between Cai Shun and his mother's coffin," then the new filial children are analogous to Cai Shun; the real coffin is analogous to the coffin within the image, and the scene within the image reappears outside of the image. At the same time that the new filial children are performing the stories of the ancient filial children, the images of the ancient filial children become a map for the new filial children in the form of shadows on the stone coffin. Regardless of the descendants' level of filiality, at least under the combined influence of the images and rituals, they had already played the part of a filial son.

Perhaps the image of Cai Shun is merely a special example; indeed, the link between the majority of images of filial piety stories and new filial children does not need to be so mechanical or complex. The meaning encompassed by filial piety tales can easily be transplanted to the person of the new filial son. The names of the ancient filial children that are in the inscriptions in the cartouches of the images on the stone coffins are plainly evident to the eye – there is no way to strip them of their deeds. Nevertheless, the new filial children can be placed on a par with these ancient exemplars. When contemporaries praise the moral behavior of the new filial children they can at any time make use of the words employed to celebrate the feats of ancient filial children, just like history books used the past achievements to clothe the actions of the new filial children.

The anecdotes lost importance when the interests of both the manufacturers and viewers in many ways changed the direction of the filial piety images, so that they became a meeting place of shared meanings. The complexity is that, if the original stories' protagonists' status, events, dates, and situations became watered down, then as soon as another force intervened, the filial piety stories would never again have their original power and the their images' meanings would be offset.

IV

The other party with interests in the burial equipment was the dead themselves.

The filial conduct of filial children during the funeral is a one-time performance, as seen in expressions such as, "to reside in a hut near the tomb for three years," "to not change the ways of one's father for three years," as well as sacrificing at fixed times. Although to a certain degree one could extend the amount of time in which filial conduct is performed, nonetheless at some point the funerary equipment together with the deceased must enter into the other world. Perhaps by means of the images of the ancient filial children, the filial conduct of new filial children obtains permanent value; thereby, forever accompanying and staying by the side of the deceased in an effort to ease the loneliness of the other world.[49] Nonetheless, from the standpoint of Han Dynasty people, the living have homes, while the dead have vaults and coffins: the two do not mutually interfere with each other. Now, after they have been buried, what use did the filial piety stories on the funerary equipment have? How did they serve the interests of the deceased?

We have already discussed how the Guo Ju tale "changed its shape." In fact, this type of occurrence was commonplace. Machira Akira has called attention to the fact that, in regard to the pictorial bricks with the images of the Seven Sages of the Bamboo Grove and Rong Qiqi found in the Southern Dynasties tomb in Wujiacun, Danyang County, Jiangsu, the figures within have all been portrayed as aged. He points out that, "This is nothing else than taking the actual recluses of the Seven Sages of the Bamboo Grove and turning them into the recluses and "masters of recipes" (*fangshi*) of an ideal realm." "To a large extent, the meaning of the mural has been transformed into praise for immortals." In connection with the confusion appearing in the tomb inscriptions from Jinjiacun and Wujiacun, he has stated, "In regard to the fact that importance is not attached to the name of each figure, does this not establish that we should view the whole as an idealized picture of recluses?"[50] Zhao Chao has in the past also noted that, during the Six Dynasties period, the forms of the Seven Sages of the Bamboo Grove became depicted as immortals. He tells us that, "Due to popularity of Daoism, the embellishments of people of the world, as well as the fact that the "The Seven Sages of the Bamboo Grove" embraced the tradition of the *Laozi* and *Zhuangzi* and advocated "The Study of the Mysteries" (*Xuanxue*), this is what caused them to be divinized and made into religious idols of Daoism."[51] I have also discussed the change in the meaning of the subject matter of recluses in the burials of the Six Dynasties period; I have pointed out that these exemplars of culture who received the people's adoration during the Six Dynasties period can be viewed as the companions or fellow travelers of the tomb lord, as he ascends to become an immortal. They thus lost their original meaning.[52] The motif of people

49 As Sheng-Chih Lin has pointed out, the images of filial piety stories can serve as a link between the living and the dead; at the same time, they replace the living in serving the tomb lord within the grave. See his "Hokuchō jidai ni okeru sōgu no zuzō to kinō."

50 Machida Akira, "Nan-Qi diling kao", Lao Ji, trans. *Dongnan wenhua* 2 (1987), 51.

51 Zhao Chao, "Cong Nanjing chutu de Nanchao zhulin qixian bihua tan kaiqu", *Zhongguo dianji yu wenhua* 3 (2000), 4-10.

52 Zheng, *Wei-Jin Nanbeichao bihuamu yanjiu*, 209-235.

sitting under a tree on the Yuan Mi stone coffin is by no means unique to filial piety stories. Images of recluses in Six Dynasties tombs often have this type of seated figures under a tree (Fig. 20).[53] Even though one can detect slight differences between the recluses on the pictorial bricks from the Xishanqiao tomb in Nanjing, however, they are a collective portrait: their mutually shared special characteristics are particularly obvious.[54] The goal of expressing the pursuit of immortality was realized through the process of continuous copying, weakening the special characteristics of each recluse. As for the images of recluses in Northern Qi tomb of Cui Fen, which was found in Haifushan, in Linqu County, Shandong, there is no way to differentiate the status of each individual, much less know their unique tales. All we see are figures that are more or less identical sitting under a tree (Fig. 21).[55] This type of trend closely resembles the examples on the Yuan Mi stone coffin.

Interwoven in the image of the Guo Ju tale, on the screen of the stone coffin bed in the Shenzhen Museum, there are some details that are worthy of our attention, such as the figure who appears in the C area of the screen (See fig. 15). Similar examples to this figure are seen on the screen of the stone coffin bed published by Wang Ziyun (Fig. 22),[56] and the screen of the stone coffin beds found in Japan's Tianri Museum, and the San Francisco Asian Art Museum.[57] Nagahiro said that the last of those pictures is "an image of freedom gained by transcending the world."[58] I suspect that these are the comings and goings of recluses or immortals in the mountains and forests. In an unpublished paper, Li Xiaoxuan has noticed that, on the pictorial brick from the Southern Dynasties tomb in Xuezhuang, Dengxian, Guo Ju's wife has a lofty topknot and is wearing splendid clothing. Her appearance is no different than the image of Dong Yong's wife on the Nelson filial piety coffin. She explains this phenomenon as the "transference" of models of figures that had been taking place since the Han Dynasty.[59] In addition to this, the phenomenon of an original character changing shape beyond the parameters of the story should have an extra layer of significance. These alterations of the filial piety tale images perhaps indicate that the narratives' characters were meant to play the same role as the immortals: as companions of the deceased who would stay by his side; thereby, causing the funerary equipment and the tomb to be transformed into the passageway for the deceased to paradise.[60]

In large scale Southern Dynasties tombs, such as the one at the Hexian'ao in Danyang, Jiangsu,[61] the Jinjiacun tomb in Jianshan,[62] and the Wujiacun tomb in Huqiao,[63] the rear part of the tomb chamber has images of the Seven Sages of the Bamboo Grove and Rong Qiqi, whereas the front section has many immortals who are guiding the Green Dragon and the White Tiger (Fig 23). On the side of the brick carved characters read, "Big dragon," and "Big tiger." The dragons and tigers

53 In the tomb in Kangye, this type of configuration is used to display the figure of the tomb lord. See Zheng Yan, "Shizhe de 'mianju': Lun Bei-Zhou Kangye mu shiguanchuang huaxiang" (revised draft), in *Cong kaoguxue dao meishushi: Zheng Yan zixuan ji* (Shanghai: Shanghai renmin chubanshe, 2012), 124-130.

54 Audrey Spiro, *Contemplating the Ancients* (Berkeley: University of California Press, 1990), 98.

55 Linqu Museum, *Bei-Qi Cui Fen bihua mu* (Beijing: Wenwu chubanshe, 2002).

56 Wang, *Zhongguo gudai shike hua xuanji*, pictures 5.7 & 5.9; for other relevant photographic plates of this stone coffin bed, once again see Huang, *Luoyang Bei-Wei shisu shike xianhua ji*, 79-90, pictures 87-98; Zhou, *Zhongguo huaxiangshi quanji: Volume 8*, 67-68 and pictures 86-87. This photographic plate explains that, "The original stone has been lost to the United States."

57 Nagahiro, *Rikuchō jidai bijutsu no kenkyū*, photographic plates 29-34, p.148, and picture 41.

58 Ibid, 148.

59 Li Xiaoxuan, "Shilun Zhongguo zaoqi huihua zhong renwu xingxiang de zailiyong", *Zhongguo meishu yanjiu* 16 (2015), 25-33.

60 Deng Fei researches the relationship between becoming an immortal and the filial piety images found in Song and Jin Dynasty tombs. See her "Guanyu Song Jin muzang zhong xiaoxingtu de sikao." The relationship between these changes and the images of filial piety tales on Northern Dynasties' funerary equipment and stone coffin beds deserves even more contemplation.

61 Nanjing bowuyuan, "Jiangsu Danyang Huqiao Nanchao damu ji zhuanke bihua", *Wenwu* 2 (1974), 44-56.

62 Nanjing bowuyuan, "Jiangsu Danyang Huqiao, Jianshan liangzuo Nanchao muzang", *Wenwu* 2 (1980), 1-17.

63 Ibid.

witnessed in the large tombs of the Southern Dynasties can also be seen in the images on Yuan Mi's coffin. The change witnessed on the latter is merely that the filial piety tales have replaced the Seven Sages of the Bamboo Grove; nevertheless, in both cases the picture is that of people under a tree united together with a large dragon and tiger. The images are quite similar; consequently, their meaning is not fundamentally different.

Many of the Northern Wei stone coffins unearthed in Luoyang decorated with dragons and tigers also add feathered men to guide one from the beginning to end – this resembles the Southern Dynasties' tombs. For example, in 1977, in a northern suburb of Luoyang at a brick and tile factory in Shangyao Chanhe, a stone coffin was excavated. Carved on it was the tomb lord riding a dragon and a tiger ascending to immortality among cries of support from immortals, musicians and strange beasts (Figs. 24, 25).[64] On the surface, this set of images is different from the filial children material. Yet, if we think of the images it shares with Yuan Mi's coffin, such as the dragons and tigers and strange beasts and then transform the shape of the filial piety tales into depictions of immortals, then this is even more of an ingenious linking method. This type of image of immortals riding dragons and tigers and strange beasts can also be seen in the murals of the Northern Qi Cui Fen tomb. The only difference is that the ones they are accompanying on the screen are merely recluses (See fig. 21).

Dragons and tigers are the mounts of immortals and feathered men are the guides and guards of those who seek immortality. After they are depicted as otherworldly beings, recluses and filial children are all on the same path in seeking immortality, just as the deceased is. At the start, filial piety images were meant for the glory and honor of the descendants. However, after the transformation, the pictorial scenes once again became tied together with the interests of the deceased. On both the stone coffin bed unearthed in Luoyang in 1977 and the stone coffin bed screen now held in the Shenzhen Museum, there is the simultaneous existence of images of the filial piety stories and depictions of the tomb lord. Even if we cannot find an image of the tomb lord, these burial furnishings were interred together with the corpse within the tomb.

The artisans that created these burial goods with images could use their marvelous techniques to create one meaning on each piece or double-meanings on each piece. The artist might burnish the deceased's descendants' reputation for filial piety or give prominence to the deceased's interest in becoming an immortal, or both. In this way, no matter whether it was in the interests of the deceased, or the glory of the descendants, both of these goals could emerge through funerary equipment images. Artisans did not create situations in which the images were set against each other or were split apart from each other.

In terms of intellectual history, the concepts of filiality and immortality communicated through these images do not surpass much of the substantial development of these notions that occurred in previous eras. The images of filial children and immortals are all stereotypes. The images of filial piety stories were decorative materials that had been popular since the Han. Likewise, in terms of content, the images of immortality lacked any innovations. It is only necessary to compare for a moment this situation with that in the Han Dynasty. If we do so, then we realize that the Northern and Southern Dynasties material concerning immortals was intellectually somewhat bland. Although Han Dynasty written records have not clearly left us with systemic theories concerning Han Dynasty ideas about the afterlife or immortality, nevertheless, within the tomb and offering shrine, we can still see that Han Dynasty people used every type of art form to construct a system of images related to beliefs about immortality. Perhaps at the beginning, these images appeared in neither the tomb nor the offering shrine; however, they truly had a profound effect on funerals. Looking at the preliminary period, this system of representation in general had three aspects. The first takes the Queen Mother Goddess of the West as its nucleus and uses each type of immortal as aiding the system of the godhead. The second concerns descriptions and musing about paradise, which includes

64 Luoyang Bowuguan, "Luoyang Bei-Wei huaxiangshi guan", *Kaogu* 3 (1980): 229-241.

motifs such as the Island of the Immortals, Mt. Kunlun, Heaven's Gate, pavilions, etc. The third is the route to paradise, which includes heavenly horses, divine deer, jade maidens, the Liubo game, as well as processions of chariots and horses. This Han system of images was perhaps only popular in some areas or among society's middle and lower classes, surely not by everyone. Even more to the point, this system was never attained a fixed form. Even so, these exploratory pictures of the Han Dynasty are vivid and fresh and full of imagination and creativity.

Comparatively, the images of immortals on Northern Dynasties funerary equipment are contrarily faint and vacuous. Nevertheless, like the Han images, they have things like the Four Deities, the feathered people who serve as guides, each type of strange beast, as well as musicians riding dragons and the wind, etc. Images depicting concrete descriptions of paradise and information about the godhead are truly rare. New, creative motifs are even rarer! Unfortunately some scholars completely miss the mark when defining these images as the fine arts of Daoism. In truth, these images lack the systematized theories and rituals of organized religions. Therefore, these should be seen as a continuation of traditional thought. In regard to the dead, for new and more systematic theories and ideology, perhaps we should look at Buddhist stone grottoes and images. In Luoyang, Buddhist monasteries and pagodas were like a forest both inside and outside the city. At that time, the grottoes at Longmen and Gongxian were being expanded on a large scale. More and more people were praying that the spirit of the dead could enter the finely constructed paradises that numerous Buddhist scriptures and images described in great detail. In regard to the burial of the physical body of the deceased, one merely took care of it according to traditional rites and ceremonies. With the exception of some decorative patterns, such as lotus flowers, Buddhist thought, teachings, and relevant interests did not really enter into the images on burial furnishings. As for Zoroastrian beliefs, they only appear in the tombs of Sogdians who migrated to China. One can say that Northern and Southern Dynasties artisans have made a unique contribution to the creation of images of the immortals by making indistinct the lines that separated recluses from filial children, to the extent that, in some senses, these stories were absorbed into the pictographic system in which the beliefs of the immortals take center stage.

In the process of surrounding the deceased with artistic creations, lowly craftsmen struck a balance between each kind of interest. They used their intellect and talent in their work and in their search for artistic forms. Such artists were capable of taking a stuffy and boring subject and making it fruitful and colorful, so that each topic would last a thousand years. We can say that, this period had a special "artistic self-consciousness." This awareness was expressed in Eastern Jin and Southern Dynasties' discussions of painting styles, theories about painting, and the works' artistic transmission. It was also expressed through picture scrolls that have been handed down from ancient times as well as in those great masters whose names will last for a thousand years. In the same manner, artistic self-consciousness appeared deeply buried in the blue-green rocks of the Yellow Springs.

Explanations of inserted photographs:

Figure 1: The Guo Ju story outlined in gold on the multi-colored, lacquered coffin excavated from the Northern Wei tomb at the Leizumiao in Guyuan, Ningxia (Taken from Ningxia Guyuan Bowuguan, *Guyuan Bei-Wei mu qiguan hua*, the third pull-out lined drawing).

Figure 2: The image of Guo Ju story on the Northern Wei filial piety coffin excavated in Luoyang and now stored in America's Nelson-Atkins Museum of Art (A reverse-angle rubbing. Taken from Huang Minglan, *Luoyang Bei-Wei shisu shike xianhua ji*, p.7, Figure 9).

Figure 3: The image of Guo Ju story on the screen of the stone coffin bed from Kuang Seng'an tomb, dated to 524. It is now stored in Japan's Kubozo Art Museum (Sketched by Zheng Yan).

Figure 4: The picture of Guo Ju story on the screen of a Northern Dynasties stone coffin bed stored in the Shenzhen Museum.

Figure 5: The picture of Guo Ju story on the screen of a Northern Wei stone coffin bed, which was formerly stored at the C. T. Loo (Provided by Sheng-Chih Lin).

Figure 6: The picture of Guo Ju story on the screen of a Northern Dynasties stone coffin bed unearthed in Luoyang. It is now stored in Nelson-Atkins Museum of Art (Sketched by Zheng Yan).

Figure 7: The picture of Guo Ju story on the screen of a Northern Dynasties stone coffin bed exhibited in New York in 2004 (Sketched by Zheng Yan).

Figure 8: The picture of Guo Ju story on stone coffin of Yuan Mi, the Zhenjing Prince of Zhao Jun. This Northern Wei stone coffin was unearthed in Luoyang and dates to 524. It is now housed in the Minneapolis Institute of Arts (Sketched by Zheng Yan).

Figure 9: An image of the Guo Ju story on a brick from the Southern Dynasties tomb found in the village of Xuezhuang in Deng County, Henan (Sketched by Zheng Yan).

Figure 10: An image of the Guo Ju story on a brick from the Southern Dynasties tomb unearthed in Jiajiachong, Xiangyang, Hubei (Taken from *Jianghan kaogu* 1 [1986], 21).

Figure 11: An image of the Guo Ju story on the foundation of the Northern Dynasties stone coffin bed stored at the Shenzhen Museum.

Figure 12: An image from the stone coffin of Yuan Mi, the Zhenjing Prince of Zhao Jun. This Northern Wei stone coffin was unearthed in Luoyang and dates to 524. It is now housed in the Minneapolis Institute of Arts (Taken from Kaka 5 [1939], inserted photograph).

Figure 13: The picture of Guo Ju story on the screen of a Northern Wei stone coffin bed unearthed in Luoyang (The rubbing comes from Zhou Dao *et al. Zhongguo huaxiangshi quanji*: Volume 8, p. 55, picture 74; the line drawing was sketched by Zheng Yan).

Figure 14: The picture of Guo Ju story on the screen of a Northern Wei stone coffin bed unearthed in Luoyang (The rubbing comes from Zhou Dao *et al. Zhongguo huaxiangshi quanji*: Volume 8, pp. 56-59, pictures 75-78).

Figure 15: An image from the foundation of the Northern Dynasties stone coffin bed stored at the Shenzhen Museum.

Figure 16: An image of the Northern Wei filial piety coffin that was excavated in Luoyang and is now stored in America's Nelson-Atkins Museum of Art (William Watson, *The Arts of China to AD 900* [New Haven & London: Yale University Press, 1995], p. 156, fig. 252)

Figure 17: The image of Guo Ju story on the Northern Wei filial piety coffin excavated in Luoyang and is now stored in America's Nelson-Atkins Museum of Art (A reverse angle rubbing. Adopted from Huang Minglan, *Luoyang Bei-Wei shisu shike xianhua ji*, p. 4, Figure 6).

Figure 18: A pictorial stone from the Fu Jia tomb completed in 573 from Qingzhou in Shandong (Sketched by Zheng Yan).

Figure 19: A filial son and a filial piety coffin (Sketched by Zheng Yan).

Figure 20: A mosaic mural composed of bricks of the Seven Sages of the Bamboo Grove with Rong Qiqi from a Southern Dynasties tomb at Gongshan in Xishanqiao, Nanjing, Jiangsu (Taken from Yao Qian and Gu Bing, *Liuchao yishu* [Beijing: Wenwu chubanshe, 1981], pictures # 162 & 163).

Figure 21: A mural from the west wall of Cui Fen's tomb, which dates to 551 and is located in Haifushan, Linqu, Shandong (Sketched by Zheng Yan).

Figure 22: An image of a figure on the screen of a Northern Wei stone coffin bed excavated in Luoyang (Taken from Wang Ziyun, *Zhongguo gudai shike hua xuanji*, pictures #5.7 & 5.9).

Figure 23: A mosaic mural composed of bricks of the white tiger from the Southern Dynasties tomb in Jinjiacun, Danyang, Jiangsu (Sketched by Zheng Yan).

Figure 24: An image of the tomb lord becoming an immortal on the left side of a Northern Wei stone coffin excavated in Shangyao, Luoyang, Henan.

Figure 25: Part of an image of the tomb lord becoming an immortal on the left side of a Northern Wei stone coffin excavated in Shangyao, Luoyang, Henan (Taken from Zhou Dao *et al* ed., *Zhongguo huaxiangshi quanji*: Volume 8, p. 45, Figure 60).

(Translated by Keith N. Knapp, Professor of the Citadel College)

关于深圳博物馆展陈北魏石床的孝子传图

——阳明本孝子传的引用

黑田彰
（日本佛教大学　教授）

一

2011年5月18日，深圳博物馆展出了一套石床，该石床的制作时间被认为是北魏晚期(以下简称为“深圳北魏石床”)。该石床的围屏部分描绘有以墓主人为主，包括马、牛车等十二幅不同的画面，其中四幅画面绘有极其珍贵的孝子传图（图版16、17）。这些孝子传图是把当时众所周知的三个孝子故事图像化，其中两幅是郭巨图（图版17），另外两幅分别是老莱子和董黯的图画（图版16）。这几幅孝子传图包含有众多研究孝子传图所不可忽视的重要内容，其中最令人吃惊的是该石床上绘制的董黯图（有关董黯的图画保存下来的数量极少），并且这几幅孝子传图上都有文字(榜题两个、题记两则)。除去画面本身，这两则题记对于该石床孝子传图的研究最为重要，可以看作是从后文提到的阳明本孝子传中引用而来的。阳明本孝子传是日本尚存的两种完整本古孝子传中的一种，此例正可以证明其与孝子传图有紧密的关系。像该石床这样的带有题记的孝子传图，以笔者的管见，是以前从未发现过的。小稿尝试对这个珍贵的石床上的孝子传图进行解读。

中国的孝子传图、二十四孝图，以闻名世界的东汉武氏祠画像石（武梁祠第1、3二石2层）所描绘的孝子传图为代表[1]，还有和林格尔东汉壁画墓（中室西、北壁1层）等[2]，以东汉、北魏时期作品为主，大量质量上乘的画作保存了下来。以唐代为界，宋辽金以来，二十四孝图的制作开始流行起来，并取代了孝子传图。[3]现在这类主题的出土文物以及新发现不断出现。多数被图像化的孝子传图、二十四孝图都应该有其绘制的粉本，并且应该有作为粉本说明来引用的孝子传和二十四孝的文本。[4]所以对该石床孝子传图内容的说明，自然要从孝子传图和其引用的孝子传的关系入手。

日本尚存的两种完整本古孝子传，关于其文学史价值，西野贞治先生在他的论文《关于阳明本孝子传的特点以及与清家本的关系》中进行了这样的阐述：“自古中国的家族制度就极其发达，为了将家族制度维持下去，针对孝行的教化是十分彻底的。一些以实例的孝子传、孝子图为题材的书，与孝经一起作为儿童的必修书，到六朝末期，就出现过十几种以上。这些书的盛行有种种资料可以证明。尚存的记录以南宋郑樵的《通志略》为下限，稍后的晁公武、陈振孙等藏书家就不再见到，也许很多都是因为南宋的战火而失传”[5]。确如西野先生所言，中国大陆自古就有刘向孝子传、萧广济孝子传等十余种孝子传作为幼儿教育而被大量制作。但是现在这些古孝子传基本上都已经失传，只能从众多

[1] 参考容庚先生《汉武梁祠画像录》，考古学社专辑13，北平燕京大学考古学社，1936年。关于孝子传图，参阅拙著《孝子伝の研究》Ⅱ一、二，佛教大学鹰陵文化专言5，思文阁出版，2001年。

[2] 内蒙古自治区文物考古研究所、日本幼学会：《和林格尔汉墓壁画孝子传图辑录》，文物出版社，2009年。关于和林格尔东汉壁画墓的孝子传图，参阅拙著《孝子伝図の研究》Ⅰ二2，汲古书院，2007年。

[3] 比如五代宋初的遗物有敦煌出土的二十四孝押座文（S七刻本等）。关于二十四孝图，参阅拙著《孝子伝の研究》Ⅱ三。

[4] 关于作为范本的孝子传，参阅拙著《孝子伝の研究》Ⅰ一。关于二十四孝同样参阅Ⅰ二。

[5] 西野贞治：《陽明本孝子伝の性格並に清家本との関係について》，《人文研究》，1956年7月。

书籍中引用的只言片语来窥测其内容。[6]可是在作为丝绸之路东端的日本，却奇迹般地保存下来了两种完整本的古孝子传。保存至今的孝子传[7]（阳明本孝子传和船桥本［清家本］孝子传，下文以两孝子传代称[8]）仍能窥见其过去的面貌。两孝子传应是从共同的祖本衍生而来的，总的来说，阳明本保存了更多的古态。[9]正如前文所述，以中国作为幼儿教育而广泛流传的纸本孝子传为基础，以东汉武氏祠画像石（武梁祠第1、3二石2层）所描绘的孝子传图为代表，可见以东汉、北魏时期作品为主的孝子传图制作的盛况。但是，这里就出现了一个问题，在欲对这些孝子传的内容进行具体的考察时，这些纸本孝子传的失传便成为影响考察的决定性障碍。例如，宋代发现后就不再见到，直到清代乾隆五十一年（1786）因黄易而再次被发现的武梁祠1、3二石2层所绘孝子传图，经过将近千年的研究，对于其画面的解读仍没有完全的进展，最大的原因就是因为纸本孝子传的失传。所以，小稿尝试对该石床孝子传图的解读，是以日本尚存的两种完整本古孝子传，尤其是阳明本孝子传为基础的。

深圳北魏石床是北魏时期石棺床的典型样式，即“冂”字（冂结构）型的，“冂”字左右的竖笔画处分别有石板一块，正上方横笔画处石板两块，四块石板的边缘用金属连接，各石板纵向按围栏轮廓分为三面背屏，共分割成十二幅图案，用线刻或浅浮雕描绘出墓主人、孝子传图等图像。该石床的图像分布结构如图一所示（孝子传图以［1］~［4］来表示，空白部描绘的是侍者等图像）。

日本尚存的两孝子传根据孝子名一共分为四十五篇，其目录详见表一。

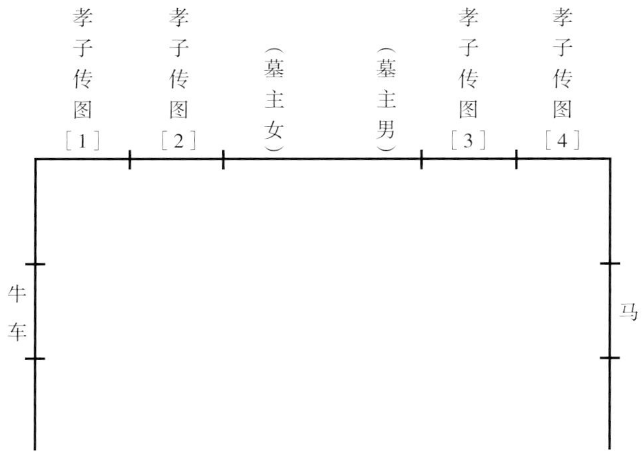

图一　深圳北魏石床示意图（一）

表一　两孝子传编目

序

1舜　2董永　3刑渠　4伯瑜　5郭巨　6原谷　7魏阳　8三州义士　9丁兰　10朱明　11蔡顺　12王巨尉　13老莱之　14宗胜之　15陈寔　16阳威　17曹娥　18毛义　19欧尚　20仲由　21刘敬宣　22谢弘微　23朱百年（上卷）24高柴　25张敷　26孟仁　27王祥　28姜诗　29叔先雄　30颜乌　31许孜　32鲁义士　33闵子骞　34蒋诩　35伯奇　36曾参　37董黯　38申生　39申明　40禽坚　41李善　42羊公　43东归节女　44眉间尺**船45**　45慈乌**船44**（下卷）

［6］关于古孝子传，参阅拙著《孝子伝の研究》Ⅰ-1，以及拙著《孝子伝図の研究》Ⅰ一。关于刘向孝子传（图），不可能是西汉刘向制作的，应是六朝以后制作。另一方面刘向著有列女传，与列女传图的制作有很深的联系。参阅拙著《列女伝図の研究——和林格爾後漢壁画墓の列女伝図—》，《京都语文》15，2008年11月。

［7］关于两孝子传图，参阅拙著《孝子伝の研究》Ⅰ—2。

［8］关于两孝子传的正文，参考收集的幼学会《孝子伝注解》（汲古书院，2003年）翻刻、注解、影印。赵超先生著《日本流传的两种古代<孝子传>》（《中国典籍与文化》，2004年第2期），是中国首次对该书进行的介绍，注意到了其与伯奇图之类的孝子传图的关系。他还著有《关于伯奇的古代孝子图画》（《考古与文物》2004年第3期）、《关于汉代的几种孝子图画》（《中国汉画学会第九届年会论文集》中收录，中国社会出版社，2004年）等论文。

［9］关于阳明本的成书时期，西野贞治先生曾经有六朝末期成书一说（注［5］中提到的论文）。但是阳明本孝子传全四十五条的内容，经过详细的探讨，武梁祠的孝子传图全十七图中的十四幅图都与阳明本一致，并且与和林格尔东汉壁画墓中室的孝子传图全十三图中的十一幅图也是一样的，至于东汉乐浪彩箧的孝子传图全四幅图都被阳明本所包含。从与汉代孝子传图的关系来看，阳明本的某些部分受到汉代流行的孝子传影响，并且与汉代流行的习俗、礼节的关联是阳明本的根本部分。这种礼俗在汉代很早就已经形成，而阳明本的现行本应该是在六朝齐末梁初时改编的。详细的论述参阅拙稿《陽明本孝子伝の成立》，《京都语文》14，2007年11月。

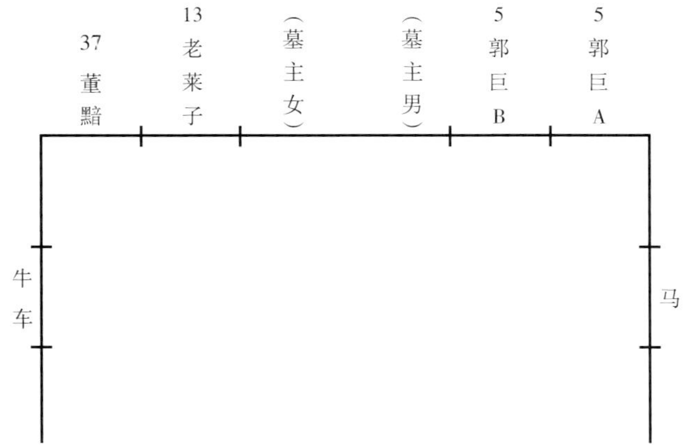

图二　深圳北魏石床示意图（二）

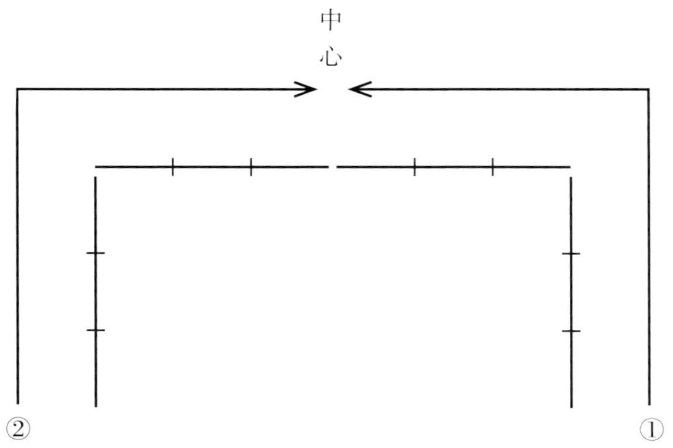

图三　孝子传图排列示意图

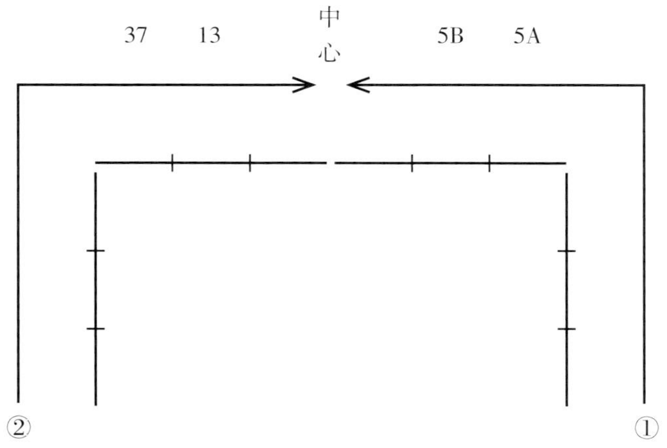

图四　深圳北魏石床孝子传图排列示意图

图一中深圳北魏石床的孝子传图［1］~［4］都有榜题，后文证明这四幅画面是根据三个孝子传的故事进行图像化的（孝子名前面的阿拉伯数字是表一中阳明本的目录编号）。

孝子传图

［1］—37 董黯

［2］—13 老莱子（之）

［3］—5 郭巨 B

［4］—5 郭巨 A

这里将图一孝子传图的［1］~［4］替换成上述的三个孝子名，该石床的示意图就变成了图二这样。

最近，林圣智（LIN Sheng-chih）著有论文《关于北朝时期葬具的图像和功能——以石棺床围屏上的墓主人肖像和孝子传图为例》，文中证明关于北朝时期石棺床围屏上描绘孝子传图的排列有重要的规律。[10]这个规律是，以北魏为主的石棺床的图像都是以墓主人肖像为中心，周围分布的孝子传图的顺序是按照日本尚存的两孝子传的目录（表一），先由右外侧向中心（男性墓主人），再由左外侧向中心（女性墓主人）排列（也有用马、牛车的图像代替两个墓主人像的情况）。笔者再次确认了林先生所指出的规律。[11]现在，根据林先生所言，将该石床孝子传图的排列顺序用简单易懂的示意图表示出来，就是图三这样。也就是说，根据表一中两孝子传编目的顺序，该石床所描绘的众孝子传图的排列顺序是，首先按照右边箭头①的顺序，然后按照左边箭头②的顺序排列。如此，图二所示该石床孝子传图的排列顺序就可以形成图四这样。即向着男墓主人右箭头①的方向，顺序排列着 5A（郭巨）、5B（郭巨），向着女性墓主左箭头②的方向，顺序排列着 37（董黯）、13（老莱子），可以算是对林先生所说原理的补充。图四中，唯一的例外是左箭头的 37 → 13 是逆着顺序的。关于这个逆序，按照林先生的原理，紧邻女性墓主人的左侧描绘的 37 董黯图，应该是不孝者王奇（寄）图（与该图酷似，纳尔逊美术馆藏北齐石床的图中有“不孝王寄”的榜题）。但这样看是不妥当的，也就是说，该石床

［10］林圣智：《北朝時代における聰具の図像と機能—石棺床囲屏の墓主肖像と孝子伝を例として—》，《美術史》154<52.2>，2003 年。

［11］拙著：《孝子伝図の研究》Ⅰ二 3。

的制作者讨厌那样不孝的行为，为了避免这样的状况发生，用对年岁已高的双亲尽孝的老莱子图（13）代替了不孝者王奇（寄）图。

下文，对该石床所描绘的孝子传图进行解读。解读的顺序按照图二所示从左侧开始，即按37董黯、13老莱子、5郭巨图进行。

二

首先，图五所示的是深圳北魏石床的董黯图[12]。然后，列出作为其出处的阳明本孝子传37董黯的正文[13]（作为参考，船桥本孝子传的原文一并列出）。

【阳明本】（为方便阅读，原书异体字均改为简体正字）

董黯家贫至孝。虽与王奇并居，二母不数相见。忽会篱边，因语曰黯母：汝年过七十，家又贫，颜色乃得怡悦如此何？答曰：我虽贫，食肉粗衣薄，而我子与人无恶，不使吾忧故耳。王奇母曰：吾家虽富，食鱼又嗜馔，吾子不孝，多与人恐，惧罹其罪，是以枯悴耳。于是各还。奇从外归。其母语奇曰：汝不孝也。吾问见董黯母，年过七十，颜色怡悦，犹其子与人无恶故耳。奇大怒，即往黯母家，骂云：何故谗言我不孝也？又以脚蹴之。归谓母曰：儿已问黯母，其云：日日食三斗。阿母自不能食，导儿不孝。黯在田中，忽然心痛，驰奔而还。又见母颜色惨惨，长跪问母曰：何所不和？母曰：老人言多过矣。黯已知之。于是王奇日杀三牲。旦起取肥牛一头杀之，取佳肉十斤、精米一斗熟而荐之。日中又杀肥羊一头，佳肉十斤、精米一斗熟而荐之。夕又杀肥猪一头，佳肉十斤、精米一斗熟而荐之。便语母曰：食此令尽。若不尽者，我当用鉾刺母心，用戟钩母头。得此言，终不能食，推盘掷地。故孝经云：虽日用三牲养，犹为不孝也。黯母八十而亡。葬送礼毕，乃叹曰：父母仇不共戴天。便至奇家斫奇头以祭母墓。须臾监司到，缚黯。黯乃请以向墓别母。监司许之。至墓启母曰：王奇横苦阿母，黯承天士，忘行己力，既得伤仇身，甘菹醢，甘监司见缚，应当备死。举声哭。目中出血。飞鸟翳日，禽鸟悲鸣，或上黯臂，或上头边。监司具如状奏王。王闻之叹曰：敬谢孝子董黯。朕寡德统荷万机。而今凶人勃逆，又应治剪，令劳孝子助朕除患。赐金百斤，加其孝名也。

【船桥本】

董黯家贫至孝也。其父早没也。二母并存。一者弟王奇之母。董黯有孝也，王奇不孝也。于时，黯在田中，忽然痛心，奔还于家，见母颜色，问曰：阿娘有何患耶？母曰：无事。于时王奇母语子曰：吾家富而无宁，汝与人恶，

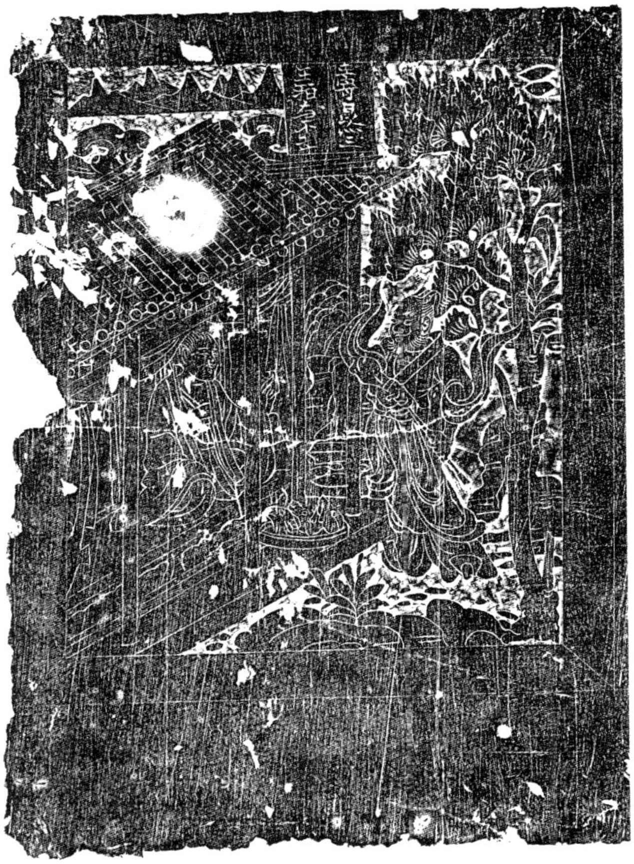

图五　深圳北魏石床董黯图

[12] 图五是Wu Qianghua先生提供的该石床拓本的照片（下同。并且，后面图六之类的该石床的局部图也是同样由Wu Qianghua先生提供的照片）。

[13] 两孝子传的正文，引用自幼学会《孝子伝注解》。下同。

而常恐离其罪，寝食不安，日夜为愁。董黯母者贫而无忧，为人无恶，内则有孝，外则有义，安心之喜，实过千金也。王奇闻之，大忿，杀三生作食，一日三度，与黯之母尔。即曰：若不吃尽，当以锋突汝胸腹，转载（戟）刺母颈。母即闷绝，遂命终也。时母年八十。葬礼毕后，黯至奇家，以其头祭母墓。官司闻之，曰：父母与君敌不戴天。则奏具状，曰：朕以寡德，统荷万机。今孝子至孝，朕可助恤，则赐以金百斤也。

晋时，虞预的《会稽典录》中还引用董黯传，除此之外还有些许章节残存，但是孝子传中记载董黯传的只有两孝子传[14]，并且船桥本中有大量的省略及改写，丧失了董黯传的原貌。

图五的上部有两行题记："王寄日杀三/生犹为不孝。"

王寄（奇）是董黯传的另一个主人公，于是可以了解该图的内容正是董黯传。更令人瞩目的是，该图的题记原样出现在阳明本孝子传正文中的画线部分[15]（三牲也称太牢，是天子供奉社稷时用于祭祀的三种牲畜——牛、羊、猪。这个三牲，在该图的题记中写作"三生"，并且在船桥本的画线部分也能看到）。这个事实是非常重要的，像该题记这样直接引用阳明本孝子传，以前从未被证实过。另一方面，该图的题记也是证明阳明本孝子传的祖本是出自北魏后期以前孝子传的极其重要的资料。同样的，如后文所述，与该石床郭巨图的题记相关，体现了该石床在孝子传图研究史上的划时代意义。特别是该题记的后半"犹为不孝"这句，是根据阳明本"故孝经云：虽日用三牲养，犹为不孝也"而来的，阳明本的画线部分所引用《孝经·纪孝行章》的"事亲者，居上而不骄，为下不乱，在丑不争。居上而骄则亡，为下而乱则刑，在丑而争则兵。三者不除，虽日用三牲之养，犹为不孝"。并且董黯传中王奇的母亲因担心儿子的品行而说的"吾子不孝，多与人恐，惧罹其罪"，正符合《孝经·纪孝行章》中所谓不孝者的条件，"三者不除"尤其是"在丑而争则兵"，在可以肯定阳明本引用孝经有其特定理由的同时，也可以断定阳明本引用孝经这种形式是在该石床制作之前出现的。

图五画面左侧描绘的是王奇的家以及屋内背靠屏风的王奇的母亲。画面右侧描绘的是站在庭院中的王奇。对王奇家屋顶上的瓦的描绘，又大又气派，体现出有钱人的感觉。与该石床老莱子的家（没有瓦）以及郭巨的家相比，对比十分明显。郭巨的家似乎是茅草屋。王奇和母亲相对，母亲的面前摆放着盛放三牲的盆。王奇分腿而立，左手握着挂在腰间的剑，右手使劲握住剑柄，一副威胁母亲的样子（敦煌本《事森》引用的《会稽典》中收录的董黯故事有这样的记载"寄……拔刀胁抑令吃之"）。只见头戴冠的王奇眉头紧锁，瞪大双眼，嘴角紧绷。左右衣袖上扬，飞舞的衣袖是对王奇的愤怒强有力的表现。相对于王奇，母亲的手掌向着王奇的方向，就像在制止王奇的逼迫。母亲的头上没有什么装饰物。

那么，该图的图案与其他的董黯图有什么样的关系呢？据笔者管见，目前所见董黯图有以下几件：

（1）美国明尼阿波利斯美术馆藏北魏石棺

（2）美国波士顿美术馆藏北魏石室

（3）美国纳尔逊美术馆藏北齐石床

以上（1）（2）（3）的董黯图为图六、图七、图八所示，分别作简要的说明[16]。首先，图六是明尼阿波利斯美术馆藏北魏石棺的董黯图（题记"孝子董懴［黯］与父犊［独］居"）。描绘的是董黯（左）与他的母亲（右）相对而坐的场景[17]。图七是波士顿美术馆藏北魏石室的董黯图（题记"董晏［黯］母供王寄［奇］母语时"）。这个图的图案比图六

[14] 和董黯图一起成为其依据的董黯传，也曾经做过探讨（详细请参阅拙著《孝子伝図の研究》Ⅱ－3）。

[15] 关于董黯传中提到的三牲，西野贞治先生这样指出（注［5］中提到的论文）："这里的三牲是王侯的礼，是庶民所不能触及的，孝经所言的只是比喻。比如太康起居注（御览八六三）中'石崇崔亮母疾、日赐清酒粳米各五升、猪羊肉各一斤半'，重臣的母亲病重，才赐予二牲。所以，这个故事中罗列的三牲，可以说是贫与富、孝与不孝的夸张对比，特别是将不孝子的愚蠢作为夸张的部分插入进故事。"

[16] 图六是照片。图七见《中国美术全集绘画编》19《石刻线画》图六，上海人民美术出版社，1988年。图八参考长广敏雄：《六朝時代美術の研究》图五六、五五、五四，美术出版社，1969年。

[17] 这幅图就像后述一样，似乎会与董永图相互弄混。

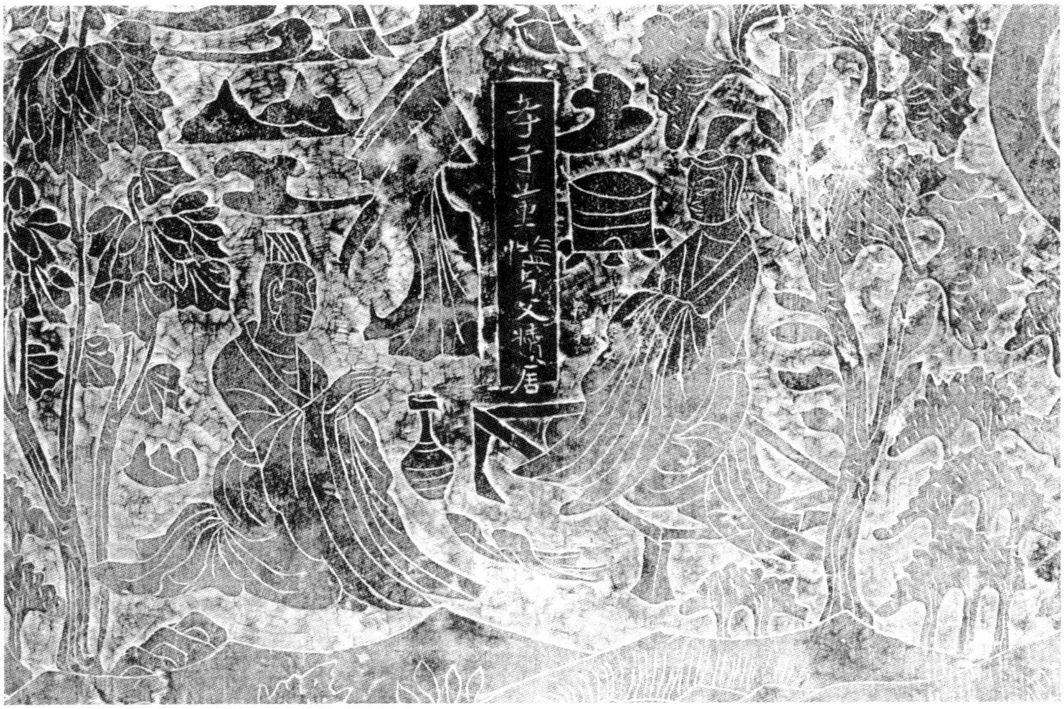

图六　美国明尼阿波利斯美术馆藏北魏石棺董黯图

图七　美国波士顿美术馆藏北魏石室董黯图

(A) (B) (C)

图八　美国纳尔逊美术馆藏北齐石床董黯图

的稍微复杂些，两人的家都有描绘，其中右侧是董黯家（正面和侧面的帘子都卷起），左侧是王奇家。右侧的屋内，董黯的母亲面向左侧坐着，画面右端董黯站在家的侧面。母亲未带发饰，仅头发在头顶盘起，董黯双髻。左侧的屋内王奇的母亲面向右侧坐着，左手持团扇，遮挡住脸。看来是王奇的母亲作掩面状，而董黯母亲的表情温柔平静，这样的描绘，形成了很好的对比。王奇母亲前面的方盒中盛放着三牲。面向着母亲、像是倚靠在柱子上的人是王奇。王奇也是双髻，眉八字集中，怒目而视。画面左端面向右站立的女性应该是侍女。这个图与深圳北魏石床的董黯图相比，左半部符合王奇家的造型，并且可以看出两幅图的整体结构是一致的。同时，深圳北魏石床的董黯图符合图七的左半部，所以图五描绘的只是这类图画的一部分。像图六这样将右半的内容图像化的，是十分难得的。图八是纳尔逊美术馆藏北齐石床的全部四块石板中，正、左、右三面。这三块石板全部用来描绘董黯的故事，可以说是三连的董黯图[18]（榜题“不孝王寄［奇］”［2面］）。该图按照（A）（B）（C）的顺序从左开始，（A）描绘的是董黯的家，（B）描绘的是王奇的家（有“不孝王寄”的榜题），（C）描绘的是母亲去世后，以王奇的头来供奉母亲之墓的董黯，向监司（刺史）乞求最后去母亲的坟墓祭拜的场景。（A）的登场人物从左开始，屋内坐着面向右侧的董黯的母亲，母亲的对面是面向左侧跪在庭院中的董黯，面向左手捧食物、运送饭食的是两个双髻侍女。（C）中面向墓右向跪倒的是董黯（董黯的下方有两个猎人）。最接近深圳北魏石床董黯图的是（B）中所描绘的画面。（B）中的登场人物，坐在垂帘前右手持杖、左手掌心向上的年老的女性是王奇的母亲，两侧面向母亲站立的是两个侍女（左边朝向后的侍女双髻，右手持团扇），面对着母亲、腰间佩剑、可以看到两足并列站立的是儿子王奇，王奇的右侧正面站立的是随从，同时绘有装饰过的马。这些表现出了王奇家的富有。母亲面前摆放的是三牲。与（A）董黯的母亲温柔平静的表情相对，这里王奇母亲嘴唇紧绷，眉眼上挑，疲倦的表情，一副已经说不出什么

［18］这个石床的复原以及董黯图，参阅注［10］中提到的林先生的论文，拙著《孝子伝図の研究》Ⅰ二3。并且关于这个三连图的董黯图，参阅拙著《孝子伝図の研究》Ⅱ－3。

指责的话的样子。并且王奇的下巴突出，一副傲慢的态度精准地表现出来。深圳北魏石床的董黯图与此图相比，值得注目的是将阳明本孝子传的正文中“王奇日杀三牲”这样记载的三牲（牛、羊、猪），一起出现在图中。图九将两者对比，左图是深圳北魏石床董黯图的三牲，右图是纳尔逊美术馆藏北齐石床的三牲图像。左图是盛放在盆里的三牲的头，左边是羊（有卷角）、中间是牛（有角）、右边是猪（有牙）。右图左边是牛、中间是羊、右边是猪（被捆绑起来），象征着母亲面前摆放的食物是三牲。

该图符合长广敏雄先生曾经提出的孝子传图的特点之一：“被熟知的传说孝行亲子的身边都有些小道具，作为孝子的特征，巧妙的象征着故事。”[19]这两幅三牲图，都可以从旁证明这些图是董黯图。深圳北魏石床的董黯图没有描绘侍女、随从等，王奇和隔着食物面向王奇的母亲是两幅图所共有的基本构图，在此之上，佩剑的王奇和三牲的表现之类的近似地方有很多。深圳北魏石床的董黯图与纳尔逊石床的董黯图相比更为写实，所以创作时间应该更早。前述深圳北魏石床的题记中“王寄日杀三生，犹为不孝”是出自阳明本孝子传，纳尔逊美术馆石床的榜题“不孝王寄”也类似深圳北魏石床的题记。从这一方面来看，深圳北魏石床的原典性和先行性，使其具有极高的资料价值。

以上是笔者关于深圳北魏石床董黯图（图五）浅薄的见解，将董黯图（1）~（3）（图六~八），所描绘的内容进行整理后，概括一览，并对董黯的图像在图中的位置进行验证。现在从场景数最多的（3）纳尔逊美术馆藏北齐石床的董黯图开始。自左边开始有

（一）董黯的家（A）

（二）王奇的家（B）

（三）董黯母亲的坟墓（C）

这样三个场景，从构成角度来看，图六~八以及图五都具有上述三个场景。根据主要的登场人物，可以概括出表二。表中的箭头表示各图中的对应关系。

表二中，最上面的董永图是指 C. T. Loo 旧藏北魏石棺床的董永图，其题记为：“孝子董永与父犊（独）居”。这个题记与图六明尼阿波利斯美术馆藏北魏石棺的董黯图题记“孝子董慥（黯）与父犊（独）居”酷似，仅仅只有“永”和“慥”一字之差，从这一点来看图六的题记很可能是误用或是转用了董永图的题记。[20]从表二来看，图六描绘是发生在董黯家的场景，图七是董黯的家和王奇的家两个场景表现

图九　三牲图像

[19] 长广敏雄：《六朝時代美術の研究》八章 180 页。

[20] 图六的题记中“父”字的出现十分奇怪（应该是母字）。这也是这个题记与该图不相符的一个证据。围绕父亲，转用董永图的题记是确凿无疑的事实。关于董永图和董黯图的关系，西野贞治曾经指出这样的事实：波士顿美术馆藏北魏石室的董永图是在董黯图的基础上描绘的，传说董黯是有名的董仲舒的六世子孙（唐，崔殷《重修董孝子庙记一》），并且有董永是董仲舒的父亲一说（董永变文之类）。也就说，董黯和董永是有很深的家族联系的，两人的图上下相配是有这样的背景的。西野贞治：《董永伝説について》，《人文研究》6.6，1955 年。西野先生所指出的是非常重要的关于董永图和董黯图的题记，出现这种关联的理由就很明显了。参阅拙著：《孝子伝図の研究》Ⅱ–3。

表二　董黯图场景一览

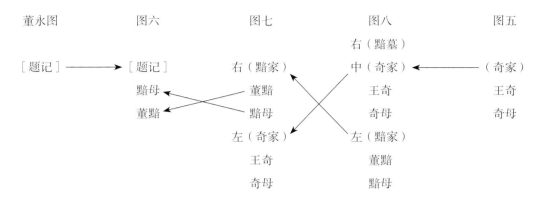

董永图	图六	图七	图八	图五
			右（黯墓）	
［题记］	［题记］	右（黯家）	中（奇家）	（奇家）
	黯母	董黯	王奇	王奇
	董黯	黯母	奇母	奇母
		左（奇家）	左（黯家）	
		王奇	董黯	
		奇母	黯母	

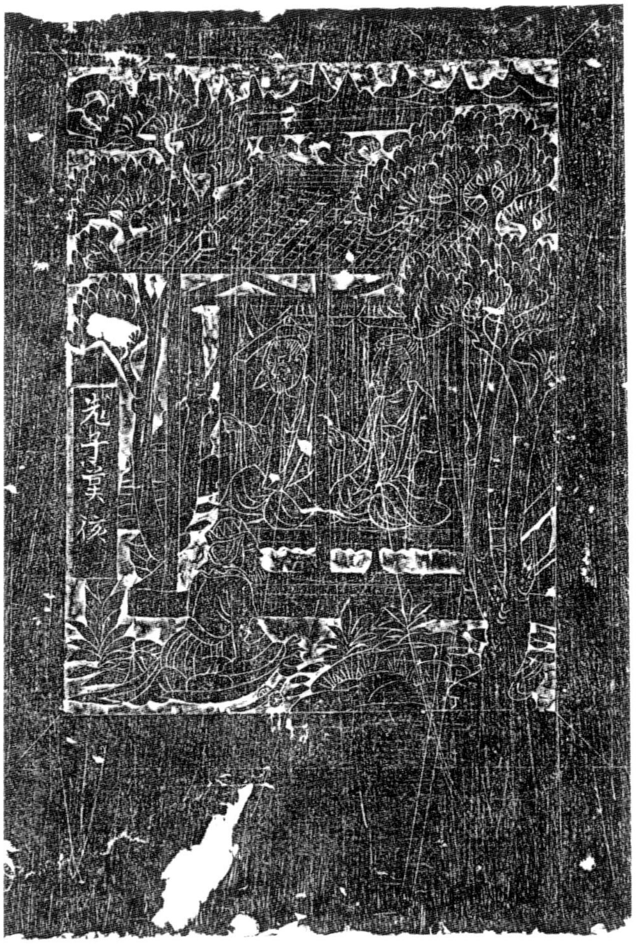

图一〇　深圳北魏石床老莱子图

在同一个画面中（但是和图六相比，家中的董黯和母亲的左右位置是相反的），图八与图七比，（一）董黯的家（A）与（二）王奇的家（B）的左右位置相互调换，再加上（三）董黯母亲的坟墓（C），图的场景多了。可见，深圳北魏石床图（图五）描绘的确实是图八中间的王奇的家，并且没有描绘图八左边王奇的家之外的场景。

三

接下来，图一〇是深圳北魏石床的老莱子图。下面是老莱子图所引用的阳明本孝子传老莱之（子）的正文（船桥本孝子传也一并列举）。

【阳明本】

楚人老莱之者，至孝也。年九十，犹父母在。常作婴儿，自家戏以悦亲心，着斑斓之衣而坐下竹马。为父母上堂取浆水，失脚倒地，方作婴儿啼，以悦父母之怀。故礼曰：父母在，言不称老，衣不纯素。此之谓也。赞曰：老莱至孝，奉事二亲。晨昏定省，供谨弥勤。戏倒亲前，为婴儿身。高道兼备，天下称仁。

【船桥本】

老莱之者，楚人也，性至孝也。年九十而犹父母存。爰莱着斑兰之衣，乘竹马游庭。或为供父母赍浆堂上，倒阶而啼，声如婴儿，悦父母之心也。

深圳北魏石床的老莱子图左边稍微靠下的地方有题记："老子萸（叹）侅"。"老子"就是老莱子。"萸"应是简略的表示叹息，"侅"是哽咽的意思，叹侅就是因为哀伤而哽咽。老莱子叹侅，自己年事已高，而父母的年事更高，忧郁充满喉头（后文中参考了明尼阿波利斯美术馆藏北魏石棺的老莱子图的题记"老来［莱］子年受百岁哭闷"）。

深圳北魏石床老莱子图（图一〇），画面中央面向左而坐的是老莱子的父母（左侧的是父亲、右侧的是母亲）。父母在有着几级高的屋内坐着，这是用来表现前厅（堂［两孝子传］）的（C. T. Loo旧藏北魏石床的题记“老莱子父母在堂”）。父母的背后描绘有屏风。画面左下面向右的人物是老莱子。老莱子像是跌坐一样，右手撞向地面。父母一起向上抬起右手，应该是要表现老莱子突然摔倒时两人同时吃惊的反映。该图是将阳明本孝子传中老莱子“为父母上堂取浆水，失脚倒地，方作婴儿啼，以悦父母之怀”的场景图像化。父亲头戴巾，母亲将头发梳成发髻。老莱子戴着有很多山形的覆盖住耳朵的帽子，有可能是阳明本孝子传中“着斑斓之衣”之类的儿童衣物。斑斓，指丰富的色彩，可能是幼儿的穿着。有趣的是，老莱子的右手下面描绘有雏鸟车的玩具。关于这个会在后文继续探讨。

孝子传图中老莱子图是很有名的，后世的二十四孝图当然也有传承，有很多残存的图像。据笔者的管见，老莱子图有以下几个。

（1）东汉武氏祠画像石（武梁祠一石）

（2）东汉武氏祠画像石（前石室七石）

（3）和林格尔东汉壁画墓

（4）美国明尼阿波利斯美术馆藏北魏石棺

（5）日本和泉市久保惣纪念美术馆藏北魏石床

（6）C. T. Loo旧藏北魏石床

（7）洛阳古代艺术馆藏北魏石床

（8）邓县彩色画像砖

（9）美国纳尔逊美术馆藏北齐石床

作为参考，现将其中的五幅图：（2）、（3）、（4）、（8）、（9）列出，分别为图一一～一五[21]。图一一是东汉武氏祠画像石的前石室七石所描绘的老莱子图（榜题从右开始是“老莱子”和“□［老］莱子父母”），这幅图与图一二都是汉代的老莱子图，图一三及以后的三幅是六朝时期的老莱子图。

首先看图一一，画面左侧的横向台子上，坐着的是老莱子的父母（面向右），画面右侧描绘着跌坐似的老莱子（面向左）。父母的座席有屏风围绕，父母的上方有低垂的帷幕，这里或许是表现之前提到过的堂。父亲头戴进贤冠，母亲头戴帼。老莱子头戴呈三个山形的巾帽，左手的鸠杖很突出，表现老莱子本人

图一一　东汉武氏祠画像石老莱子图（前石室七石）

［21］图一一见《“中央研究院”历史语言研究所所藏汉代石刻画像拓本精选集》，“中央研究院”历史语言研究所，2004年。图一二是内蒙古自治区文物考古研究所提供的照片。图一三是照片。图一四见《邓县彩色画像砖墓》图版一八，文物出版社，1958年。图一五见长广敏雄：《六朝時代美術の研究》图四七。

图一二　和林格尔东汉壁画墓老莱子图

图一三　美国明尼阿波利斯美术馆藏北魏石棺老莱子图

也已是高龄。再向左，有盛放着一些食器的盆子，描绘的应该是“取浆水”的场景。父亲两手上举，面向着拱手的母亲（左），两人像是在谈笑。应该是运送食物的老莱子摔倒的样子十分可笑。武梁祠第一石与这幅图有基本一样的图像。图一二是和林格尔东汉壁画墓的老莱子图（榜题，从左开始是“来［莱］子父”、“来［莱］子母”、“老来［莱］子”<下>）。这幅图中，描绘有坐在建筑物中老莱子的父母和其下已经严重损坏的摔倒的老莱子。这个建筑物不用说是对堂的描绘，说不定老莱子就是从堂的台阶上摔下的。图一三是明尼阿波利斯美术馆藏北魏石棺的老莱子图。这幅图与图一一、图一二之类的汉代画像相比有很大的不同，比如不见对建筑（堂）的描绘，用童子的形象表现老莱子等。堂上的双亲，及其前面的老莱子是汉代以来老莱子图的基本构图形式，其后的变化很小，从六朝时期的老莱子图来看，部分比较符合汉代的图像，但也有一些显著的变化。根据六朝时期的老莱子图的变化可以总结出以下的三点（附有含有这些特征的老莱子图的编号）：

（一）老莱子是童子的形象

a 老莱子有动作：（4）（6）（8）

b 老莱子没有动作：（5）（7）

（二）老莱子是老人的形象：（9）、图一〇

（三）没有描绘建筑（堂）：（4）（5）（7）（9）

（一）中老莱子是以童子的形象表示的，但是这个老莱子也有能看出动作的 a 类图和看不出动作的 b 类图。b 是 a 的象征化，b 中的双亲也是以立像（坐像）来象征化，看不出动作的占大多数。（二）是与（一）b 相对，老莱子以老人的形象进行描绘。图一〇也具有这样的特征。（三）没有描绘建筑（堂），因而描绘的老莱子的双亲是坐在榻上的。（三）和（一）b 一样，是对老莱子图进行大胆的象征化而出现的结果。现在话题回到图一三。

图一三有：“老来（莱）子年受百岁哭闷”这样的题记，与图一〇的题记相关，前文中就已经提到了。就像这个题记中提到的一样，很罕见地注明老莱子的年龄有百岁，而两孝子传记载是九十岁，一般七十岁的说法比较多。这幅图，画面的右侧，坐在榻上的是老莱子的父母（面向左），画面的左侧以儿童形象表现的是老莱子（面向右）。父亲头戴进贤冠，母亲头发用发带挽成结，发带末端的两条，在身后扬起。父亲拱手，母亲合掌。老莱子的头发扎成双鬟，被描绘成童子形。可以看出是将阳明本孝子传的赞中的“为婴儿身”直接图像化。就像跟着老莱子一起移动的雏鸟车，在画面中十分突出。从老莱子的姿势来看，向着父母的方向挥动，就好像正向左边跳起，呈现出不可思议的姿势。老莱子姿势的结局是记载中的“失脚倒地”（阳明本），图像表现的没有过分变形。有趣的是，老莱子的动作看起来像是在优雅的舞蹈游戏（参考图一四），图中的母亲像是在用手打着拍子。六朝时期接受了这种形象的老莱子。实际上，后世的二十四孝图中

图一四　邓县彩色画像砖老莱子图

关于老莱子的动作有“戏舞”（见《全相二十四孝诗选》）这样的解释。邓县彩色画像砖的老莱子图（图一四），画面右侧是老莱子的父母（面向左），左侧是童子形的老莱子（头发扎成双鬟，面向右）。父母坐在像亭子一样的堂中，父亲头戴进贤冠，母亲头发用发带挽成结，发带的末端做飘荡状。老莱子在比堂低一级的台阶上，左手捧着食器摔倒，右手碰到台阶。老莱子双膝朝下，两腿上翘，上半身抬起，脸朝着双亲的方向，父母一起，像拍手一样，双手打开，表现的是运送食物的老莱子突然摔倒，让两人同时吃惊了。图一四和图一三，都和汉代的画像不同，洋溢着浓郁的优美的六朝风格。图一五是纳尔逊美术馆藏北齐石床的老莱子图。这幅图中，画面右下是老莱子（面向左），其上位于画面中央偏左的是老莱子的父母。没有描绘建筑（堂）。父亲头戴呈两个山字形的巾，右膝立起，面向右坐。父亲稍微靠下的是母亲，头发用发带挽成结，左手拿着食器，面向左坐着。老莱子是老人的形象，有趣的是像是扎着很小的双鬟，双手和左膝盖触地，脸面向正面稍偏左。这幅图被视为北齐时的，也没有描绘建筑物，拥有象征化这一特点。将图一三和图一四相比较的话，以对人物等的写实性的描绘作为其时代特征（老莱子的双鬟有意识的被描绘的较小），北魏晚期的老莱子图拥有相同的画风，可以看作是这幅图（图一五）的先例。从这点来看，包

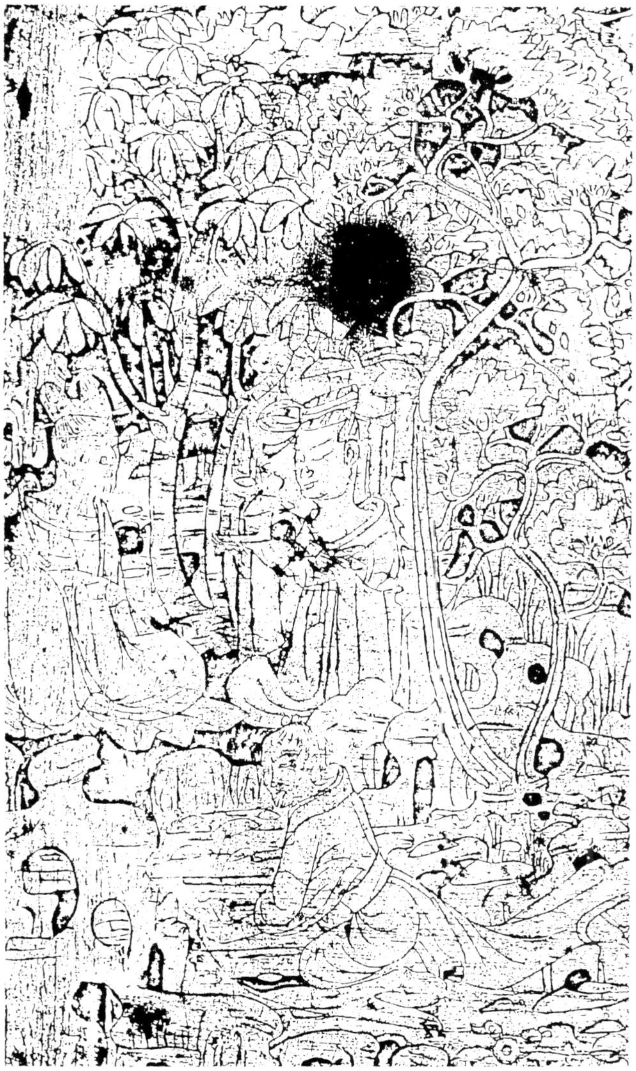

图一五　美国纳尔逊美术馆藏北齐石床老莱子图

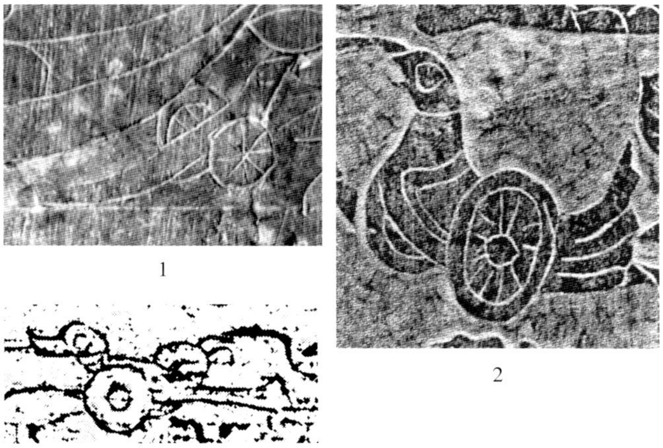

图一六　雏鸟车

含深圳北魏石床在内，直至纳尔逊美术馆藏北齐石床等，是了解北魏后期到北齐时期孝子图发展的不可或缺的资料。

观察图一五的右下方，长广敏雄先生曾经指出："更值得注意的是，老莱子放在地上的左手，握着一个细长绳的前端，这个绳子连接着画面右下方小小的鸟形物品。小鸟形象是玩具一般，有车轮。"[22]这里有对雏鸟车的描绘。这是在深圳北魏石床老莱子图和图一三中都能看到的，图一六将这些放在一起（1是图一〇、2是图一三、3是图一五的雏鸟车）。虽然这种描绘在两孝子传中没有见到，但可以见到如佚名《孝子传》（《初学记》卷十七所引）中所说："老莱子……弄雏鸟于亲侧"，还有《列女传》佚文（《艺文类聚》二十所引。今本《列女传》不见）中"老莱子……或弄乌鸟于亲侧"之类的记载，可能是两孝子传中脱落的部分。这种雏鸟车是把雏鸟跟在亲鸟身后走路的习性象征化的可爱的玩具。

四

最后，图一七是深圳北魏石床的郭巨图。下文列出该图所引用的阳明本孝子传正文（船桥本孝子传也一并列举）。

【阳明本】

（家贫养母）

郭巨者，河内人也。时年荒。夫妻昼夜勤作，以供养母。其妇忽然生一男子。便共议言：今养此儿，则废母供事。仍掘地埋之。忽得金一釜。釜上题云：黄金一釜，天赐郭巨。于是遂致富贵，转孝蒸蒸。赞曰：孝子郭巨，纯孝至真。夫妻同心，杀子养亲。天赐黄金，遂感明神。善哉孝子，富贵荣身。

【船桥本】

郭巨者，河内人也。父无母存，供养勤勤。于年不登，而人庶饥困。爰妇生一男。巨云：若养之者，恐有老养之妨。使母抱儿，共行山中，掘地将埋儿。底金一釜。釜上题云：黄金一釜，天赐孝子郭巨。于是因儿获金，不埋其儿。忽然得富贵，养母又不乏。天下闻之，俱誉孝道之至也。

深圳北魏石床的郭巨图（图一七）是该石床孝子传图中唯一使用两幅连续的画面进行描绘的。这二连图在该石棺床的位置是正面右石板的男性墓主人右侧的两面（图一孝子传图［3］［4］）。二连图的顺序按照前述林圣智所说从右开始，以A→B的顺序（图二、郭巨A→B）进行。现在以这个顺序来探讨该图，用郭巨图对林圣智说法的正确性进行更加具体的说明。

该图A的左上和B的右下共有两个题记（图一八）分别是：

"孝子郭柜杀儿养母"（A）

"孝子郭柜"（B）

值得注意的是与前述董黯图的题记（图六）一样，这两个题记也是根据孝子传郭巨正文中的赞里面画线部分文字而来。孝子传中说："赞曰：孝子郭巨……杀子养亲"

母字，根据赞中押韵各字，真、亲、神、身（上平声，十一真韵），亲应该是正确的，柜是音同，并且儿与子、亲与母比较，从意义上来看，更加易懂。这些都可以看作是深圳北魏石床所做的改动。这么看来，就出现了令人吃惊的事实，深圳北魏石床的三幅孝子传图的题记中，有两幅图的题记都可

[22] 长广敏雄：《六朝時代美術の研究》九章997页。

B　　A

图一七　深圳北魏石床郭巨图（A、B）

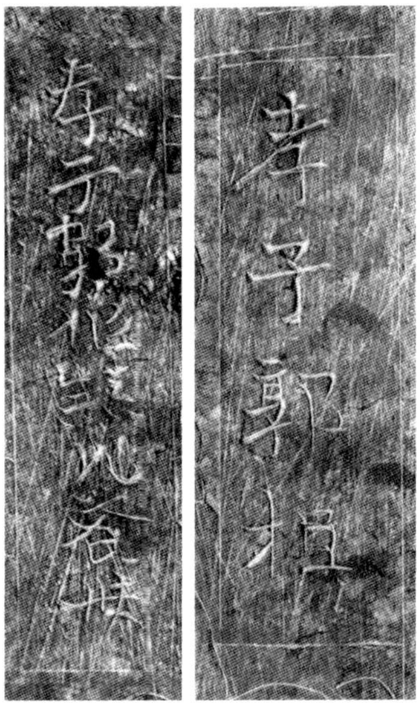

A　　B

图一八　深圳北魏石床郭巨图题记

以证实是从阳明本孝子传中引用而来的。这已经不是单纯偶然的一致了，于是可以得出，深圳北魏石床的制造者所使用的《孝子传》原本，即便不是系统的阳明本也是极其接近阳明本的。这个事实也是不可动摇的证据，证明北魏时期阳明本孝子传已经开始流传这个事实。回溯研究史，半个世纪以前，西野贞治先生有名的论文《关于阳明本孝子传的特点以及与清家本的关系》中，就曾经预言过这一点。现在深圳北魏石床的出现，使之变成了可以证明的事实。在这层含义下，前文中所述的深圳北魏石床是具有极高学术价值的遗物，无疑是正确的。该郭巨图（图一七）与董黯图（图五），有与该石床学术价值相关的重要的题记，所以，这里对图像的内容再次确认一下。

图一七右A与题记一样描绘的是贫穷的郭巨夫妇将要把儿子埋入土中的场景。画面右侧站着的是怀抱婴儿的郭巨的妻子（面向左）。婴儿裸着，面向郭巨的方向（左）并用右手指着。画面左侧是两手握着锹，左脚用力踩在锹上的郭巨（面向右）在地上挖坑。妻子梳着发髻，郭巨头戴巾。郭巨目光看向锹右边挖出的“黄金一釜”。上天被郭巨的孝心感动，赐予郭巨黄金。这是郭巨图A的内容。向左继续，B的内容是天赐黄金之后，郭巨的母亲、儿子一起迎接免于杀子的郭巨夫妇，表现大团圆的结局。图一七左B，画面右侧，一起面向左站着郭巨（右侧）和他的妻子（左侧），画面左侧，屋里的榻上坐着郭巨的母亲和孩子。母亲梳着发髻。B中建筑物的屋顶是茅草顶，是在表现郭巨家的贫穷。屋内的榻有屏风围绕。孩子穿着婴儿装，双腿向前伸着，张着嘴。郭巨的母亲，左手拿着食器，右手在喂孩子食物。B中没有描绘A中挖出的黄金，如果按照林圣智所说的A、B两个场景的顺序，逆着解释也是可能的，也就是说B的场景并不是故事中的大团圆，反而是故事的开端。在这里不用逆着的解释，在下文中对郭巨图的排列稍做探讨并说明其原因。

孝子传图中，郭巨图与老莱子图一样都是人气很高的图像，笔者管见，尚存的遗物中有以下11图。

（1）江苏徐州佛山画像石墓

（2）宁夏固原北魏墓漆棺画

（3）美国明尼阿波利斯美术馆藏北魏石棺

（4）日本和泉市久保惣纪念美术馆藏北魏石床

（5）美国纳尔逊美术馆藏北魏石棺

（6）C. T. Loo旧藏北魏石床

（7）洛阳古代艺术馆藏北魏石床

（8）美国纳尔逊美术馆藏北齐石床

（9）邓县彩色画像砖

（10）襄阳贾家冲画像砖墓

（11）陕西历史博物馆藏三彩四孝塔式缶

上述图像中（1）是东汉的遗物，（11）是非常珍贵的唐代孝子传图的遗物。除去（1）和（11），其他都是六朝时期的遗物。[23]

通观上述（1）~（11）的郭巨图，一般都是描绘挖坑的郭巨（夫妇）和挖出黄金这两个场景中的一个，偶尔也有跟随原文的情节展开，用二连图或三连图来表现的。现将两孝子传郭巨的故事按照下面五个场景进行划分，同时考虑有郭巨图遗物的保存状况。以下是根据郭巨（夫妇）的行动进行的场景化。

①供养（开端）

②行路

③挖坑、黄金

④搬运

⑤供养（大团圆）

虽然①和⑤对于郭巨夫妇的母亲来说都是供养场景，但原则上，场景需要符合登场人物全员。⑤中一般都有描绘黄金釜，但也有省略的（后述）。在这种情况下，是很难分辨①和⑤的。②是夫妇为了埋儿子而向山中进发的场景。③是郭巨（夫妇）在地上挖坑，地里出现黄金釜的场景，这个黄金釜已经可以看作郭巨图的象征。④是两人将黄金釜往家中搬运的场景。于是把各遗物的场景分别对应到①~⑤的场景中，用表三来表示（物品名用该图的编号表示）。可以说表三是通过场景来看遗物，然后再根据每件遗物列举出遗物所包含的场景，为表四（场景的内容用上记①~⑤的编号表示）。从表三来看，郭巨图中描绘③挖坑、黄金的场景占压倒性多数，⑤供养（大团圆）为其次［（5）和（7）中都未描绘黄金釜］。描绘①供养（开端）和②行路的只有一例。描绘④搬运也只有两例。

从表四来看，以一个场景来表现郭巨图的比较多，二连图的有（6）这一例。三连图的有（2）、（4）、（5）这三例。深圳北魏石床的郭巨图（图一七）是二连图，是（6）之后的第二件遗物。

上述（1）~（11）内，其中两幅由三连图构成的郭巨图将在下文中进行介绍。图一九是（2）宁夏固原北魏墓漆棺画中描绘的郭巨图。[24]图二〇是（5）

表三　郭巨图场景一览

场面	遗物
①供养	（2）
②行路	（2）
③挖坑，黄金	（1）（2）（4）（5）（6）（8）（9）（10）图一七 A
④搬运	（4）（5）
⑤供养	（3）（4）（5）*（6）（7）*（11）图一七 B

* 无黄金釜。

表四　郭巨图遗物场景一览

遗物	场面
（1）	③
（2）	①②③
（3）	⑤
（4）	③④⑤
（5）	③④⑤
（6）	③⑤
（7）	⑤
（8）	③
（9）	③
（10）	③
（11）	⑤
图一八	③⑤

［23］最近的桥本草子就郭巨是否存在发表了很有意思的看法（《“郭巨”說話の成立をめぐって》，《野草》71，2003年）。其中的一个理由是郭巨图在汉代的画像中没有发现。比如江苏徐州佛山画像石墓等，今后需要继续关注郭巨图的出土情况。

［24］图一九见宁夏固原博物馆：《固原北魏墓漆棺画》，宁夏人民出版社，1988年。

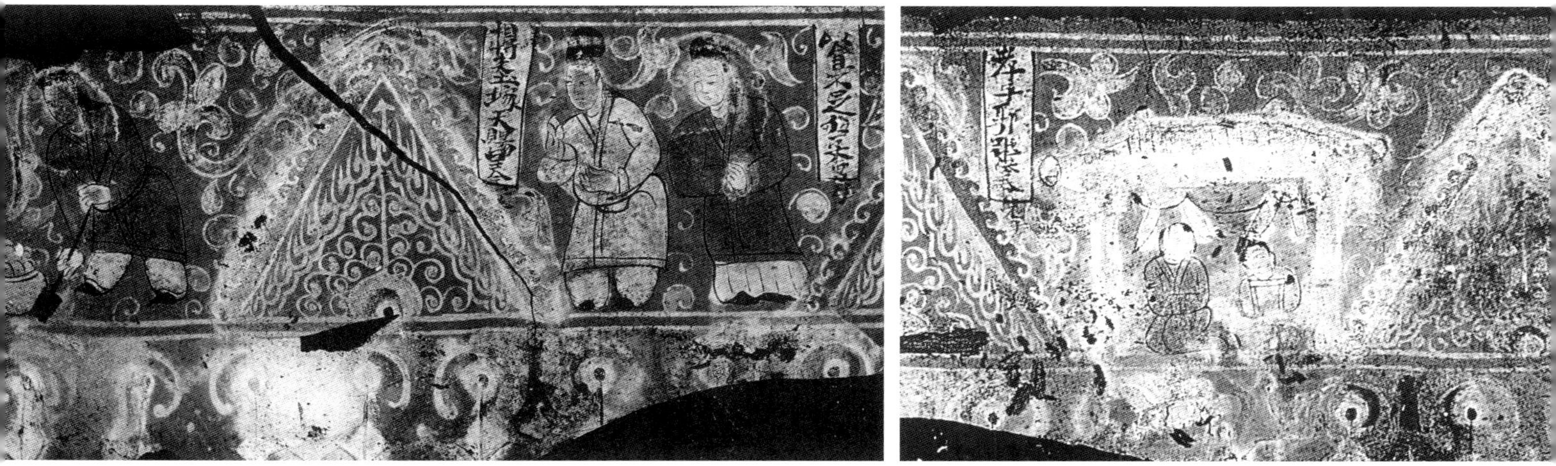

C　　B　　A

图一九　宁夏固原北魏墓漆棺画郭巨图（A~C）

纳尔逊美术馆藏北魏石棺的郭巨图。[25]

图一九是三连图构成的郭巨图，各个场面都有题记。分别为：A“孝子郭距（巨）供养老母”；B“以食不足敬□□母，相将夫土塚天赐皇今（黄金）一父（釜）”；C“官不德（得）脱（夺）私不德（得）与”。这幅图描绘在漆棺的左侧棺上栏。三连的郭巨图（从右开始以 A → B → C 的顺序），是从八连的舜图左边开始的。图中见到的三角状的山形是用来区别画面的。这幅图的左侧已经不见，很可能是原本中另一幅大团圆的场景。这个漆棺是北魏太和时期（477~499）制作，图像中独具特色的服装是当时鲜卑习俗的残留，是非常珍贵的遗物。首先，这幅图的 A 图从场景来说属于前述的①供养（开端），描绘的是郭巨的家。从题记开始，屋内左侧是郭巨的母亲，右侧是郭巨的妻子。B 图是②行路的场景。画面右侧是郭巨，左侧是妻子，妻子像是怀抱着婴儿。在众多郭巨的图像中，只有这幅图描绘有①、②的场景（参考表三）。C 图是③挖坑发现黄金的场景，描绘的是握着锹的郭巨和被挖出的黄金釜。这个 C 图与图一七 A 的内容相当。

图二〇是纳尔逊美术馆藏北魏石棺右侧棺中栏所描绘的郭巨图。榜题“子郭巨”。左侧（棺木头侧）是舜图，右侧（棺木足侧）是原谷图。以石头和树作为场景的分隔，形成三连图（顺序是 A → C）。关于这幅图，首先从 A 图来看，画面左下方描绘的是③挖坑出现黄金的场景。A 图右侧跪着的是怀抱婴儿的郭巨的妻子，左侧双手握着锹，左脚用力踩在锹上的是郭巨（两人均面向左）。锹的左侧是挖出的黄金釜，郭巨正在注视着它。A 图稍偏右上是 B 图，描绘的是④搬运的场景。郭巨夫妇把黄金往家里搬运，两人均面向右。夫妇把黄金釜绑在棍子上，郭巨在前面，右手抱着孩子的妻子在后面，两人一人右肩一人左肩抬着棍子的两端走着。B 图右侧描绘的是最后的 C 图，是⑤供养（大团圆）的场景。右侧榻上右膝立起、双手抱着婴儿坐着的是郭巨的母亲，左侧并列站立的两人是郭巨和妻子。这幅图的 A 和 C 两个场面与图一七的 A 和 B 相当。（6）C.T.Loo 旧藏北魏石床的郭巨图以及这幅图与（4）和泉市久保惣纪念美术馆藏北魏石床的郭巨图三连图（具有③、④、⑤）相比，省略了④搬运的场景（参考表四）。有趣的是，图二〇 C 中与场景⑤供养（大团圆）相关的黄金釜并没有出现在画中。如果图二〇 C 是①供养（开端）的话，从 B 中夫妇向着 C 走来看，其他的画面看起来也不自然。所以，还应该

［25］图二〇见奥村伊九良：《孝子伝石棺の刻画》，《瓜茄》4，1937年。《古拙愁眉 支那美術史の諸相》，みすず書房，1982年再録，図一。

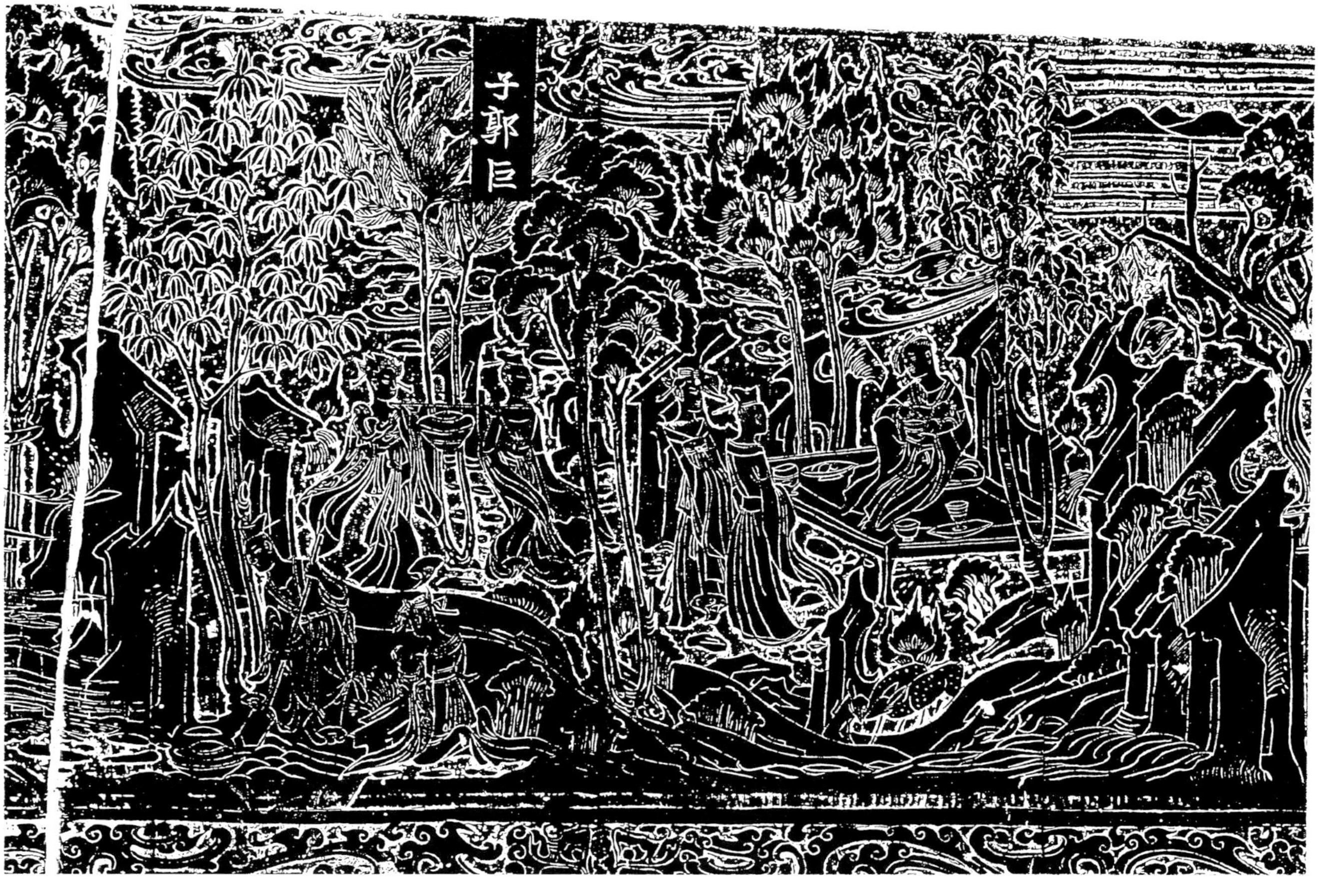

图二〇　纳尔逊美术馆藏北魏石棺郭巨图（A~C）

是⑤供养（大团圆）的场景。从这个角度来看，像图二〇 C 和（7）洛阳古代艺术馆藏北魏石床这样的郭巨图⑤供养（大团圆）的场景中有时不会描绘黄金釜。图一七 B 应该就是这种情况。

后记

在此，对给予我机会参观石床原物的 Wu Qianghua 先生深表感谢，Wu Qianghua 先生特意将在保管库中存放的四个石板搬出给我参观，对此好意，由衷难忘。小稿的写成与中国社会科学院考古研究所赵超教授的支持是分不开的，对教授的学恩深表谢意。小稿得到了平成十四年（2012）度科学研究费补助金基本研究 B 以及佛教大学特别研究费的资助。

本文由中央民族大学文博学院黄盼盼翻译成中文，特此致谢。

The Image of the Paragons of the Filial Piety on the Stone Couch of the Northern Wei Dynasty Exhibited in the Shenzhen Museum

The Quotation of Yōmei Version of Xiaozi Zhuan

Kuroda Akira
(Professor, Bukkyo University, Japan)

A set of stone sculpture artworks is exhibited in Shenzhen Museum (Pls. 16, 17). This paper mainly discusses the images of the "Paragons of Filial Piety" on one of them – a new-unearthed stone couch of the Northern Wei Dynasty and hopes to clarify their values for the research on the filial piety thought in ancient East Asia. The images of the "Paragons of Filial Piety" with inscriptions such as "Wang Ji" and so on, in the knowledge scope of the author, are never seen before the discovery of this stone couch; therefore, this paper tries to present a detailed interpretation to all of the motifs on this invaluable stone couch. These images are the visualization of the stories of the "Paragons of Filial Piety" well-known at that time. Two of these images are that of Guo Ju, the other two are that of Laolaizi, Dong An and Wang Ji, respectively. The author of this paper believes that these images of the "Paragons of Filial Piety" contained important contents which should not be neglected by the researchers on the "Paragons of Filial Piety". For example, the images about Dong An are the most striking. There have been very few images about Dong An preserved from the ancient times. The inscriptions of these two images about Dong An are the most important for the researches on the "Paragons of Filial Piety" images on this stone couch, and can be seen as directly quoted from the original texts of the stories of the "Paragons of Filial Piety" in ancient times. Since very early period, the stories about the "Paragons of Filial Piety", such as the *Xiaozi Zhuan* (Biographies of the Paragons of Filial Piety) by Liu Xiang and the *Xiaozi Zhuan* (another work in the same title) by Xiao Guangji, have been distributed widely as the reading materials for children. However, these stories have been lost at present, and their contents could only be seen from the quotations in other books. The lost of these textual stories of the "Paragons of Filial Piety" became the decisive barrier against the relevant observations. For example, the images of the "Paragons of Filial Piety" on the second registers of the stones Nos. 1 and 2 have not been interpreted through almost 1000 years of researches, the most important reason for which is that the lost of the textual biographies of the "Paragons of Filial Piety". What noticeable is, a Yōmei Version of *Xiaozi Zhuan* (Kōshi Den in Japanese) preserved in Japan has text similar to the inscriptions on this stone couch. Yōmei Version is one of the two complete versions of *Xiaozi Zhuan* (Kōshi Den) preserved in Japan, the original of which reflecting the original feature of the *Xiaozi Zhuan* in the medieval period would be introduced in Japan in the Six Dynasties or later period, so they are very valuable. The images of the "Paragons of Filial Piety" and their inscriptions on this stone couch are exactly the historic physical proof of the text of the Yōmei Version of *Xiaozi Zhuan*, and they proved the close relationship between the Yōmei Version of *Xiaozi Zhuan* and the images of the "Paragons of Filial Piety" popular in the ancient times.

Therefore, referring to the images of this stone couch and other relevant materials in the "Paragons of Filial

Piety" motifs of the Northern Dynasties and the texts in the Yōmei Version of *Xiaozi Zhuan* and other literary records, this paper made in-depth interpretation and estimation to the images of the "Paragons of Filial Piety", such as that of Dong An, Wang Ji, Guo Ju, Laolaizi, etc., reflected in this stone couch and other figures and stories with temporal characteristics. This work is helpful for the further understanding to the popularity of the images of "Paragons of Filial Piety" and the thought of filial piety.

(English abstract, translated by Ding Xiaolei, Institute of Archaeology, Chinese Academy of Social Sciences)

图版 Plates

1 **虎形基座** / Tiger-shaped Base

北 朝 / Northern Dynasties (386-581 CE)
灰 岩 / Limestone
长 度 / L. 80 cm
宽 度 / W. 29 cm
高 度 / H. 52 cm

2　兽形门枕座 / Monster-shaped Bearing Stone

北　朝 / Northern Dynasties（386-581 CE）
灰　岩 / Limestone
高　度 / H. 25 cm

3 兽形门枕座 / Monster-shaped Bearing Stone

北　朝 / Northern Dynasties (386-581 CE)
灰　岩 / Limestone
高 (左) / H.(L.) 16.5 cm
高 (右) / H.(R.) 15.5 cm

4 **兽形门枕座** / Monster-shaped Bearing Stone

北　朝 / Northern Dynasties (386-581 CE)
灰　岩 / Limestone

长（左）/ L.(L.) 82 cm	长（右）/ L.(R.) 84 cm
宽（左）/ W.(L.) 35 cm	宽（右）/ W.(R.) 37 cm
高（左）/ H.(L.) 68 cm	高（右）/ H.(R.) 66 cm

5 石辟邪 / Winged Mythological Creature

南　朝 / Southern Dynasties (420-589 CE)
灰　岩 / Limestone
长　度 / L. 104 cm
宽　度 / W. 41 cm
高　度 / H. 46 cm

6 石灯 / Stone Lamp

北　朝 / Northern Dynasties (386-581 CE)
灰　岩 / Limestone
高　度 / H. 54 cm

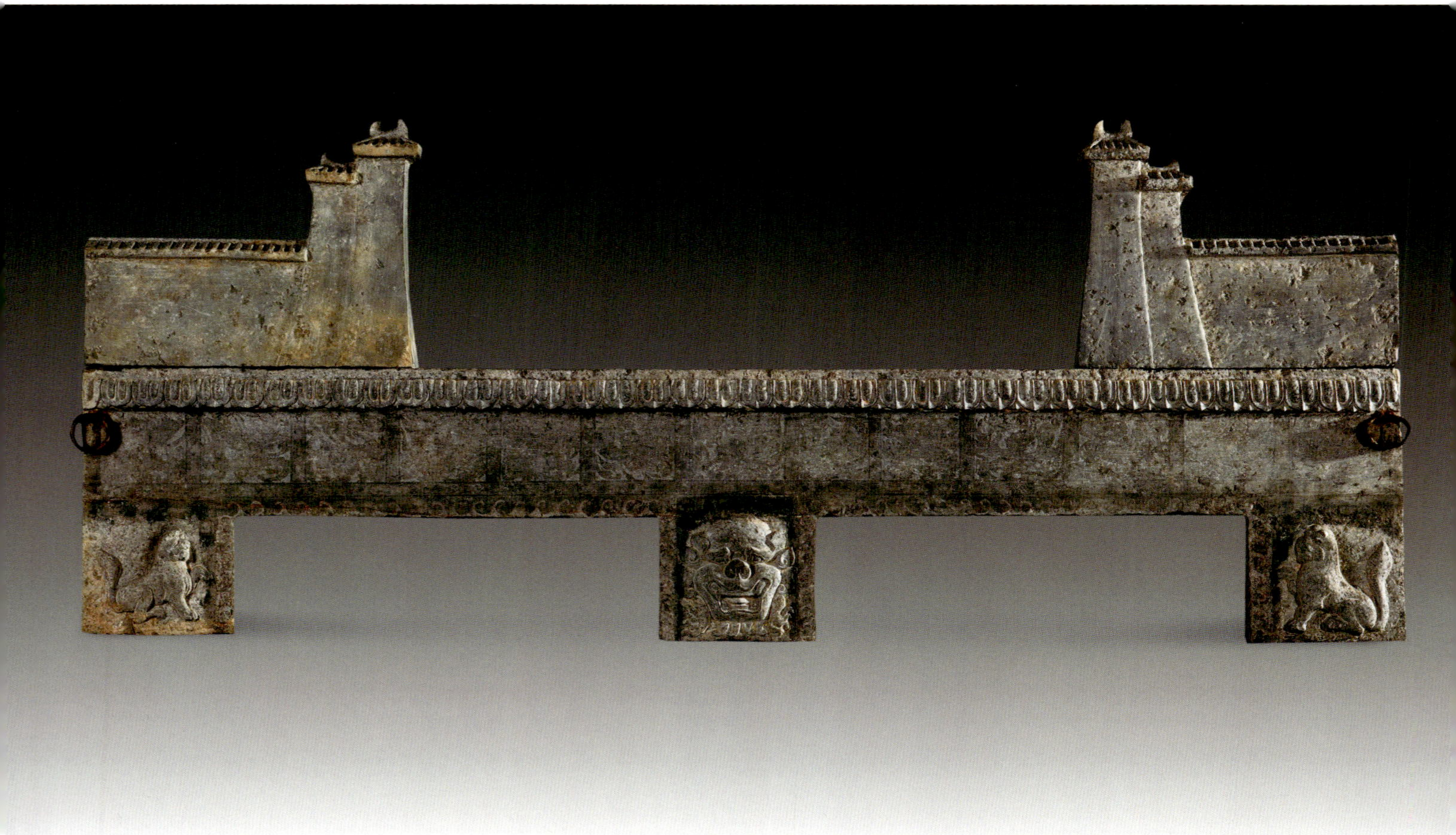

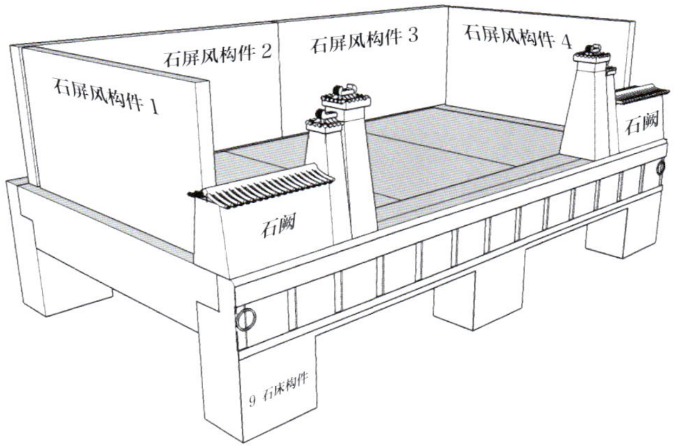

7　**石阙** / Stone Watchtower

北　朝 / Northern Dynasties (386-581 CE)
灰　岩 / Limestone
长（左） / L.(L.) 54 cm　　长（右） / L.(R.) 52 cm
宽（左） / W.(L.) 12.5 cm　　宽（右） / W.(R.) 11 cm
高（左） / H.(L.) 43 cm　　高（右） / H.(R.) 44 cm

8　**石枕** / Stone Pillow

北　朝 / Northern Dynasties (386-581 CE)
灰　岩 / Limestone
长　度 / L. 33 cm
宽　度 / W. 11 cm
高　度 / H. 8.6 cm

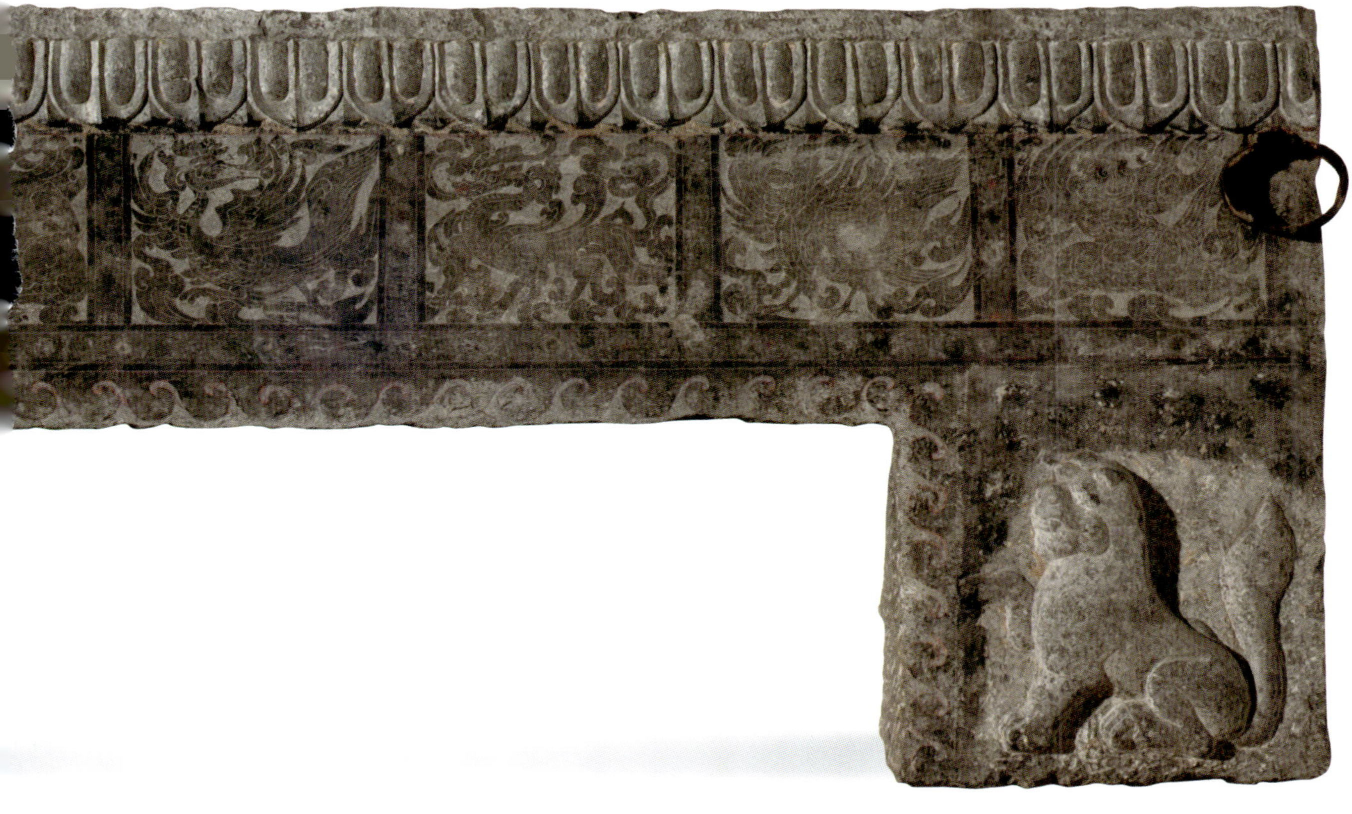

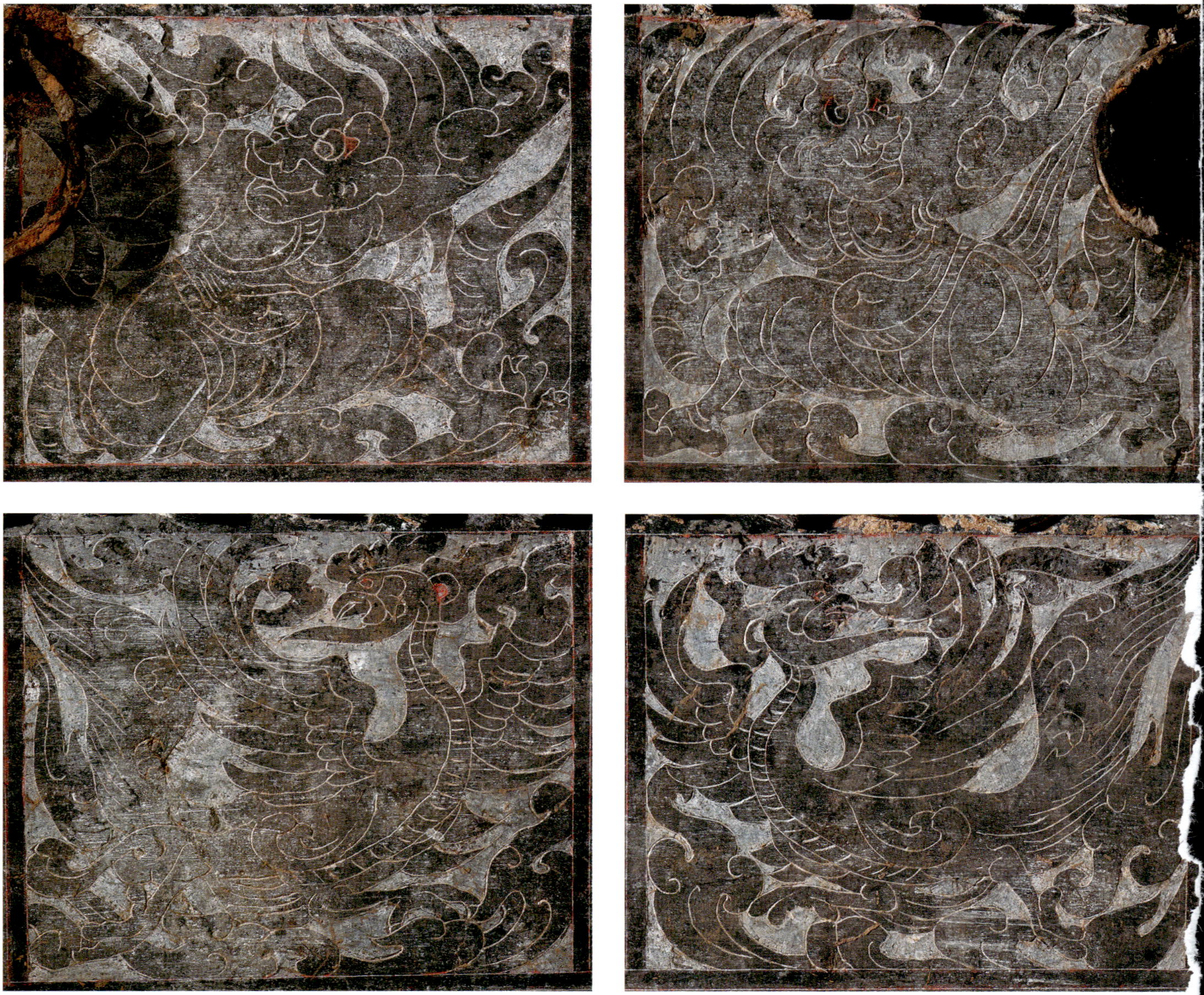

石床图案 / The Patterns of the Stone Bed

石床图案 / The Patterns of the Stone Bed

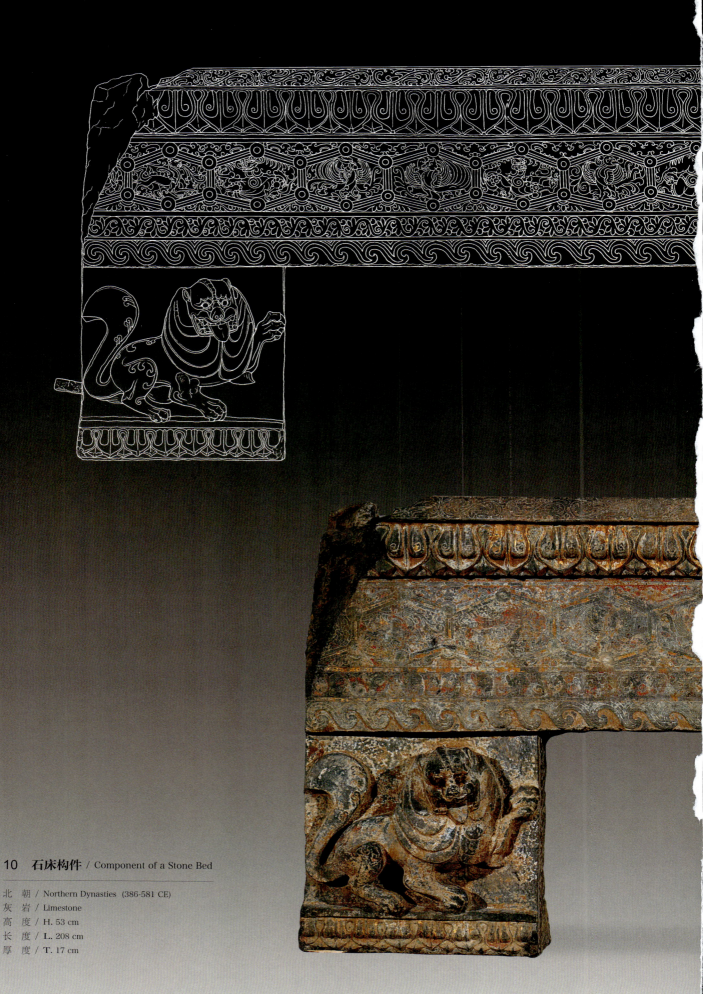

10　石床构件 / Component of a Stone Bed

北　朝 / Northern Dynasties (386-581 CE)
灰　岩 / Limestone
高　度 / H. 53 cm
长　度 / L. 208 cm
厚　度 / T. 17 cm

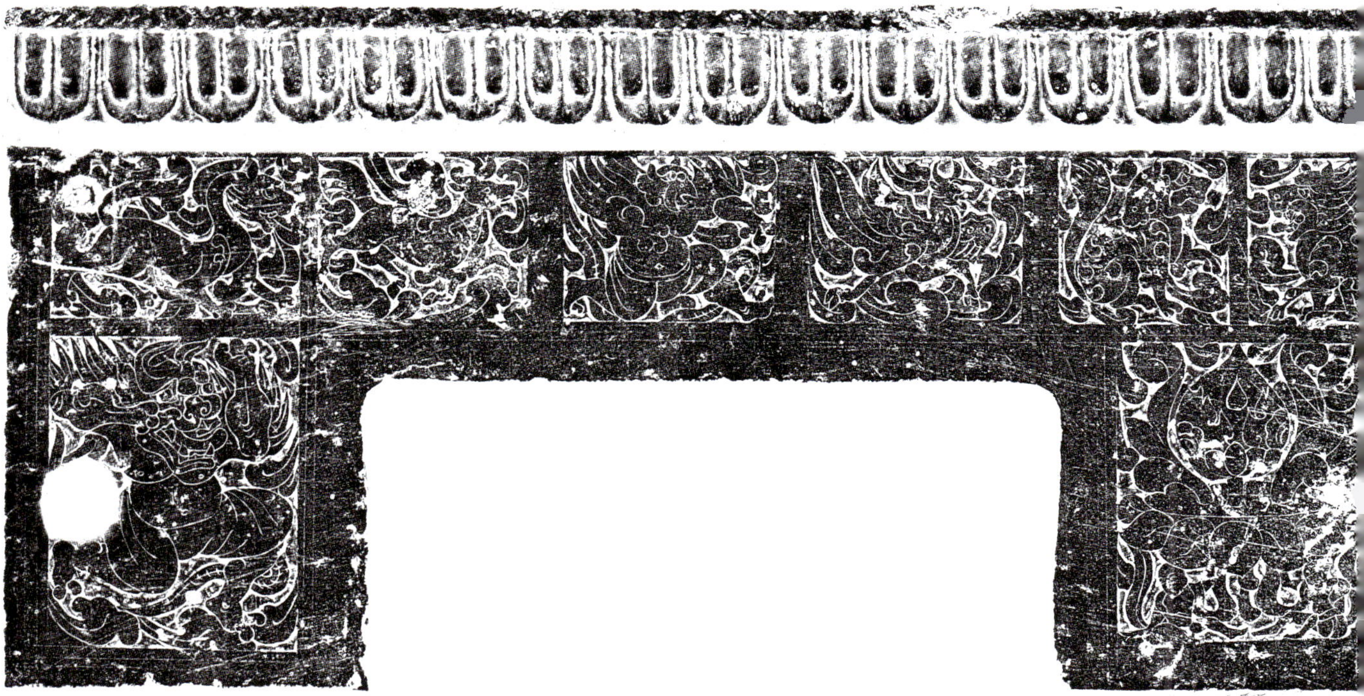

12 **石床构件** / Component of a Stone Bed

北　朝 / Northern Dynasties（386-581 CE）
灰　岩 / Limestone
高　度 / H. 57 cm
长　度 / L. 198 cm
厚　度 / T. 19 cm

興和四
年七月

11 石床构件 / Component of a Stone Bed

东　魏 / Eastern Wei (534-550 CE)
灰　岩 / Limestone
高　度 / H. 46 cm
长　度 / L. 205 cm
厚　度 / T. 17 cm

[有“兴和四年（542）”纪年 / With “The Fourth Year of Xinghe Reign Period (542)” Inscriptions]

铭文：兴和四 / 年七月 / 廿日亡人 / 朱洛石 / 泼冥记

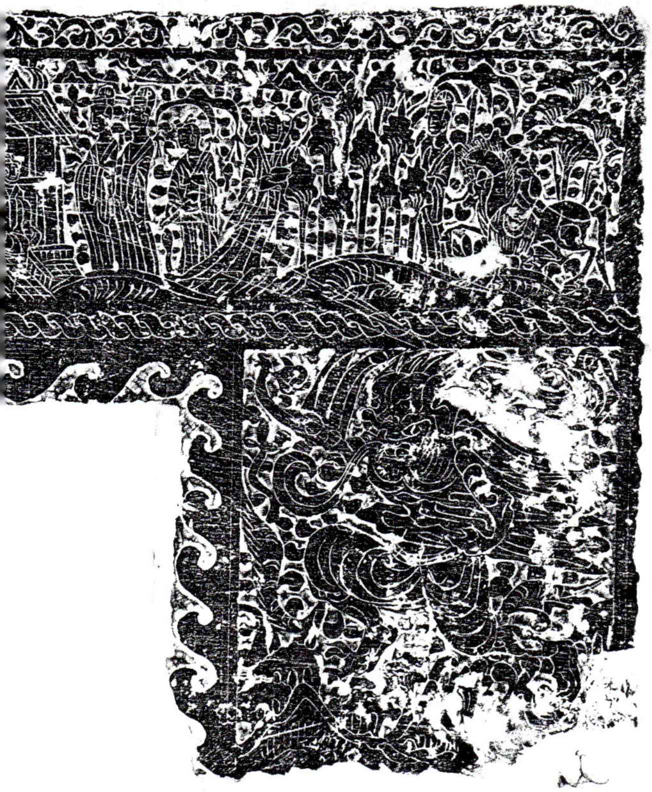

石床图案 / The Patterns of the Stone Bed

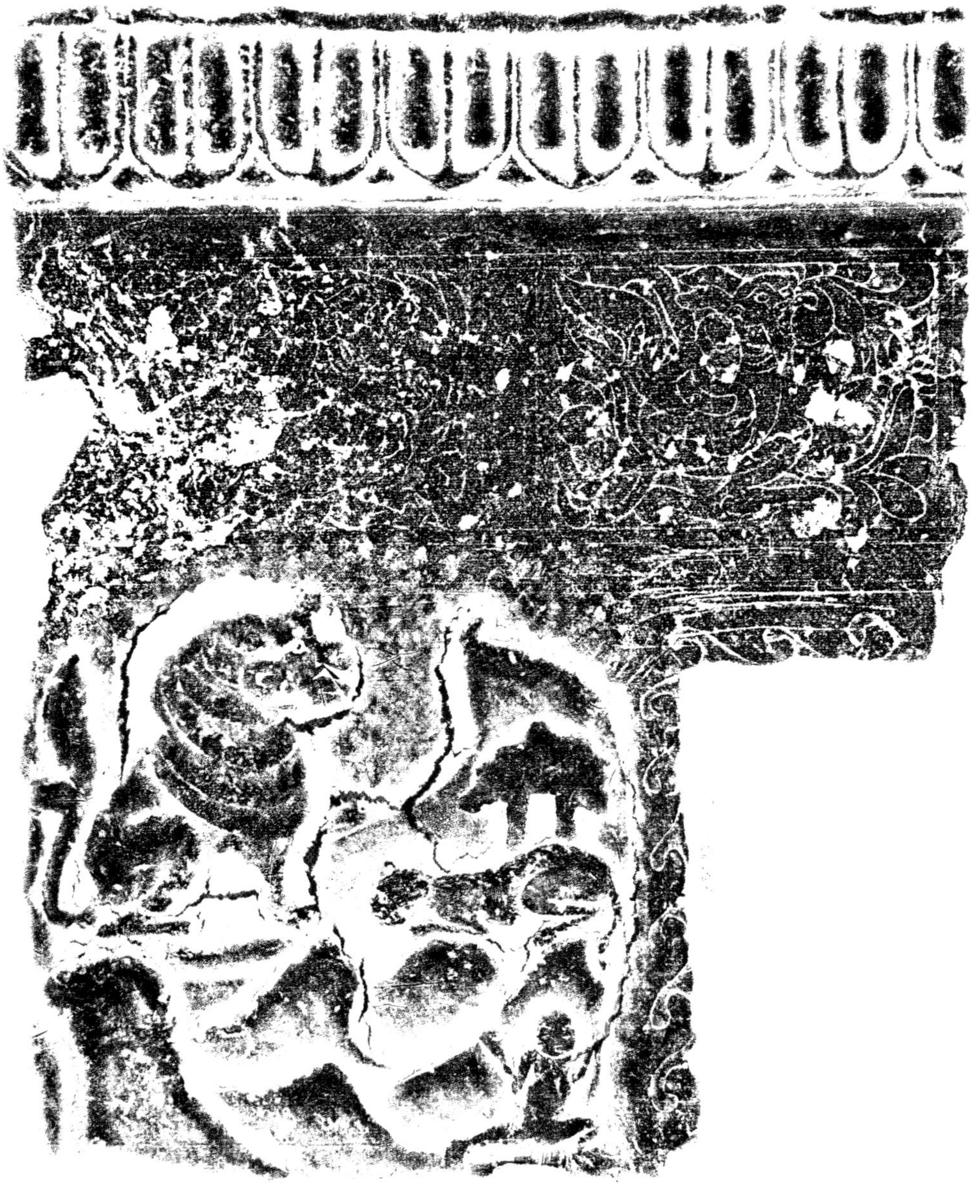

14 **石床残件** / Remnant of a Stone Bed

北　朝 / Northern Dynasties (386-581 CE)
灰　岩 / Limestone
高　度 / H. 44 cm

15 石屏风构件 1 / Component Part I of a Stone Screen

北　朝 / Northern Dynasties (386-581 CE)
灰　岩 / Limestone
高　度 / H. 46 cm
宽　度 / W. 86 cm
厚　度 / T. 7 cm
（左起依次为：侍女图、牛车图、女主人出行图）

16 石屏风构件 2 / Component Part II of a Stone Screen

北　朝 / Northern Dynasties (386-581 CE)
灰　岩 / Limestone
高　度 / H. 46 cm
宽　度 / W. 96 cm
厚　度 / T. 7 cm
（左起依次为：王寄图、老莱子图、女主人宴坐图）

铭文：王寄日煞（杀）三生（牲）犹为不孝

铭文：老子美侅（欢孩）

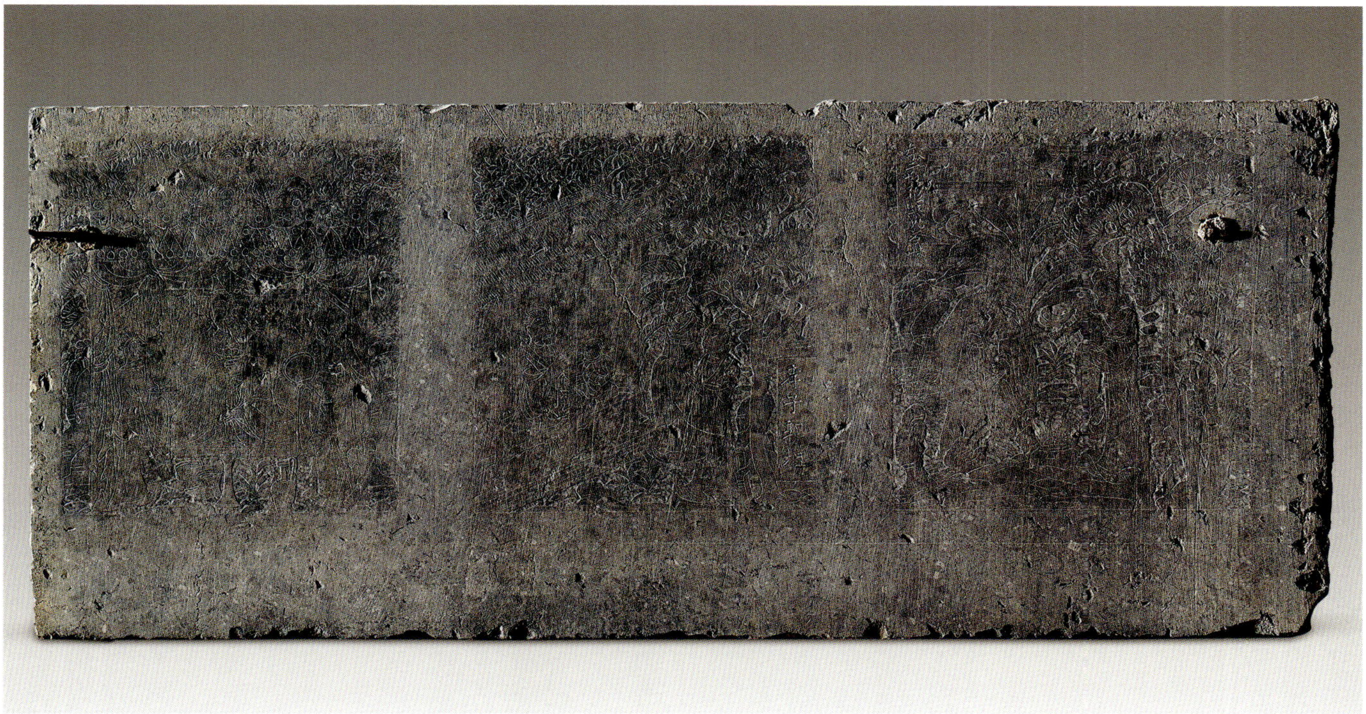

17 石屏风构件 3 / Component Part Ⅲ of a Stone Screen

北　朝 / Northern Dynasties (386-581 CE)
灰　岩 / Limestone
高　度 / H. 46 cm
宽　度 / W. 109 cm
厚　度 / T. 7 cm
(左起依次为：男主人宴坐图、郭巨图、郭巨埋儿图)
铭文：孝子郭柜(巨)
铭文：孝子郭柜(巨)煞(杀)儿养母

18 石屏风构件 4 / Component Part Ⅳ of a Stone Screen

北　朝 / Northern Dynasties (386-581 CE)
灰　岩 / Limestone
高　度 / H. 46 cm
宽　度 / W. 85 cm
厚　度 / T. 7 cm
(左起依次为：侍女图、牵马图、肩舆图)

侍女图（石屏风构件 1　左图）/ Image of Attendants (Component Part I of a Stone Screen, Left Section)

牛车图（石屏风构件 1　中图）/ Image of Ox-cart (Component Part I of a Stone Screen, Middle Section)

女主人出行图（石屏风构件 1　右图）/ Image of Hostess's Outing (Component Part 1 of a Stone Screen, Right Section)

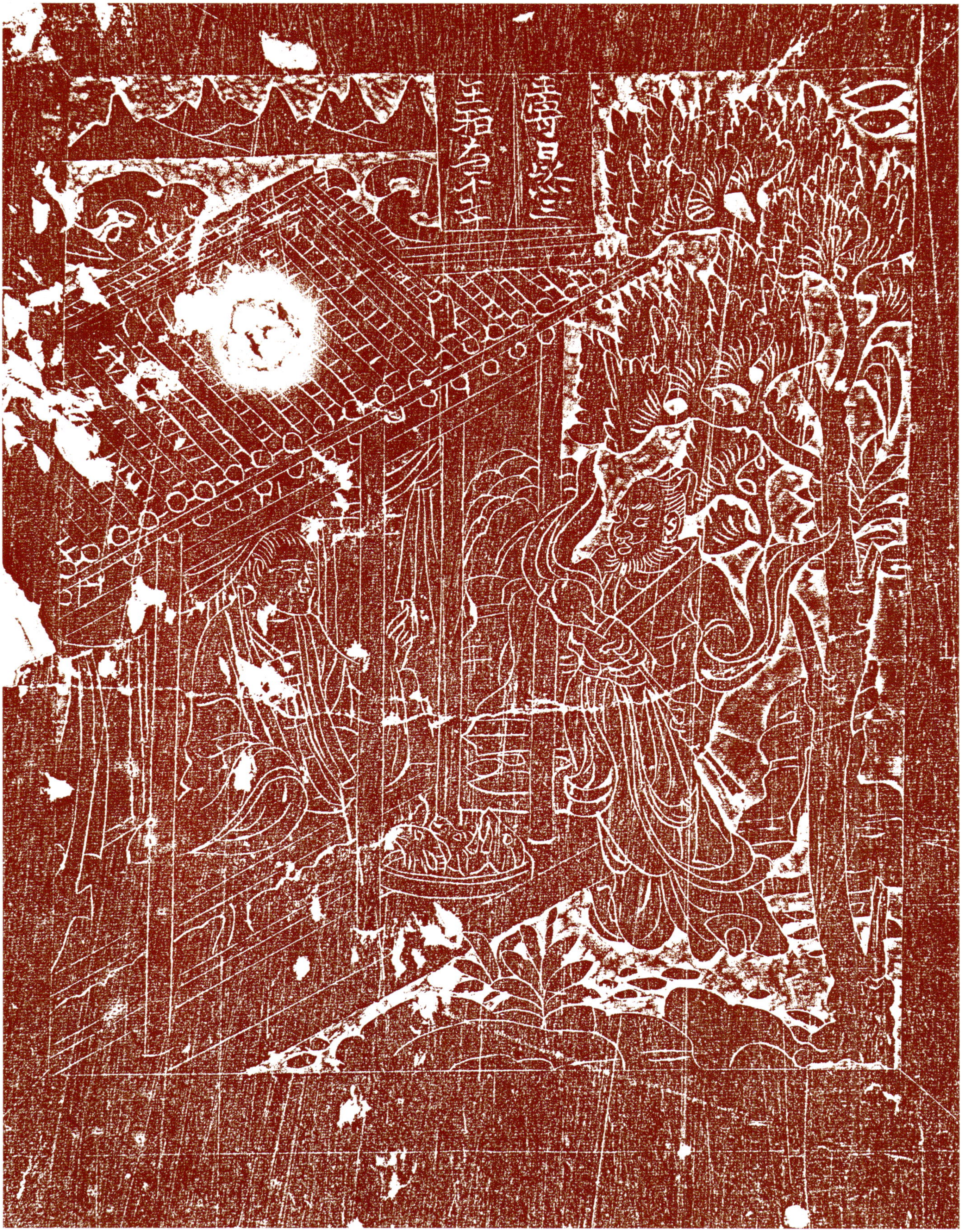

王寄图（石屏风构件 2　左图）/ Image of Wang Ji (Component Part II of a Stone Screen, Left Section)

老莱子图（石屏风构件 2　中图）/ Image of Laolaizi (Component Part II of a Stone Screen, Middle Section)

女主人宴坐图（石屏风构件 2　右图）/ Image of Hostess's Banquet (Component Part II of a Stone Screen, Right Section)

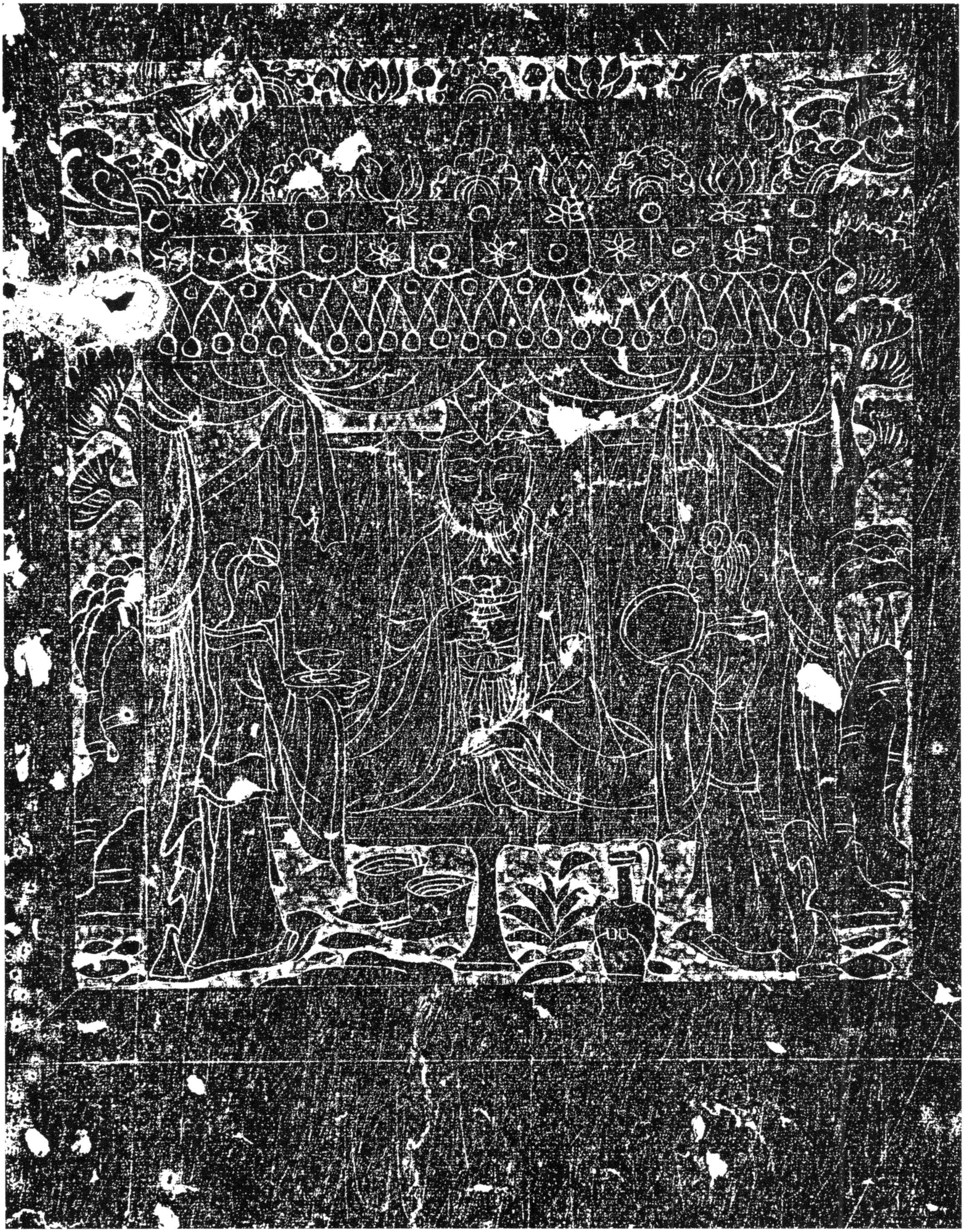

男主人宴坐图（石屏风构件 3　左图）/ Image of Host's Banquet (Component Part Ⅲ of a Stone Screen, Left Section)

孝子郭拒

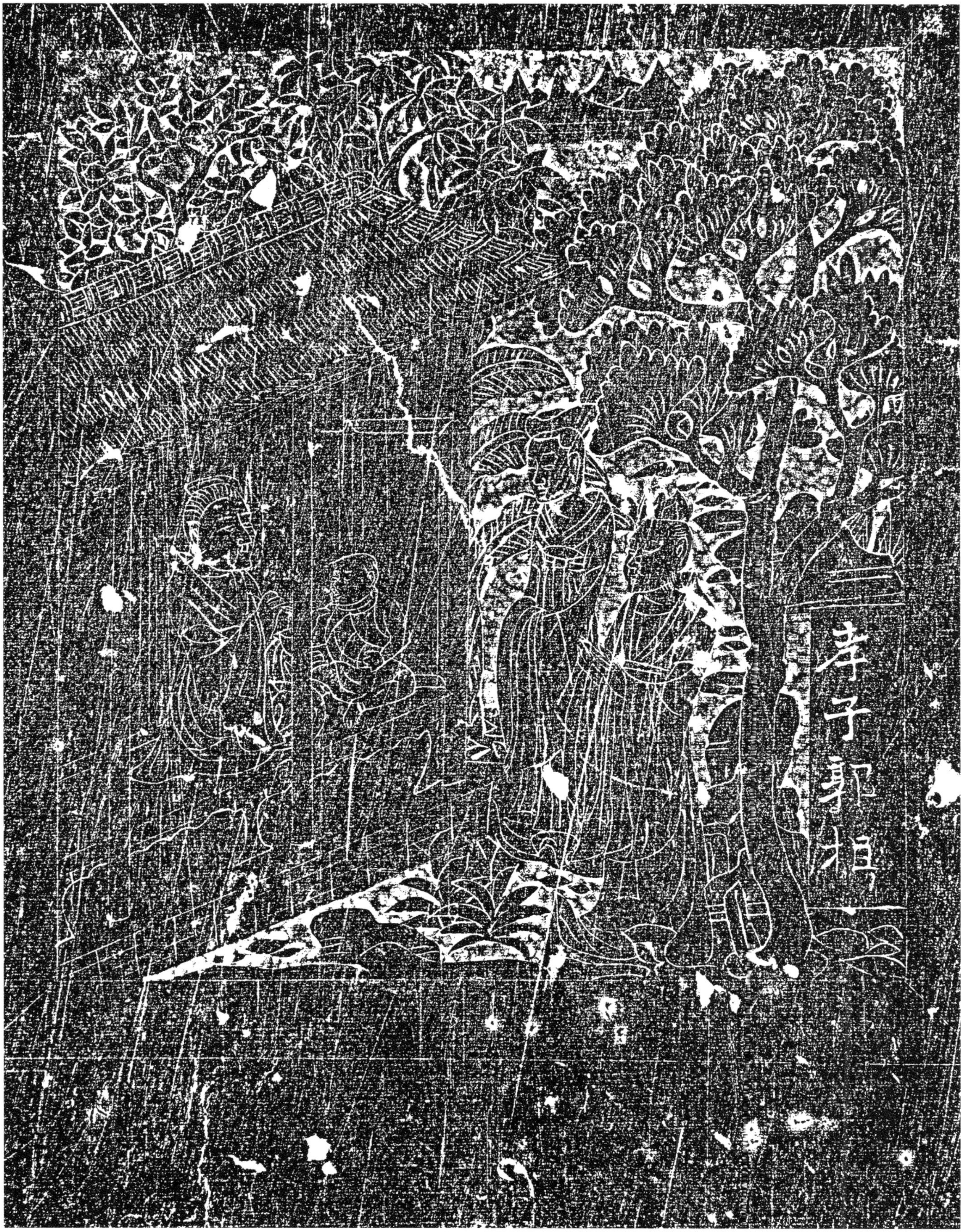

郭巨图（石屏风构件 3　中图）/ Image of Guo Ju (Component Part III of a Stone Screen, Middle Section)

郭巨埋儿图（石屏风构件 3　右图）/ Image of Guo Ju's Burying His Son (Component Part Ⅲ of a Stone Screen, Right Section)

侍女图（石屏风构件 4　左图）/ Image of Attendants (Component Part IV of a Stone Screen, Left Section)

牵马图（石屏风构件 4　中图）/ Image of Leading Horse (Component Part Ⅳ of a Stone Screen, Middle Section)

肩舆图（石屏风构件 4　右图）/ Image of Sedan-chair (Component Part Ⅳ of a Stone Screen, Right Section)

19 **佛坐像残件** / Remnant of a Seated Buddha Statue

北 魏 / Northern Wei (386-534 CE)
灰 岩 / Limestone
高 度 / H. 28 cm

20　残佛龛（存释迦、多宝二佛并坐与交脚弥勒）/ Remnant of a Niche for Seated Buddha

北　魏 / Northern Wei (386-534 CE)
砂　岩 / Sandstone
高　度 / H. 43 cm

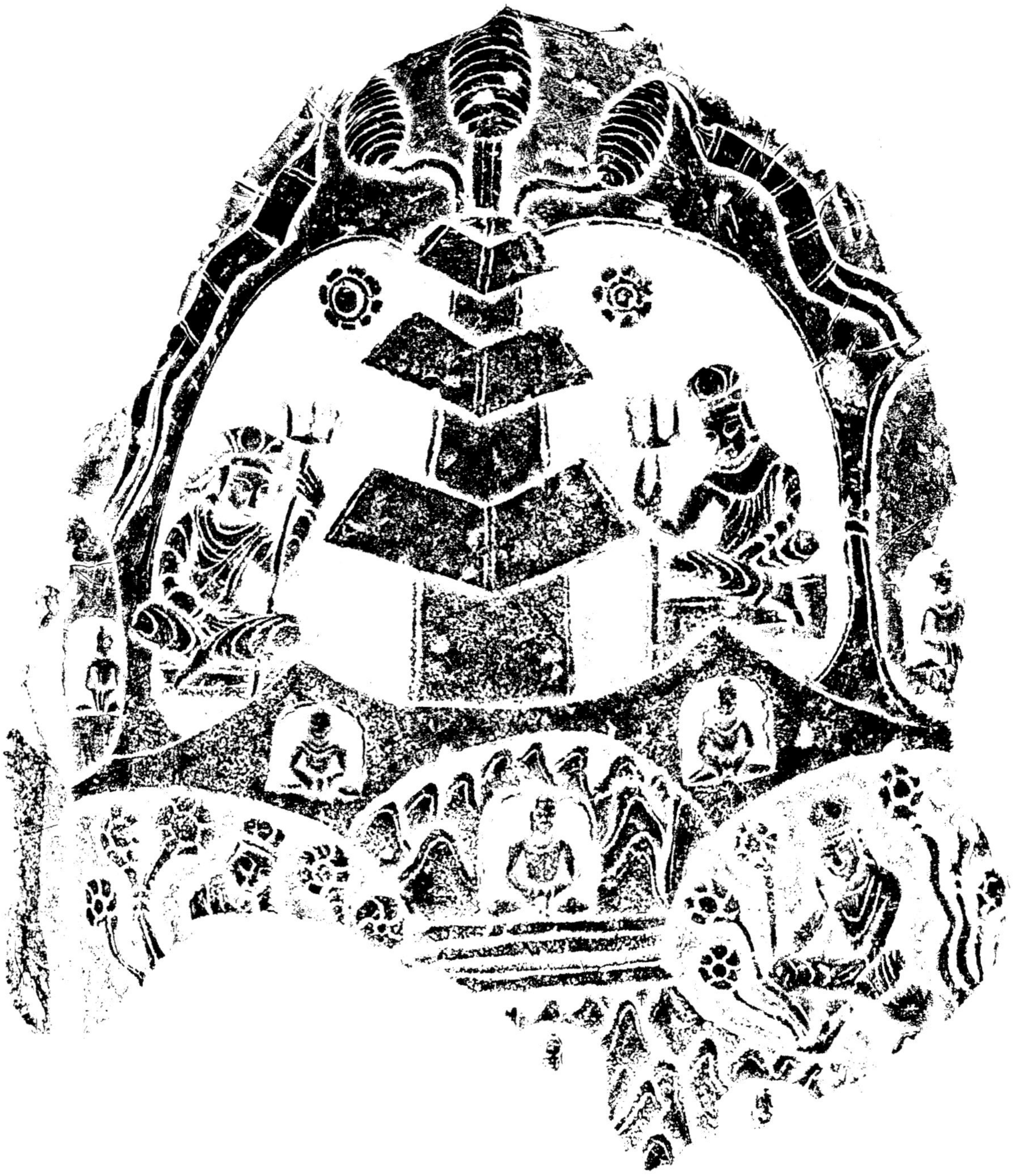

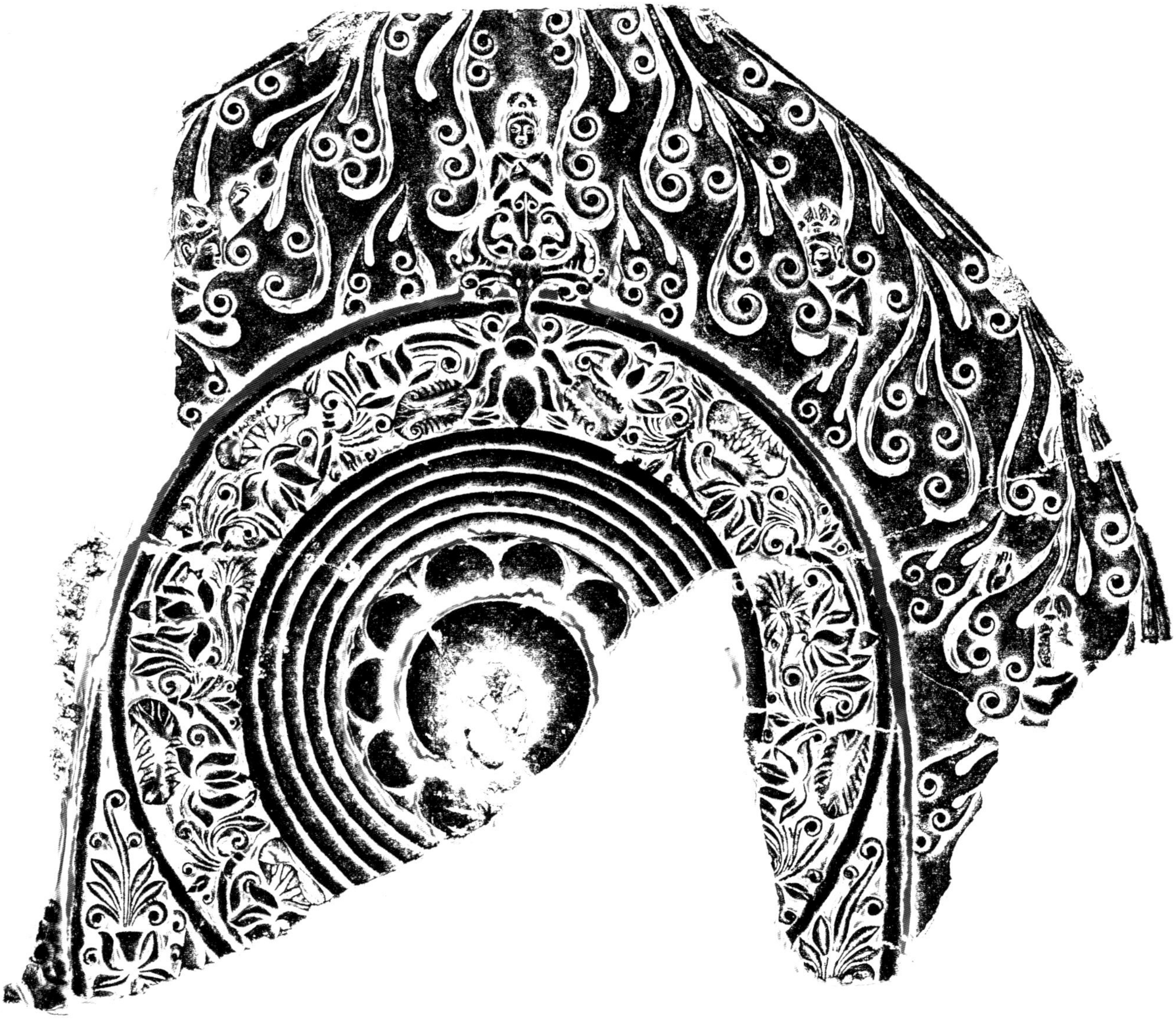

21 故正平郡君裴氏造像背屏残件 / Remnant of a Buddha Nimbus

北　齐 / Northern Qi (550-577 CE)
大理石 / Marble
高　度 / H. 57 cm

亡女
故正平
郡君裴

22 佛五尊像 / Five Buddhas Statue

北　齐 / Northern Qi (550-577 CE)
砂　岩 / Sandstone
高　度 / H. 57 cm

23 李普贤造释迦像 / Buddha Sakyamuni Statue

隋　代 / Sui Dynasty (581-618 CE)
大理石 / Marble
高　度 / H. 56 cm

［有“开皇四年（584）”纪年 / With “The Fourth Year of Kaihuang Reign Period (584)” Inscriptions］

发愿文：

左侧：开皇四年 / 岁次甲辰 / 六月八日

背面：佛弟子李 / 普贤为父 / 母及祖父 / 母造释迦 / 像一 / 区

右侧：佛弟子杨 / 和媚一心 / 供养佛

24 佛坐像残件 / Remnant of a Seated Buddha

隋 代 / Sui Dynasty (386-581 CE)
大理石 / Marble
高 度 / H. 18 cm

25 佛坐像残件 / Remnant of a Seated Buddha

唐 代 / Tang Dynasty (618-907 CE)
大理石 / Marble
高 度 / H. 21 cm

26 佛坐像残件 / Remnant of a Seated Buddha

唐　代 / Tang Dynasty (618-907 CE)
大理石 / Marble
高　度 / H. 72 cm

27 东方文贵造思惟菩萨像残件 / Remnant of Bodhisattva in Meditation

东　魏 / Eastern Wei (534-550 CE)
大理石 / Marble
高　度 / H. 32 cm

［有“天平三年（536）”纪年 / With “The Third Year of Tianping Reign Period (536)” Inscriptions］

发愿文：

天平三年岁次丙辰 / 二月壬申朔五日丙 / 子中山郡卢奴县人 / 东方文贵为一切众 / 生后为亡妻敬造白 / 石思唯像一区供养

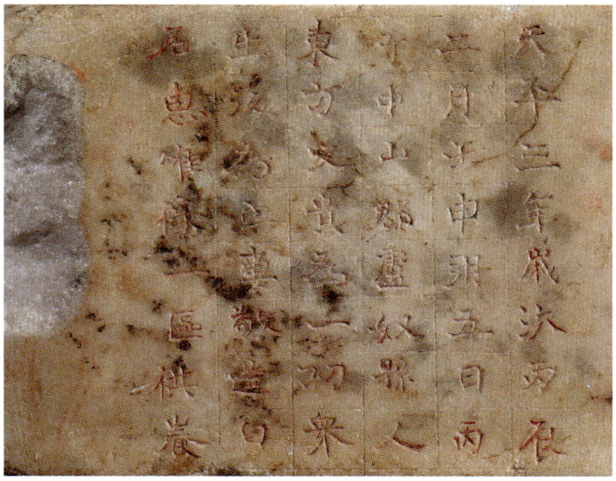

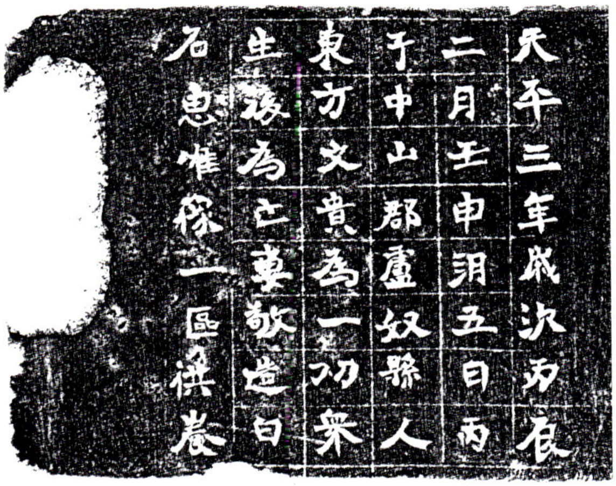
天平三年歲次丙辰
二月壬申朔五日丙
子中山郡盧奴縣人
東方文貴為一切衆
生孩為亡妻敬造白
石思惟像一區供養

28 比丘惠略造观世音菩萨像残件 / Remnant of Avalokitesvara Statue

东　魏 / Eastern Wei (534-550 CE)
大理石 / Marble
高　度 / H. 28 cm

[有"兴和元年（539）"纪年 / With "The First Year of Xinghe Reign Period (539)" Inscriptions]

发愿文：

兴和元年 / 岁在己未十 / 二月十九日尹 / 氏寺比丘惠 / 略为亡祖父母 / 亡父现存内亲 / 敬造观世音 / 像一区供养

29　观音菩萨立像残件 / Remnant of Standing Avalokitesvara

北　齐 / Northern Qi (550-577 CE)
大理石 / Marble
高　度 / H. 23 cm

30 **半跏思惟菩萨残件** / Remnant of Bodhisattva in Meditation

北 齐 / Northern Qi (550-577 CE)
灰 岩 / Limestone
高 度 / H. 28 cm

31 菩萨立像残件 / Remnant of Standing Bodhisattva

北　齐 / Northern Qi (550-577 CE)
灰　岩 / Limestone
高　度 / H. 41.6 cm

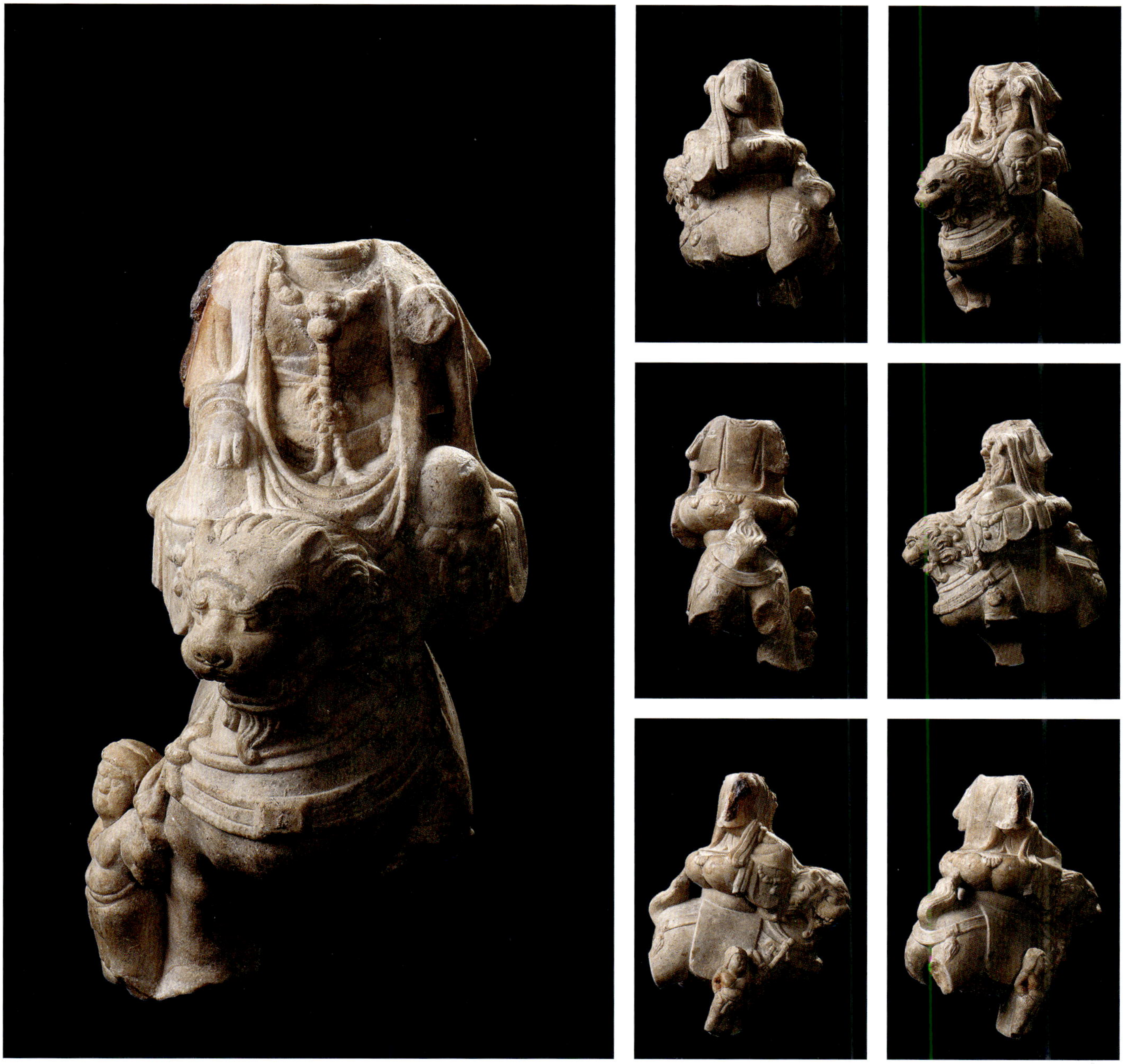

32 文殊菩萨骑狮像残件 / Remnant of Bodhisattva Manjusri

唐　代 / Tang Dynasty (618-907 CE)
大理石 / Marble
高　度 / H. 26 cm

33 供养人坐像残件 / Remnant of Seated Buddhist Provider

北　齐 / Northern Qi (550-577 CE)
大理石 / Marble
高　度 / H. 50 cm

34 **佛头** / Head of Buddha

北 魏 / Northern Wei (386-534 CE)
砂 岩 / Sandstone
高 度 / H. 60 cm

35 **佛头** / Head of Buddha

东　魏 / Easter Wei (534-550 CE)
灰　岩 / Limestone
高　度 / H. 10.8 cm

36 **佛头** / Head of Buddha

北　齐 / Northern Qi (550-577 CE)
灰　岩 / Limestone
高　度 / H. 25 cm

37 **佛头** / Head of Buddha

北　齐 / Northern Qi (550-577 CE)
灰　岩 / Limestone
高　度 / H. 23.5 cm

38 **佛头** / Head of Buddha

北　周 / Northern Zhou (557-581 CE)
灰　岩 / Limestone
高　度 / H. 11.5 cm

39 **佛头** / Head of Buddha

北　周 / Northern Zhou (557-581 CE)
灰　岩 / Limestone
高　度 / H. 21 cm

40 佛头 / Head of Buddha

唐　代 / Tang Dynasty (618-907 CE)
大理石 / Marble
高　度 / H. 9 cm

41 佛头 / Head of Buddha

唐　代 / Tang Dynasty (618-907 CE)
大理石 / Marble
高　度 / H. 9.5 cm

42　佛头 / Head of Buddha

唐　代 / Tang Dynasty (618-907 CE)
大理石 / Marble
高　度 / H. 10 cm

43　佛头 / Head of Buddha

唐　代 / Tang Dynasty (618-907 CE)
大理石 / Marble
高　度 / H. 8.5 cm

44 **佛头** / Head of Buddha

唐　代 / Tang Dynasty (618-907 CE)
砂　岩 / Sandstone
高　度 / H. 8.3 cm

45 **佛头** / Head of Buddha

唐　代 / Tang Dynasty (618-907 CE)
大理石 / Marble
高　度 / H. 7.3 cm

46 **佛头** / Head of Buddha

唐　代 / Tang Dynasty (618-907 CE)
大理石 / Marble
高　度 / H. 11 cm

47 菩萨头 / Head of Bodhisattva

北　齐 / Northern Qi (550-577 CE)
大理石 / Marble
高　度 / H. 7.5 cm

48 力士头 / Head of Warrior

北　齐 / Northern Qi (550-577 CE)
大理石 / Marble
高　度 / H. 7 cm

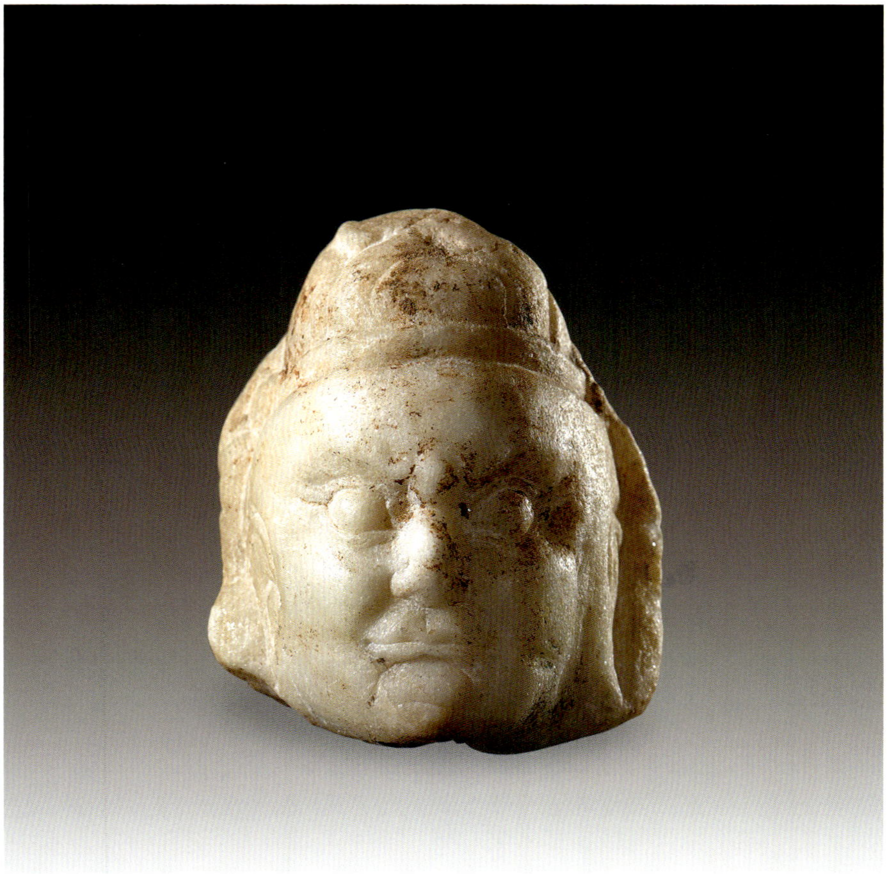

49 力士头 / Head of Warrior

北　齐 / Northern Qi (550-577 CE)
大理石 / Marble
高　度 / H. 7.3 cm

50 **供养人头** / Head of Buddhist Provider

唐 代 / Tang Dynasty (618-907 CE)
大理石 / Marble
高 度 / H. 7.9 cm

51 从次好造思惟菩萨像残件 / Remnant of Bodhisattva in Meditation

北　齐 / Northern Qi (550-577 CE)
灰　岩 / Limestone
长　度 / L. 22.5 cm
宽　度 / W. 15.5 cm
高　度 / H. 16 cm

[有"天保元年（550）"纪年 / With "The First Year of Tianbao Reign Period (550)" Inscriptions]

发愿文：

大齐天保元年岁 / 次戊寅十二月庚 / 申廿十五日甲戌 / 清信女佛弟子从 / 次好知一切诸业 / 非亡者之资归佛 / 法僧明利益于往 / 过遂敬造思萨像 / 一区冀恃此因常 / 生净国后愿师 / 僧父母存亡眷属 / 含识有形俱蒙斯 / 福也

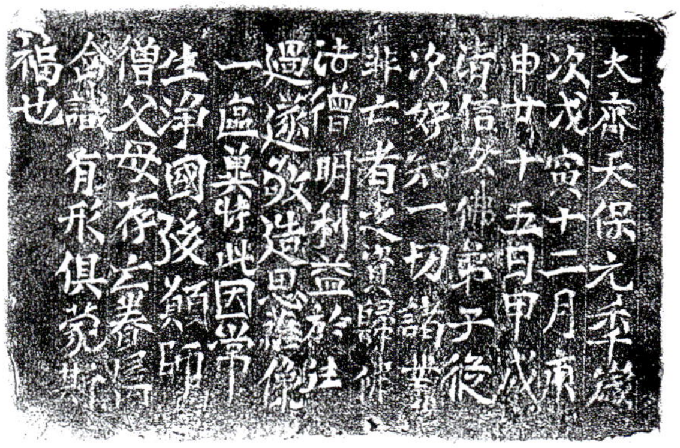

52 刘道和等十七人合邑造像残件 / Remnant of a Seated Buddha

北　齐 / Northern Qi (550-577 CE)
大理石 / Marble
长　度 / L. 32 cm
宽　度 / W. 15 cm
高　度 / H. 17 cm

[有“皇建二年（561）”纪年 / With “The Second Year of Huangjian Reign Period (561)” Inscriptions]

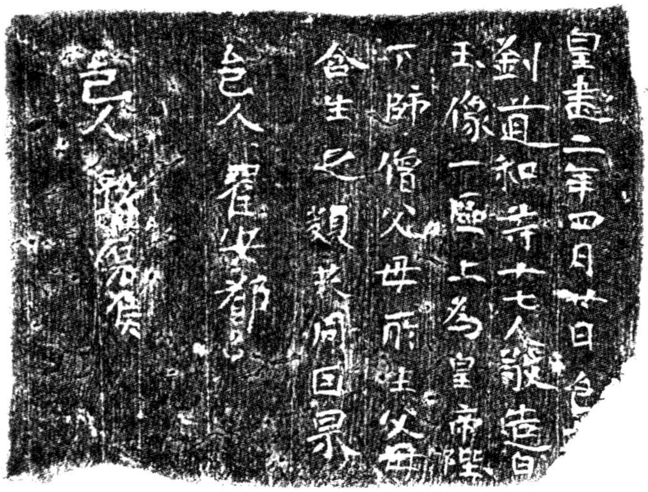

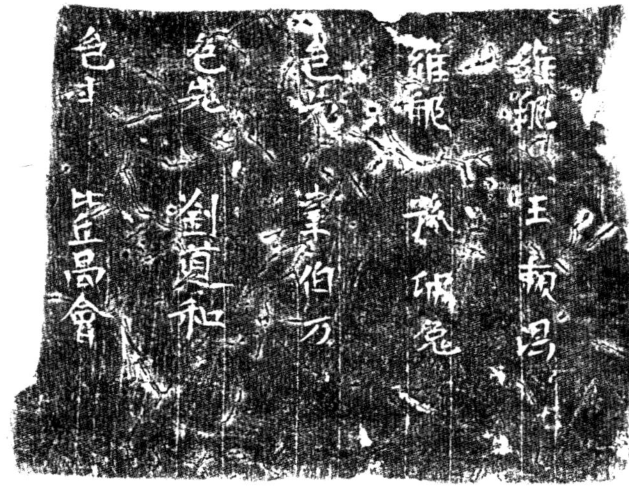

发愿文：

皇建二年四月廿日邑子 / 刘道和等十七人敬造白 / 玉像一区上为皇帝陛 / 下师僧父母所生父母 / 含生之类共同因果 / 邑人翟安都 / 邑人孙磨侯 / 邑人王市和 / 邑人业豫道 / 邑人毛遵和 / 邑人杨奴仁 / 邑人宋白瓜 / 录事光奚胡子 / 录事马贰□ / 中正王遵庆 / 中正李鸿休 / 维那聂当□ / 维那董洪智 / 维那王赖渴 / 维那孙卯兔 / 邑老韦伯万 / 邑老刘道和 / 邑主比丘昙会

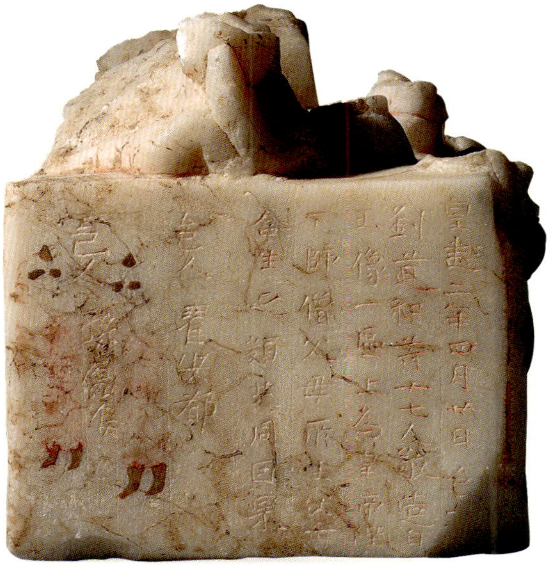

53 杨昨杨箱兄弟造释迦像底座 / Seat of Buddha Sakyamuni

东　魏 / Eastern Wei (534-550 CE)
灰　岩 / Limestone
长　度 / L. 17 cm
宽　度 / W. 16 cm
高　度 / H. 9 cm

[有“武定二年（543）”纪年 / With “The Second Year of Wuding Reign Period (543)” Inscriptions]

发愿文：

武定元年二 / 月 十八日佛 / 弟子杨昨杨 / 箱兄弟等敬 / 造释迦像一 / 躯为师僧父 / 母香火因缘 / 十善知识法 / 界有形咸同 / 斯 福

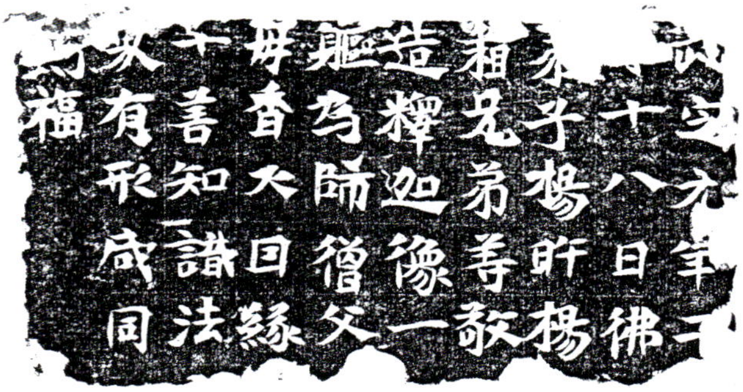

54 造像底座残件 / Remnant of a Seat of Buddha

北　齐 / Northern Qi (550-577 CE)
大理石 / Marble
长　度 / L. 33 cm
宽　度 / W. 22 cm
高　度 / H. 14 cm

发愿文：

大齐武平／□年七月／廿六日佛／弟子弥姐／相宝仰为／亡考敬造／白石阿弥／
陀像一区愿／一切法界／众生发菩／提心离苦／得乐俱时／作佛

55 弥姐相宝造阿弥陀佛像底座 / Seat of Buddha Amitabha

北　齐 / Northern Qi (550-577 CE)
大理石 / Marble
长　度 / L. 35 cm
宽　度 / W. 34 cm
高　度 / H. 16 cm

[有“武平□年（570–576）”纪年 | With “The Year of Wuping Reign Period (570–576)” Inscriptions]

56 须磨造释迦像底座 / Seat of Buddha Sakyamuni

北　齐 / Northern Qi (550-577 CE)
大理石 / Marble
长　度 / L. 10.5 cm
宽　度 / W. 10.5 cm
高　度 / H. 10 cm

[有"武平五年（574）"纪年 | With "The Fifth Year of Wuping Reign Period (574)" Inscriptions]

发愿文：武平五 / 年 (574) 二月 / 八日佛 / 弟子 / 须磨 / 为母造 / 释迦像 / 后……

57 释迦像底座 / Seat of Buddha Sakyamuni

北　齐 / Northern Qi (550-577 CE)
灰　岩 / Limestone
长　度 / L. 57 cm
宽　度 / W. 46 cm
高　度 / H. 30 cm

58 释迦像底座 / Seat of Buddha Sakyamuni

北　齐 / Northern Qi (550-577 CE)
大理石 / Marble
底　长 / L. 82 cm
底　宽 / W. 82 cm
高　度 / H. 45 cm

发原文：

□□□□灭六趣轮□□□□ / □还□□□电是以□□□ / 东乃□□身为实諦□丘阴 / 方觉□□含空朗妹□□□ / 慧徒□归信三宝□□□□ / 悕□□坼□考神鉴□外万 / □□表远慕须达□□□监 / 遂□果园造立□□□□岂 / 构□□出云暮□□□□□ / □□□乃精图□□□□竹 / 园之□慈氏来□□恋□□ / □颜□身世难殚□同川逝 / □□□□□深闺□朗兄弟 / □□□□愿号哽崩绝欲 / □□夙霄无舍□以大齐□ / □□年八月□□□□造弥□ / □像一□□□□□□慈□ / 丹誓□□□□□□□□□ / □□妙□双□□□□□父 / 丹□□□□兜□□□□以 / 去□□□□□□□□□□□ / 果□□□□□□□□现□□□ / 普□□□□□□□□□□□来 / 小□□□□□□□□□□□□ / □□□真定县令冯乘秀

59 **兽面纹力士座** / Base of Warrior with Animal Mask Pattern

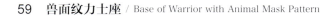

北　齐 / Northern Qi (550-577 CE)
大理石 / Marble
高　度 / H. 26.5 cm

60 陈兴绪造四天王像底座 / Base of Four Sanskrit Vajras

隋　代 / Sui Dynasty (581-618 CE)
灰　岩 / Limestone
长　度 / L. 78 cm
宽　度 / W. 78 cm
高　度 / H. 28 cm

［有“开皇六年（586）”纪年 / With “The Sixth Year of Kaihuang Reign Period (586)” Inscriptions］

发愿文：

右侧：(开)皇六年八月十五 / 日陈兴绪妻潘姬愿 / 造四天王像一区上 / 为皇帝师僧父母 / 一切含生俱时作佛

正面：孙息孟儁供养 / 孙息善相供养 / 孙息善德供养 / 象主陈兴绪供养 / 象主兴妻潘供养 / 兴妻赵供养 / 荆氏女妙晖 / 孙女万岁供养 / 孙女璎洛供养

左侧：荆氏外生文博 / 兴息季才 / 兴息叔珍 / 兴息宝贞 / 兴息淑宗供养 / 宗妻□供养 / 贞妻张供养 / 宗妻李供养 / 荆氏外生阿□

背面：曾孙善护 / 安乐郡守陈僧愍供养 / 比丘僧药供养 / 愍妻赵供养 / 愍妻成供养 / 宜息达摩供养 / 宜息长修供养 / 潘比宜供养 / 宜妻翟供养 / 比丘尼员（下泐）

61 **造像碑残件** / Remnant Stele of Buddha

北　魏 / Northern Wei (386-534 CE)
灰　岩 / Limestone
高　度 / H. 66 cm
宽　度 / W. 39 cm
厚　度 / T. 12 cm

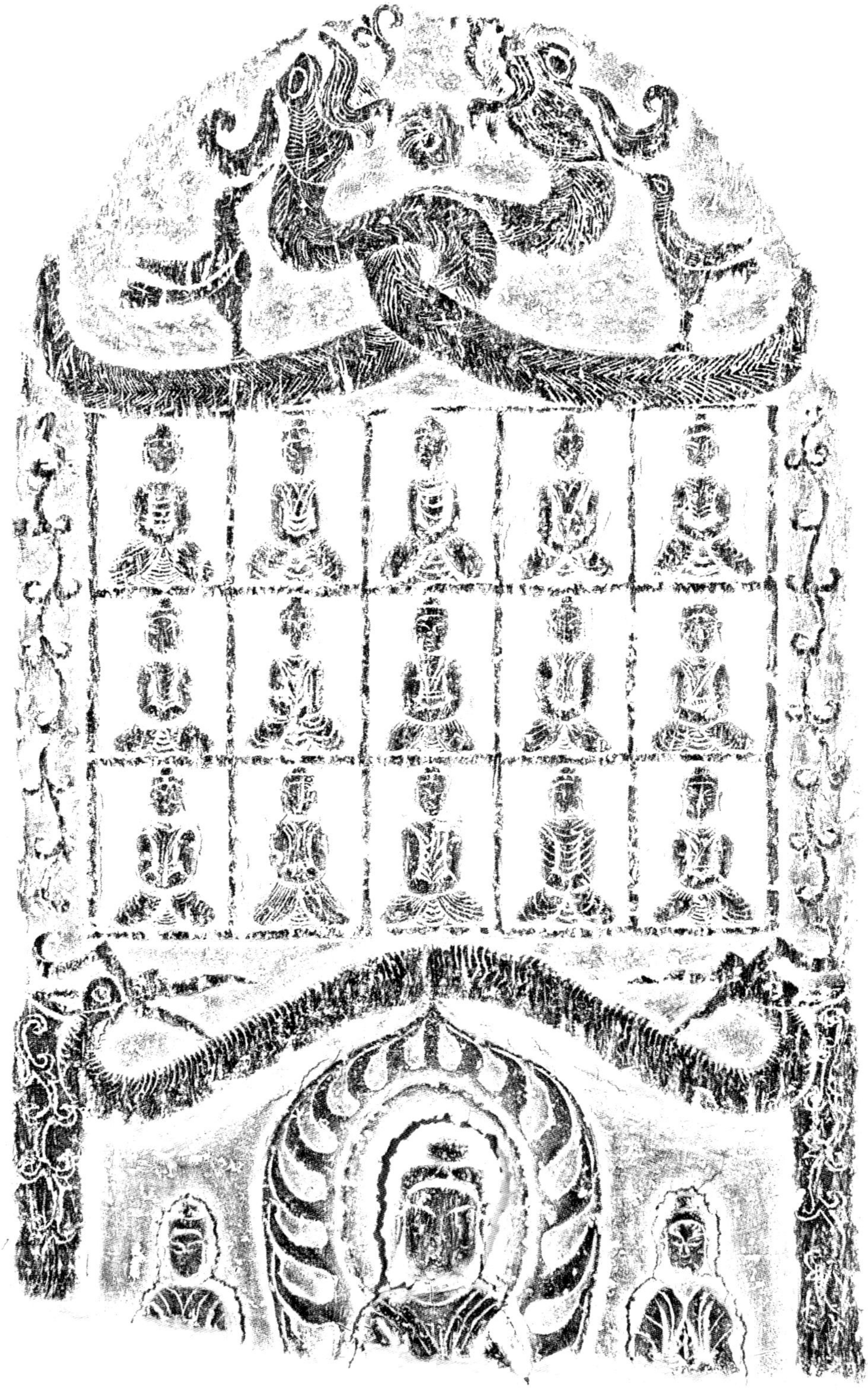

62 造像碑残件 / Remnant Stele of Buddha

北　魏 / Northern Wei (386-534 CE)
灰　岩 / Limestone
高　度 / H. 68 cm
宽　度 / W. 34 cm
厚　度 / T. 25 cm

63 造像碑残件 / Remnant Stele of Buddha

北 魏 / Northern Wei (386-534 CE)
灰 岩 / Limestone
高 度 / H. 73 cm
宽 度 / W. 39 cm
厚 度 / T. 27 cm

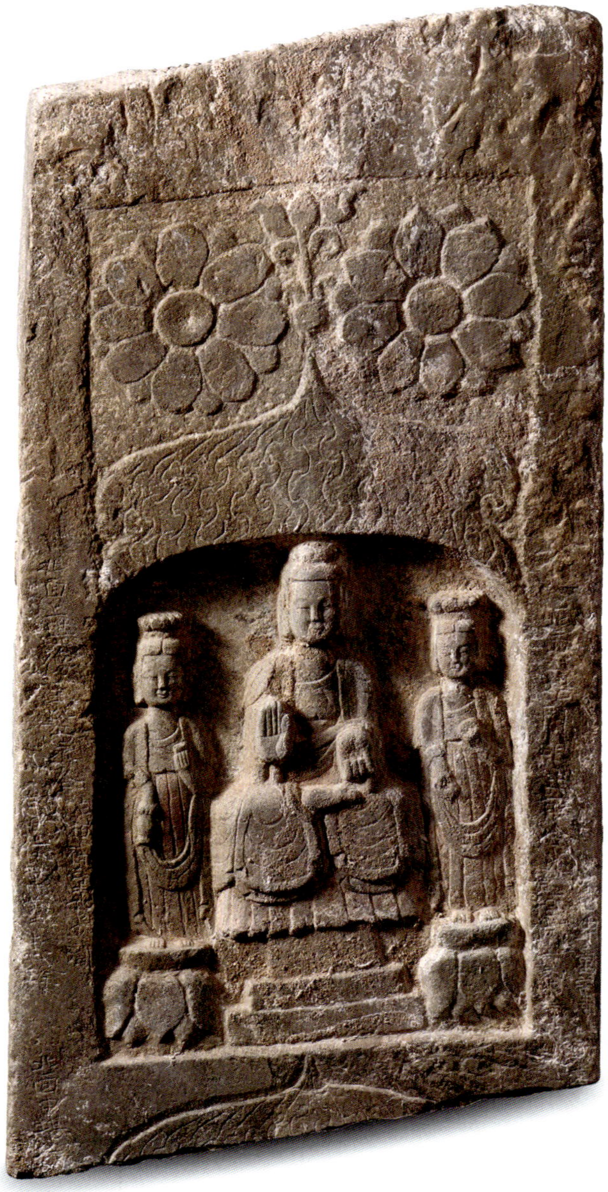

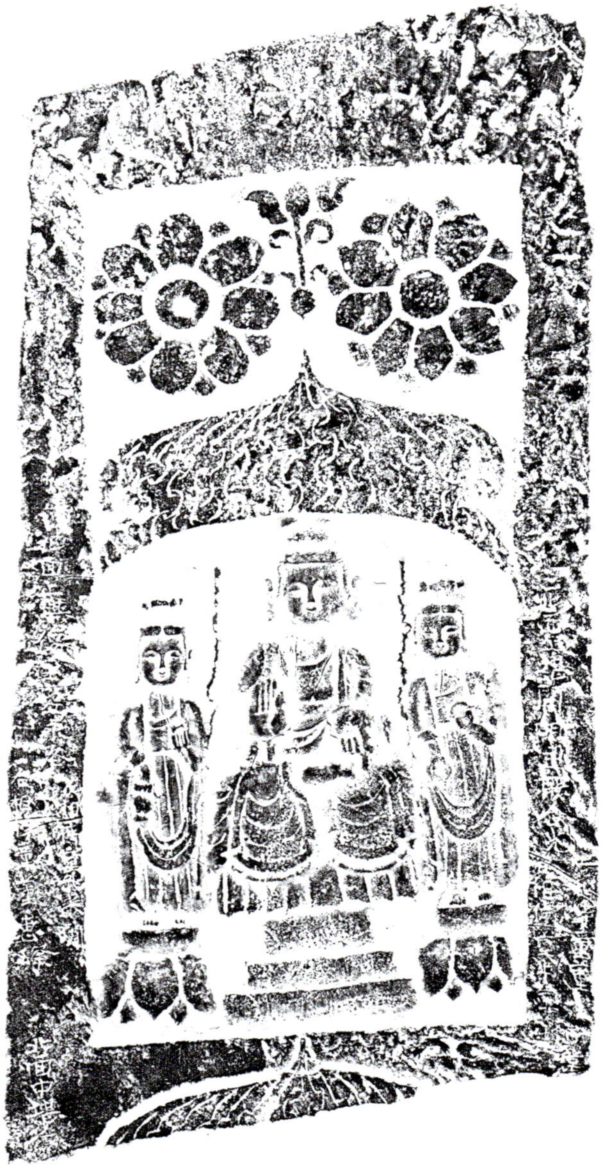

64 四面佛龛造像碑残件 / Remnant Stele of Buddha with Niche on Four Sides

北　周 / Northern Zhou (557-581 CE)
砂　岩 / Sandstone
高　度 / H. 65 cm
宽　度 / W. 32 cm
厚　度 / T. 13 cm

发愿文：

都像主林阿仲／左相侍童□□女／右相侍童王阿丑／南面上光明主尹迴胜／左相侍童王子□／右相侍童苏□／南面上堪像主吕树妃／左相侍童赵吴仁／右相侍童王三犊／宝塔主比丘僧和／左相侍童（下残）／右相侍童（下残）

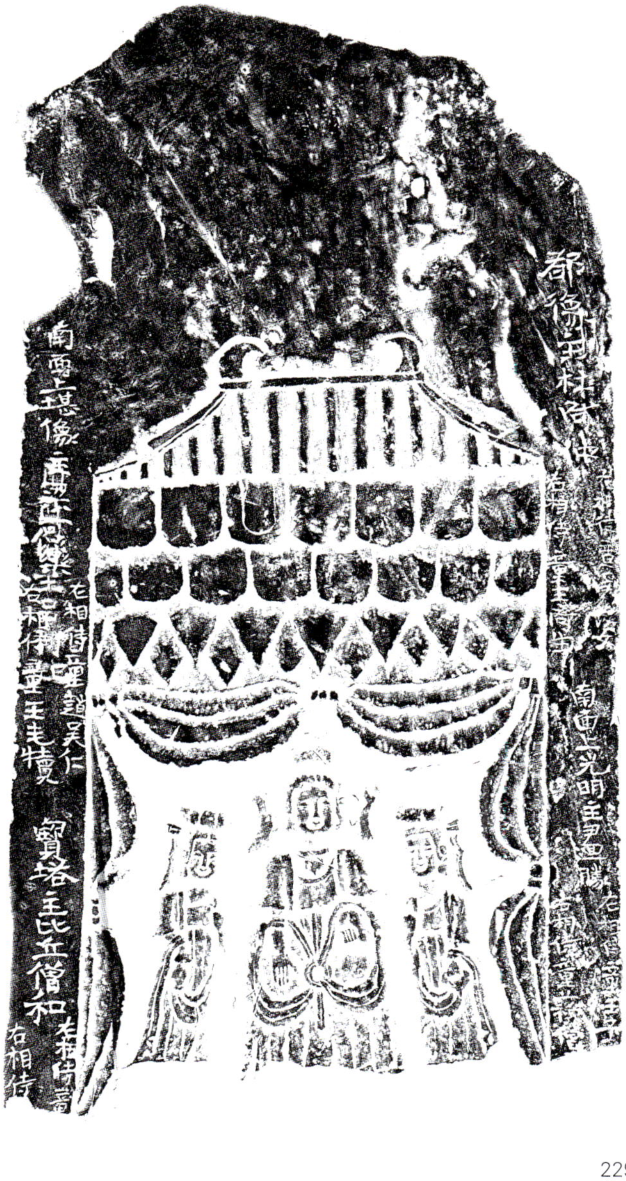

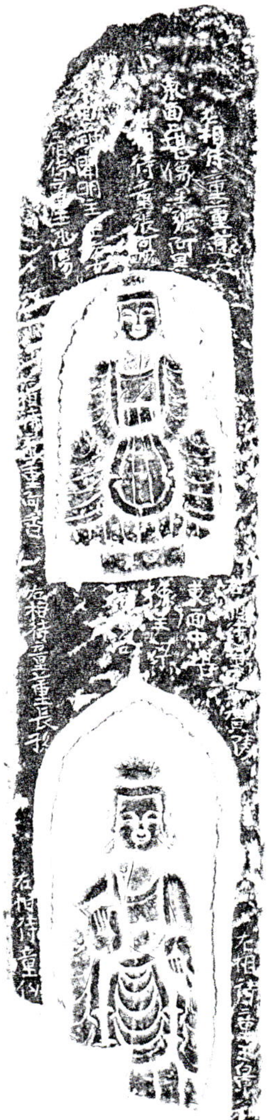

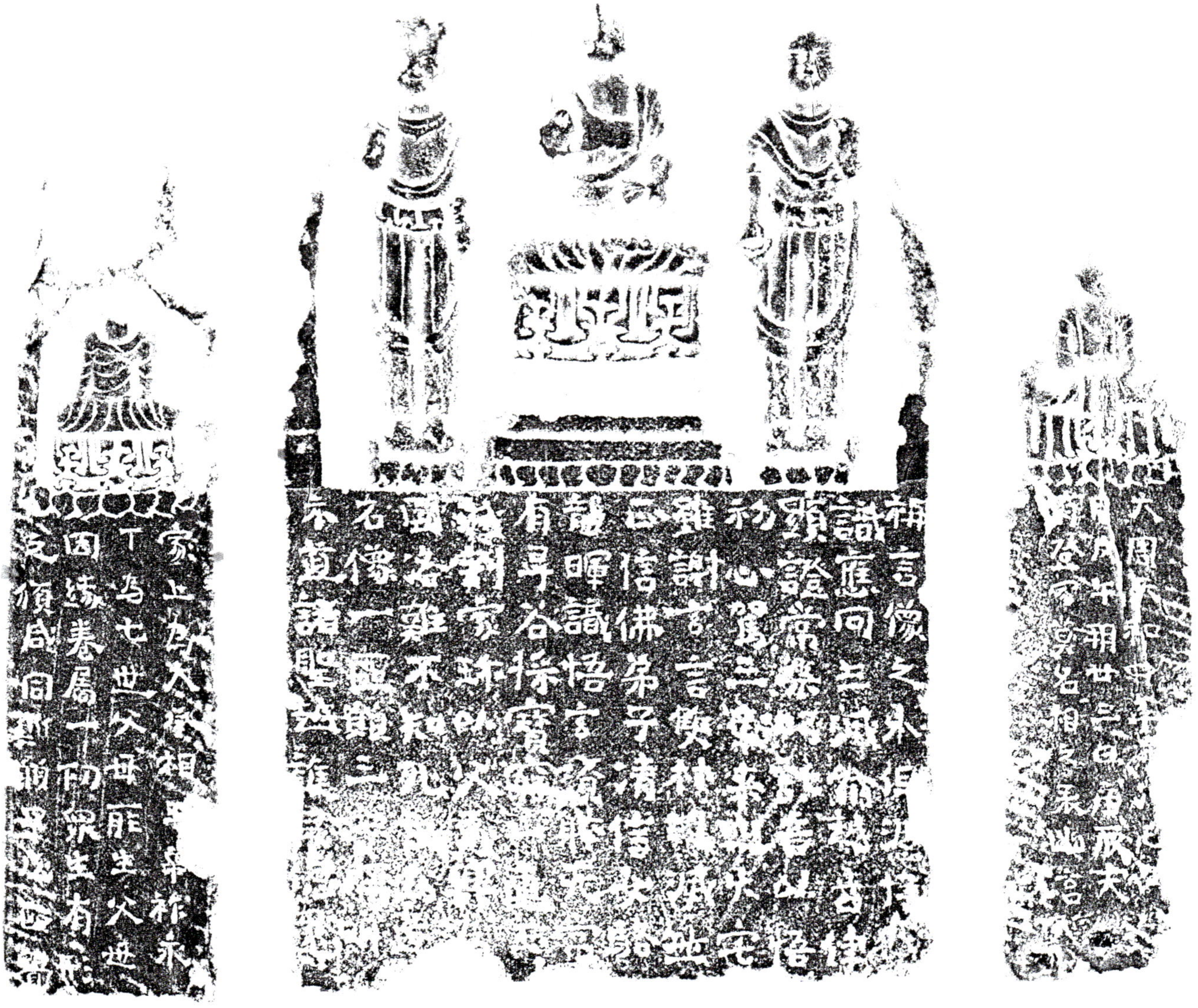

右侧发愿文：

家上为大丞相皇帝祚永 /
下为七世父母所生父母 /
因缘眷属一切众生有形 /
之类咸同斯愿早□正觉

正面发愿文：

称言像之外但泥□□ / 识应同三灭喻越苦律 / 显证常乐□托言以悟 / 初心驾三乘来□火宅 / 虽谢玄言双神□灭然 / 正信佛弟子清信女骆 / 韶晖识悟玄资体无常 / 有寻谷采宝寂山匣玉 / 减割家珍以父□兴□ / 国洛难不知死□□□ / 石像一区愿三宝□□ / 示道诸圣□谁□德□

左侧发愿文：

大周天和四年岁次　/ 月戊午
朔廿三日庚辰夫□ / 有登寂
莫名相之表幽宫□

65　一佛二菩萨造像碑 / Stele of Buddha and Two Bodhisattvas

北　周 / Northern Zhou (557-581 CE)
砂　岩 / Sandstone
高　度 / H. 53 cm
宽　度 / W. 31 cm
厚　度 / T. 12 cm

[有“天和四年（569）”纪年 / With “The Fourth Year of Tianhe Reign Period (569)” Inscriptions]

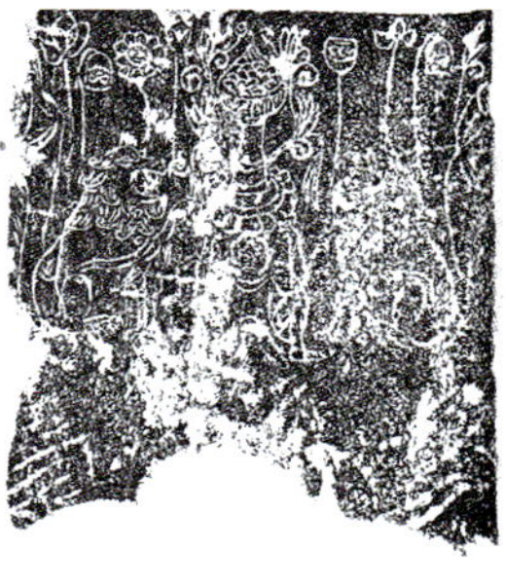

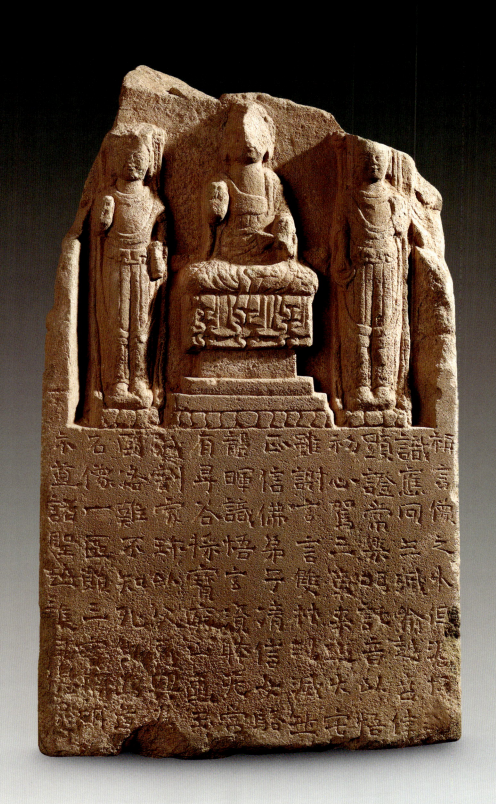

66 佛龛龛眉残件 / Remnant of Buddha Niche

隋　代 / Sui Dynasty（581-618 CE）
灰　岩 / Limestone
高　度 / H. 44.5 cm
宽　度 / W. 44 cm
厚　度 / T. 19 cm

67 飞天残件 / Remnant of a Flying Devata

北　齐 / Northern Qi (550-577 CE)
大理石 / Marble
高　度 / H. 10cm

68 飞天残件 / Remnant of a Flying Devata

北　齐 / Northern Qi (550-577 CE)
大理石 / Marble
高　度 / H. 6.5 cm

69　蹲狮 / Squatted Lion

北　朝 / Northern Dynasties (386-581 CE)
灰　岩 / Limestone
高　度 / H. 25 cm

70 狮首残件 / Remnant of Head of a Lion

东　魏 / Eastern Wei (534-550 CE)
大理石 / Marble
高(左) / H.(L.) 8.5 cm
高(右) / H.(R.) 10 cm

71　蹲狮 / Squatted Lion

北　周 / Northern Zhou (557-581 CE)
大理石 / Marble
高　度 / H. 15.2 cm

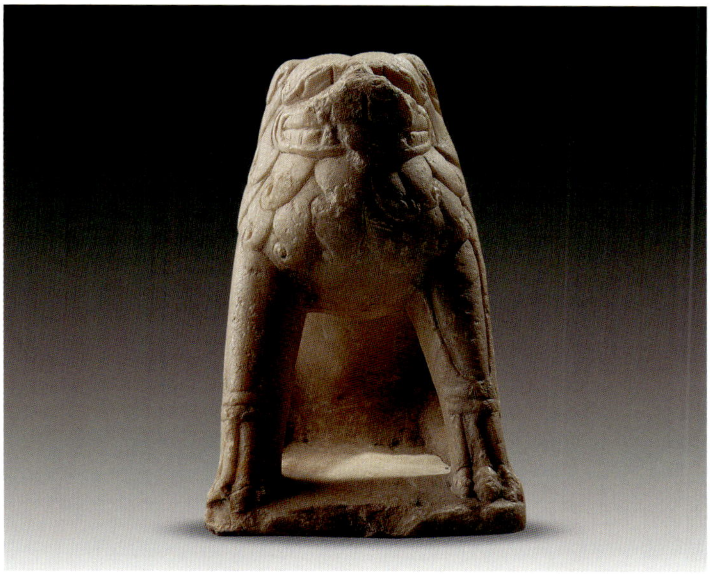

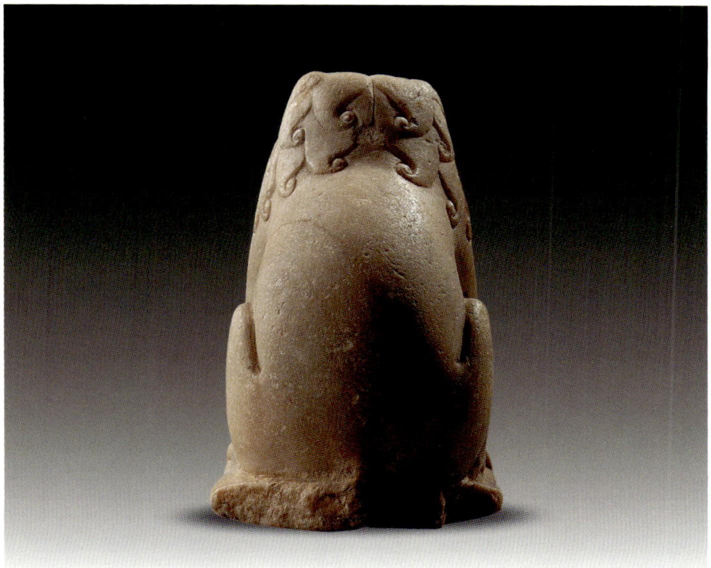

72 狮首残件 / Remnant Head of Lion Statue

唐　代 / Tang Dynasty (618-907 CE)
大理石 / Marble
高　度 / H. 11 cm

73 伎乐纹八面塔段 / Component Part of a Stupa with Music-offering Goddesses

唐 代 / Tang Dynasty (618-907 CE)
灰 岩 / Limestone
高 度 / H. 36 cm

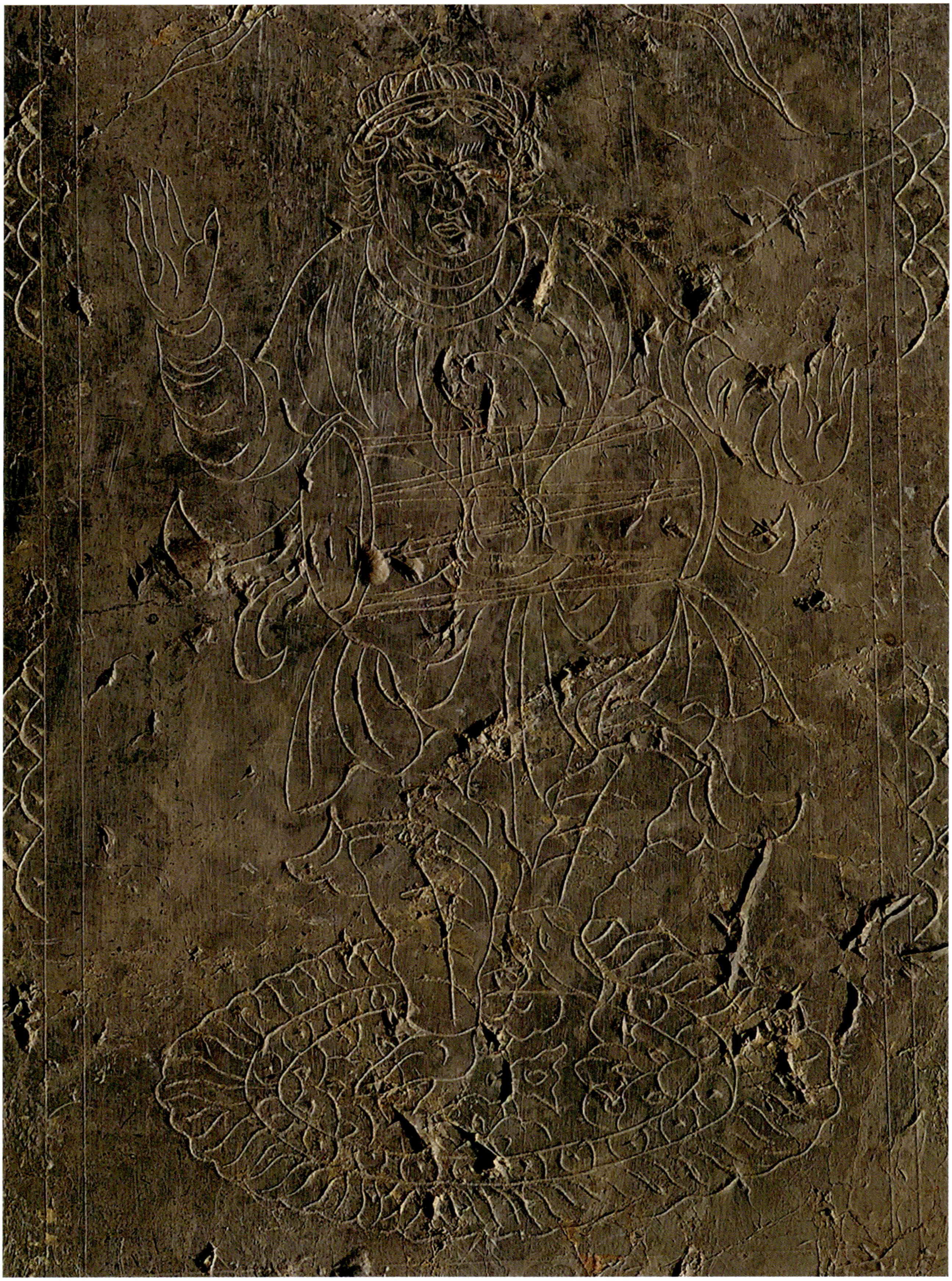

伎乐纹八面塔段图案 1 / The Patterns of the Stupa with Music-offering Goddesses, Section 1

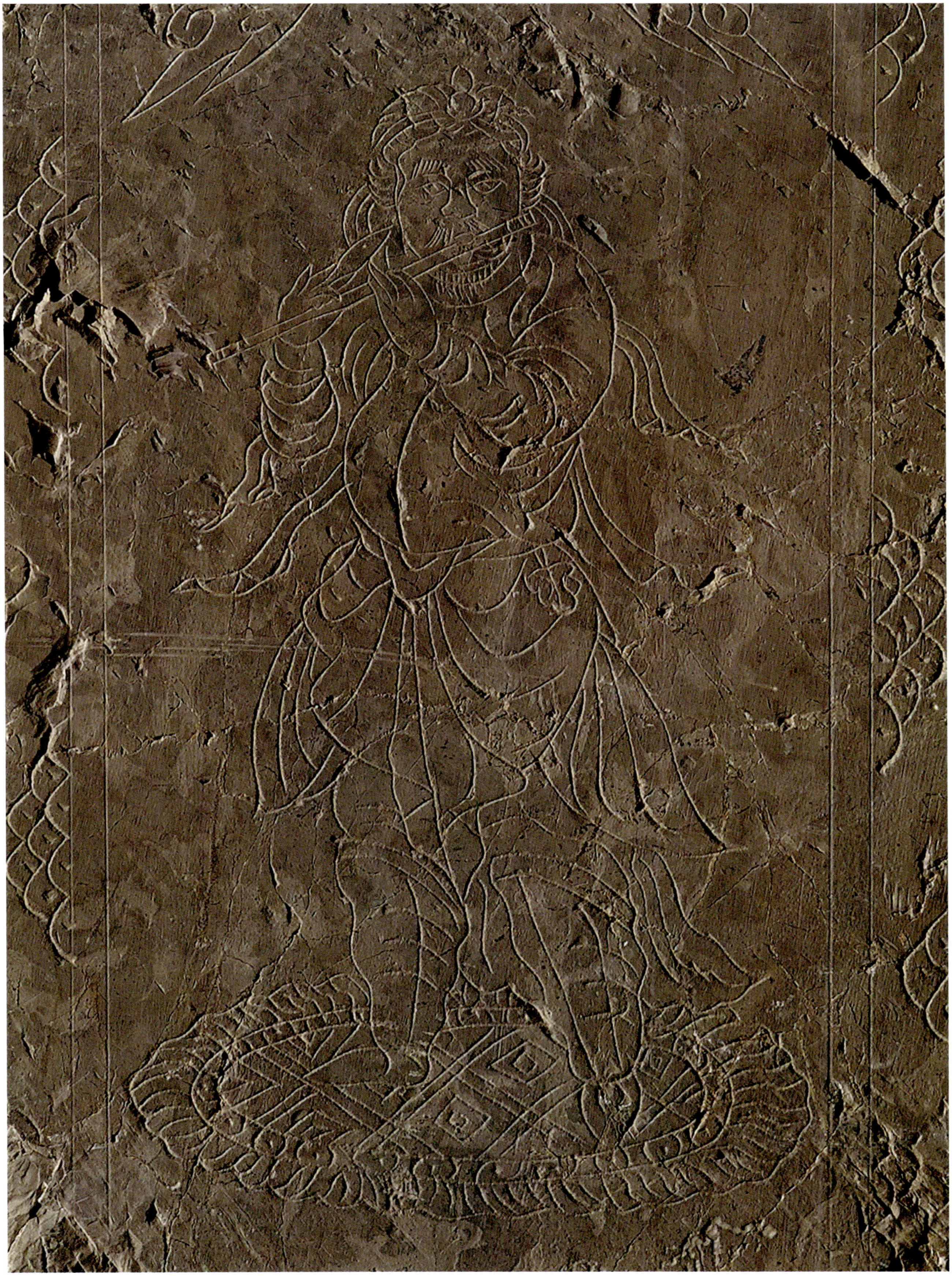

伎乐纹八面塔段图案 2 / The Patterns of the Stupa with Music-offering Goddesses, Section 2

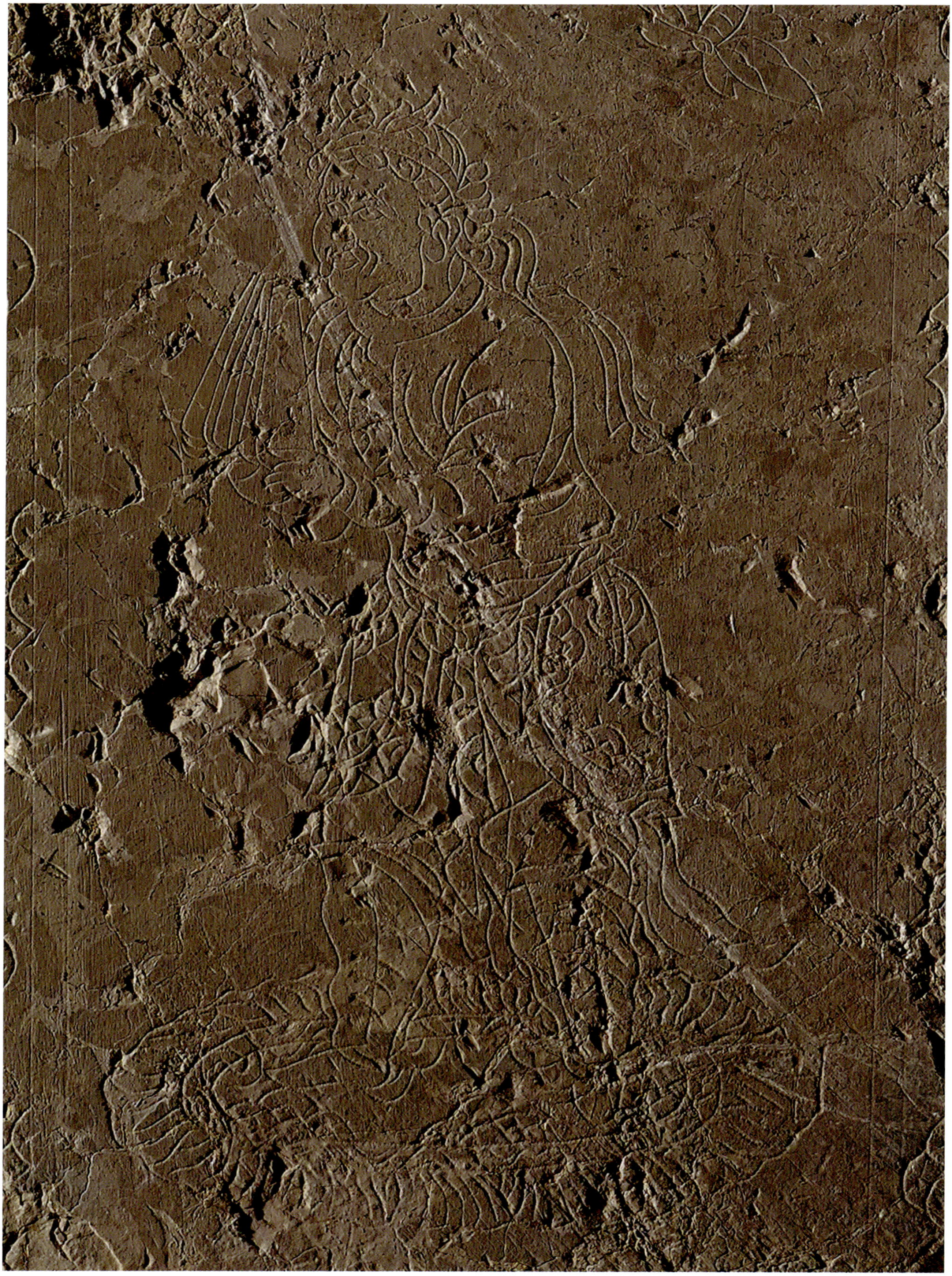

伎乐纹八面塔段图案 3 / The Patterns of the Stupa with Music-offering Goddesses, Section 3

伎乐纹八面塔段图案 4 / The Patterns of the Stupa with Music-offering Goddesses, Section 4

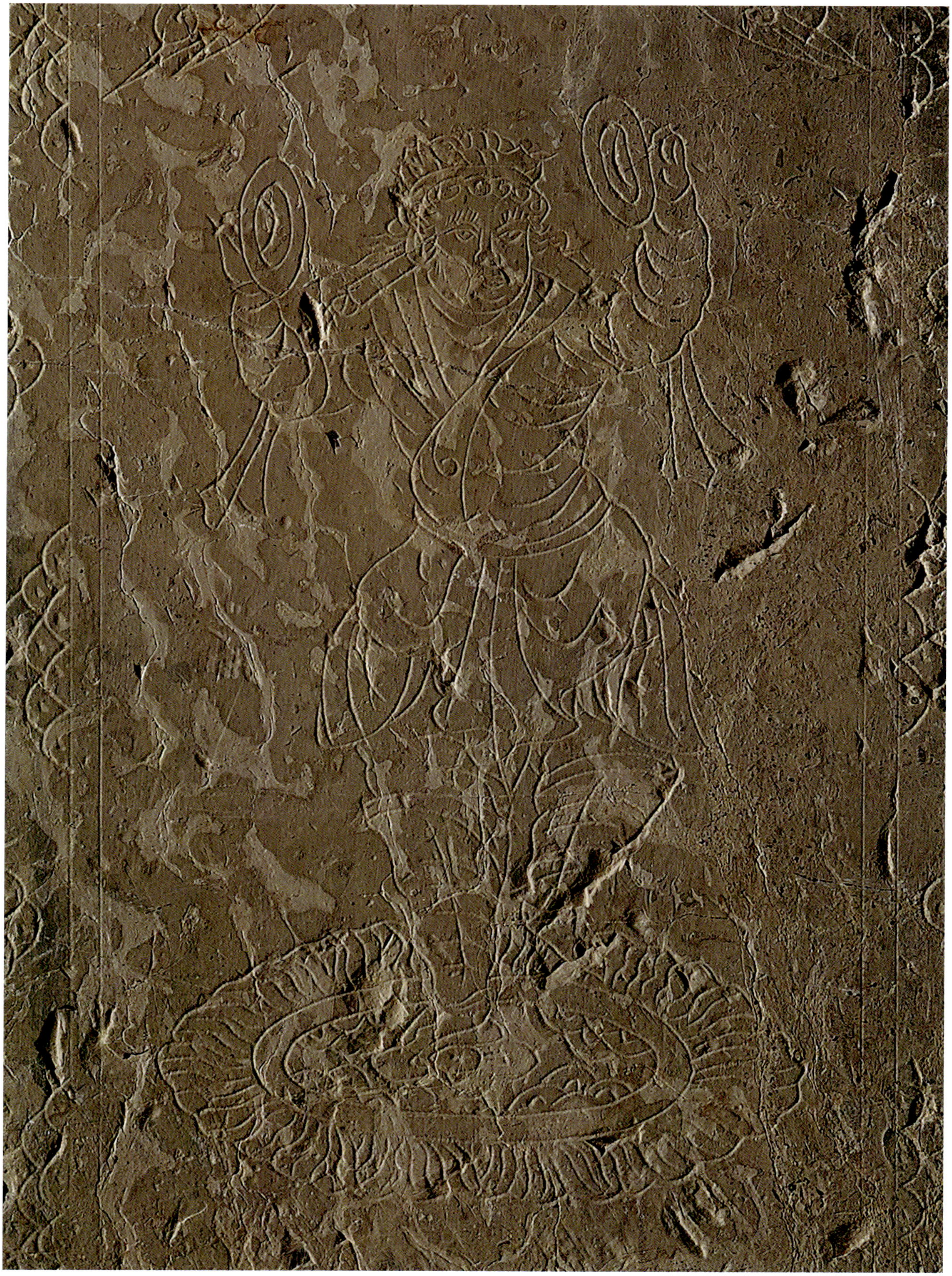

伎乐纹八面塔段图案 5 / The Patterns of the Stupa with Music-offering Goddesses, Section 5

伎乐纹八面塔段图案 6 / The Patterns of the Stupa with Music-offering Goddesses, Section 6

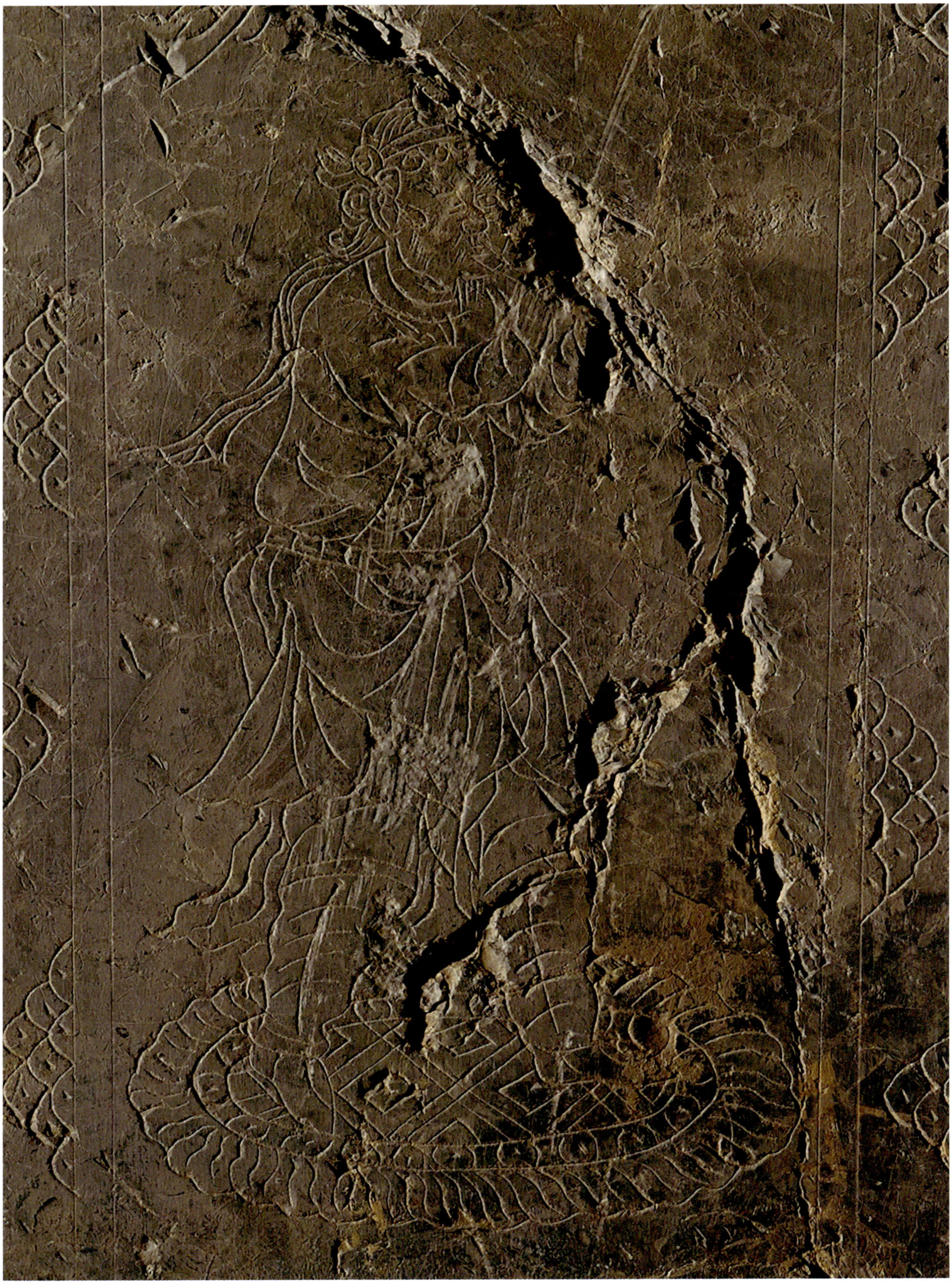

伎乐纹八面塔段图案 7 / The Patterns of the Stupa with Music-offering Goddesses, Section 7

伎乐纹八面塔段图案 8 / The Patterns of the Stupa with Music-offering Goddesses, Section 8

74 **力士四面像塔段** / Component Part of a Stupa with Four Warriors

唐 代 / Tang Dynasty (618-907 CE)
大理石 / Marble
高 度 / H. 19 cm

75 塔段 / Part of a Tower

辽　代 / Liao Dynasty (916-1125 CE)
大理石 / Marble
宽　度 / W. 66 cm
高　度 / H. 71 cm

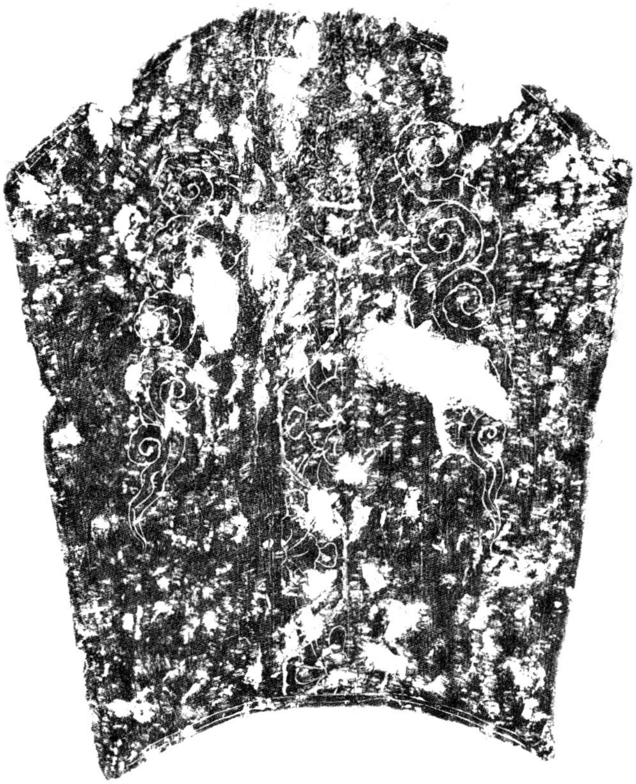

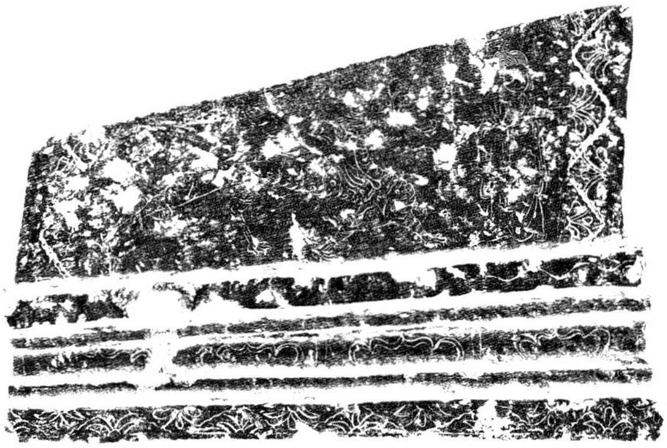

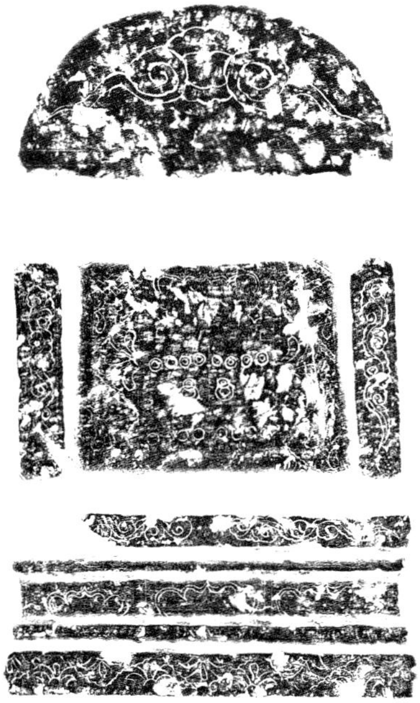

76 **舍利函** / Sarira Sarcophagus

唐　代 / Tang Dynasty (618-907 CE)
灰　岩 / Limestone
长　度 / L. 43 cm
宽　度 / W. 40 cm
高　度 / H. 26 cm

77 翼羊 / Winged Goat

南　朝 / Southern Dynasties (420-589 CE)
灰　岩 / Limestone
长　度 / L. 33 cm
宽　度 / W. 18 cm
高　度 / H. 32 cm

78 **单柄双系独流忍冬纹莲瓣壶** / Acanthus and Lotus-petal Design Ewer with Two Rings

南　朝 / Southern Dynasties (420-589 CE)
大理石 / Marble
高　度 / H. 26 cm

79 托举忍冬纹石榴盘力士覆莲座 / Base Warrior Lotus Design Seat

唐　代 / Tang Dynasty (618-907 CE)
灰　岩 / Limestone
底　长 / L. 19 cm
底　宽 / W. 19 cm
高　度 / H. 34 cm

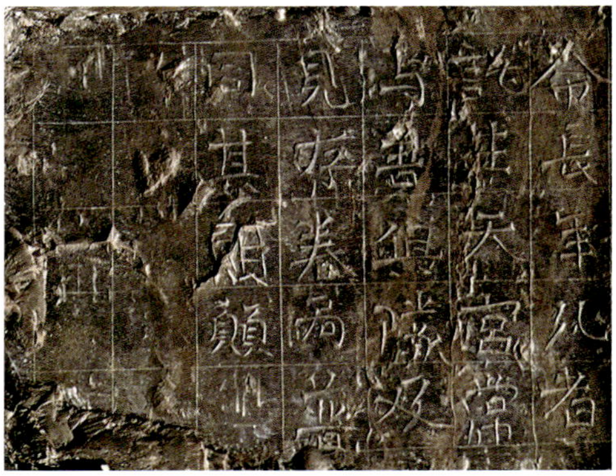

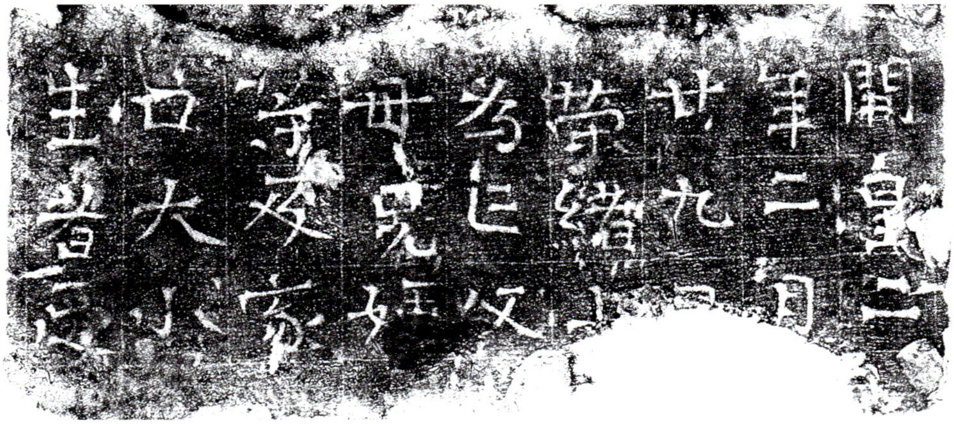

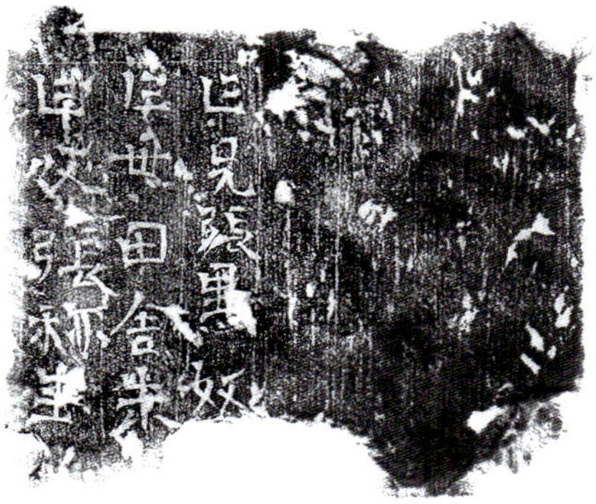

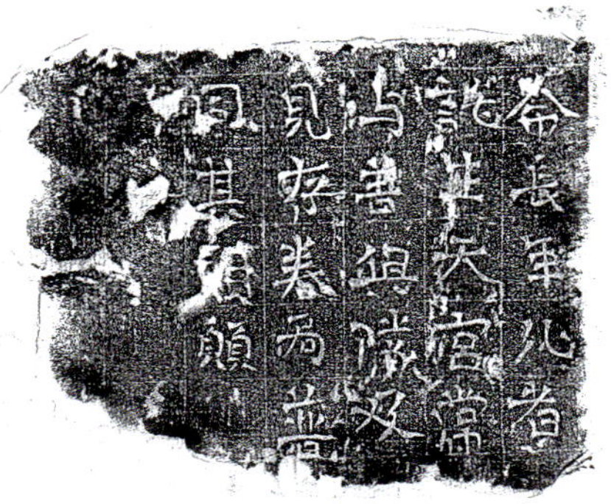

发愿文：

正面：开皇二 / 年二月 / 廿九日 / 荣绪上 / 为亡父 / 母兄嫂 / 等及家 / 口大小 / 生者受

右侧：命长年化者 / 托生天宫常 / 与善俱隣及 / 见存眷属普 / 同其□愿

左侧：亡兄张黑奴 / 亡母田舍朱 / 亡父张 称 生

80 荣绪造老君坐像 / The Supreme God of Taoism

隋　代 / Sui Dynasty (581-618 CE)
石灰岩 / Limestone
高　度 / H. 40 cm

[有“开皇二年（582）”纪年 / With “The Second Year of Kaihuang Reign Period (582)” Inscriptions]

81 **禅定佛坐像** / Seated Buddha

十六国 / The Sixteen States Dynasty (304-439 CE)
铜鎏金 / Gilt Bronze
高 度 / H. 8.3 cm

82 **禅定佛坐像** / Seated Buddha

十六国 / The Sixteen States Dynasty (304-439 CE)
铜　质 / Gilt Bronze
高　度 / H. 17.7 cm

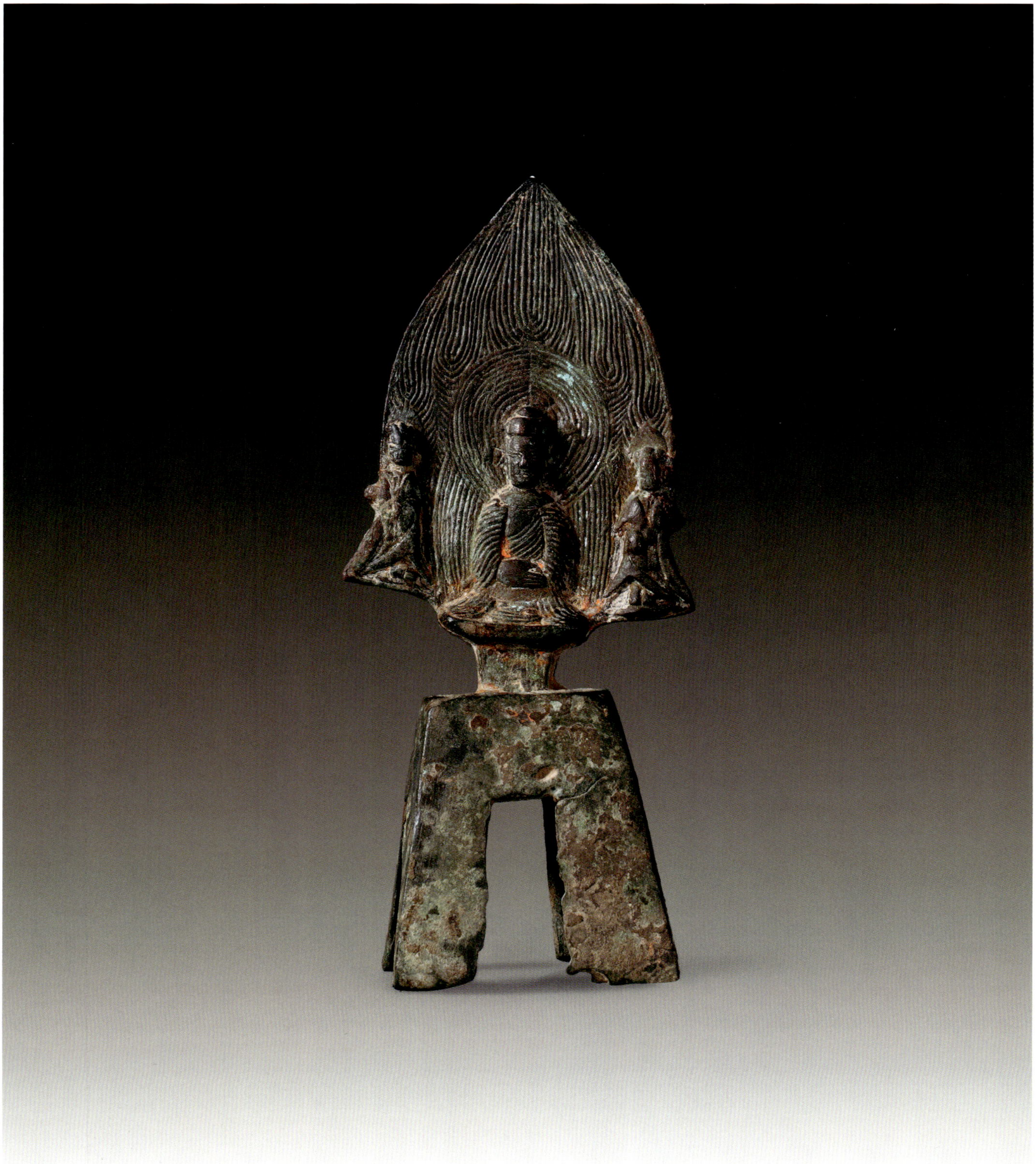

83 禅定佛三尊像 / Statue of Seated Buddha and Two Bodhisattvas

北　魏 / Northern Wei (386-534 CE)
铜　质 / Bronze
高　度 / H. 14.3 cm

84 **禅定佛坐像** / Seated Buddha

北　魏 / Northern Wei (386-534 CE)
铜　质 / Bronze
高　度 / H. 11.3 cm

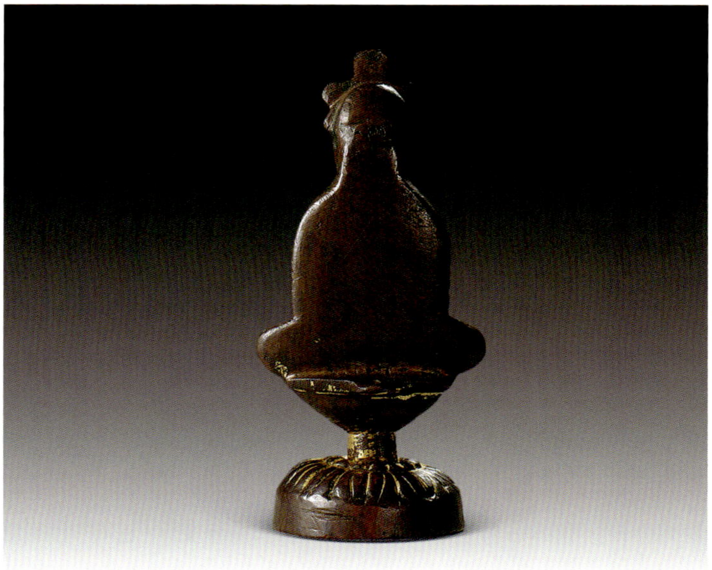

85　**禅定佛坐像** / Seated Buddha

北　魏 / Northern Wei (386-534 CE)
铜鎏金 / Gilt Bronze
高　度 / H. 10.6 cm

86 **佛立像** / Standing Buddha

北 魏 / Northern Wei (386-534 CE)
铜 质 / Bronze
高 度 / H. 18.3 cm

87 **菩萨立像** / Standing Bodhisattva

东　魏 / Eastern Wei (534-550 CE)
铜　质 / Bronze
高　度 / H. 18 cm

88 王阿胜造普贤菩萨像 / Samantabhadra Bodhisattva

东　魏 / Eastern Wei (534-550 CE)
铜鎏金 / Gilt Bronze
高　度 / H. 7.9 cm

[有“天平四年（537）”纪年 / With “ The Fourth Year of Tianping Reign Period (537)” Inscriptions]

发愿文：天平四年十月三日杜贵母王阿胜为长女阿妃造像一区

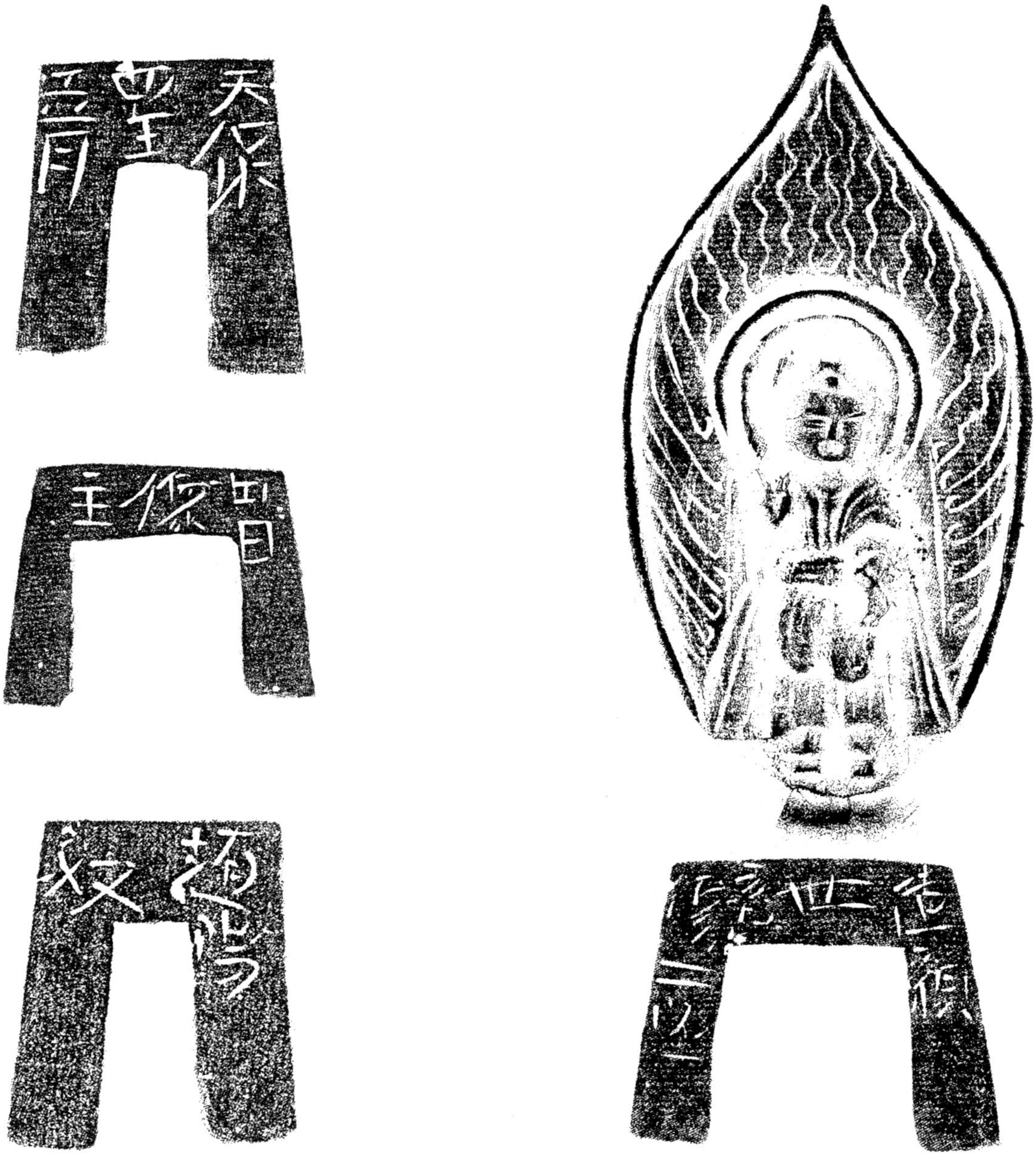

89 赵阳奴造观音菩萨立像 / Standing Avalokitesvara

北　齐 / Northern Qi (550-577 CE)
铜　质 / Bronze
高　度 / H. 16.5 cm

[有“天保四年（553）”纪年 / With “The Fourth Year of Tianbao Reign Period (553)” Inscriptions]

发愿文：天保四年五月四日像主赵阳奴造观世音像一区

90 菩萨坐像 / Seated Bodhisattva

北　齐 / Northern Qi (550-577 CE)
铜鎏金 / Gilt Bronze
高　度 / H. 10.6 cm

91　菩萨三尊像 / Bodhisattva

南　朝 / Southern Dynasties (420-589 CE)
铜　质 / Bronze
高　度 / H. 19.7 cm

92 **辟邪** / Winged Mythological Creature

北　朝 / Northern Dynasties (386-581 CE)
铜鎏金 / Gilt Bronze
高　度 / H. 4.9 cm

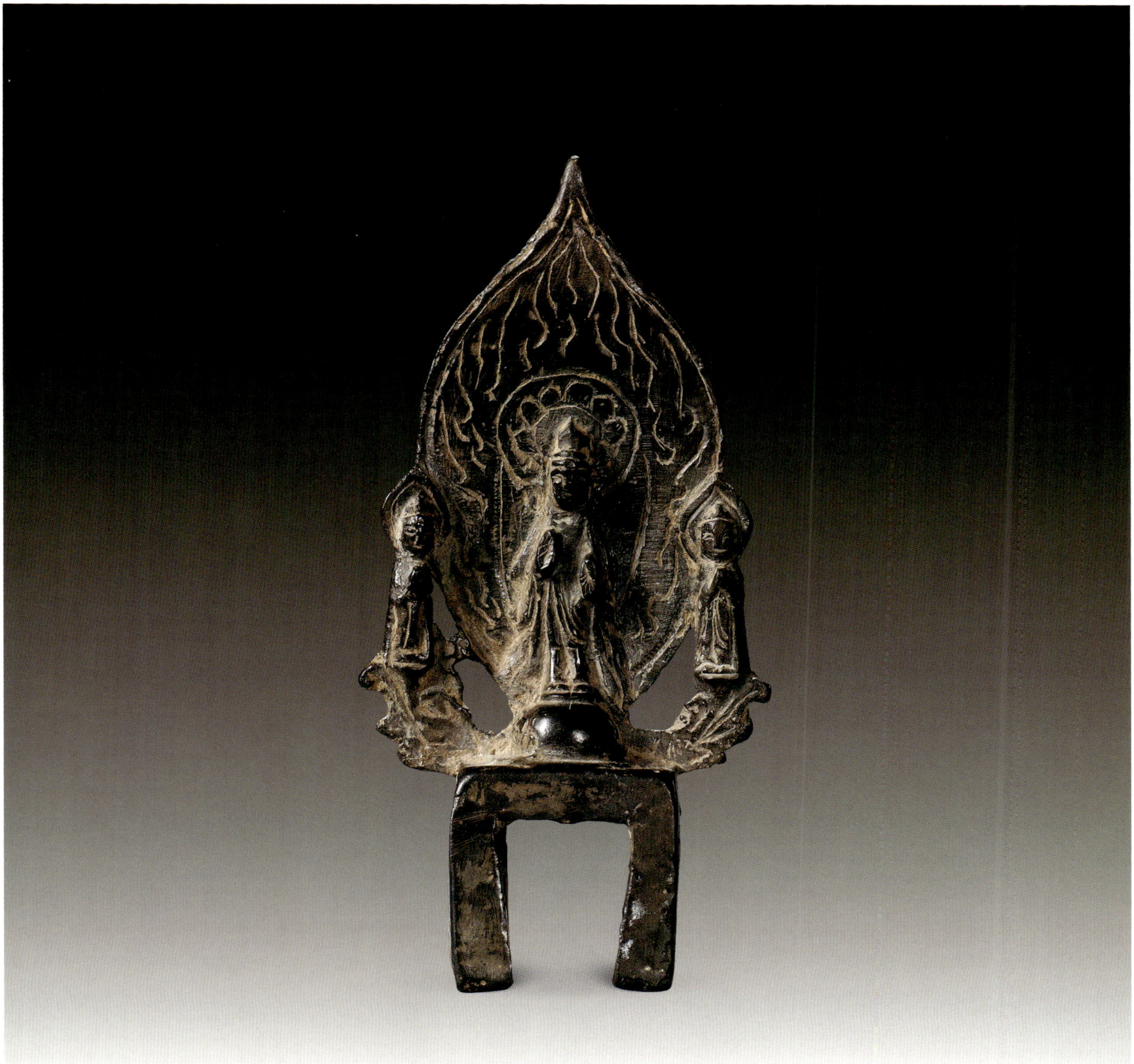

93 魏奴母赵造佛立像 / Standing Buddha

隋　代 / Sui Dynasty (581-618 CE)
铜　质 / Bronze
高　度 / H. 13.6 cm

[有“开皇八年（588）”纪年 / With “The Eighth Year of Kaihuang Reign Period (588)” Inscriptions]

发愿文：开皇八年四月 / 十六日魏奴母 / 赵愿生长安 / 子造一像区

94 菩萨立像 / Standing Bodhisattva

隋 代 / Sui Dynasty (581-618 CE)
铜鎏金 / Gilt Bronze
高 度 / H. 16.4 cm

95 佛说法坐像 / Seated Buddha

唐　代 / Tang Dynasty (618-907 CE)
铜鎏金 / Gilt Bronze
高　度 / H. 12.3 cm

96 七连佛像 / Statue of Seven Buddhas

唐　代 / Tang Dynasty (618-907 CE)
铜鎏金 / Gilt Bronze
高　度 / H. 13.4 cm

97 观音菩萨立像 / Standing Avalokitesvara

唐　代 / Tang Dynasty (618-907 CE)
铜鎏金 / Gilt Bronze
高　度 / H. 16.2 cm

98 **罗汉立像** / Standing Arhan

唐　代 / Tang dynasty (618-907 CE)
铜鎏金 / Gilt Bronze
高　度 / H. 9.2 cm

99 **天尊坐像** / Seated Taoist God

唐　代 / Tang Dynasty (618-907 CE)
铜鎏金 / Gilt Bronze
高　度 / H. 9.5 cm

100 **胡人跪像** / Kneeling Hunni

唐　代 / Tang Dynasty (618-907 CE)
铜鎏金 / Gilt Bronze
高　度 / H. 6 cm

后 记

喜欢中国古代石刻不需要理由。

依稀记得童年时在大石狮肚子底下钻来耍去的快乐情景。时光飞逝，六公园的那对大石狮卓立依旧，自己已是过“五十而知天命”。

无心插柳柳成荫。犹记得当年哲学系的王元骧老师在公共课上对真、善、美的精彩解读，被自己主观演绎为力求古器物之真、力求古器物之独特文化价值、力求古器物之独立美学价值，并成为自己内心追求的境界。

器物为大。每一件古器物所蕴含的意义，其实远比我们的眼睛所能看见的要多得多。我们固然有选器择物的权利，也有辨别真伪、判断价值、品味鉴赏的责任，更有传播并传承悠久灿烂中华文明的义务。器物为大才会心存敬畏，器物为大才能思接千古且情有所寄。

“指穷于为薪，火传也，不知其尽也。”在承载着千年文化积淀的古代器物面前，人类是如此渺小。人对这些古器物的占有、失去和再占有，远不如古器物与人类文明之间的关系来得更为深入和持久，任何人都不可能永远地占有它们。我们唯一能够回馈的，就是将蕴藏在古器物深处的文化脉络悉心挖掘梳理出来，留给下一代人，使其有机会和可能一代代地传承下去。

光阴无限，人生有期。痴迷一物者，往往不及其余。这个时代能够坐享“流传有序”的究竟凤毛麟角，更多的时候需要的是一批集腋成裘的有心人。流传有序，可以从此器此物起步；薪火相传，可以从此时此刻开始。

本书辑录了2011年5月18日在“永远的北朝——深圳博物馆北朝石刻艺术展”中展出的及部分尚未公开展陈的藏品，合计100件。展览已于2015年8月13日闭馆，历时四年有余。期间接待了无数海内外的参观者，许多参观者写下了情真意切的留言。展览使观众真切感受到了公元4~6世纪期间中国古代石刻那种撼动人心的人文之美，同时也唤醒了我们对自己所生存的时代的重新思考。

感谢深圳博物馆的领导和专家，正是因为有了你们的全力支持，这批古器物才得以长期公开展陈。

感谢金石文化的同仁们，正是因为你们多年的努力，一个继续展陈这批重要器物的深圳市金石艺术博物馆即将正式向全体市民开放。

感谢日本佛教大学教授黑田彰先生。黑田彰先生展览期间专程来了深圳三次，每一次都带来了自己对这批古器物最新的研究成果。

更要深深感谢中国社会科学院考古研究所研究员赵超先生。赵超先生在书籍的编辑、出版过程中严谨的治学态度，令我终身受益。没有他的始终如一的支持，就不会有今天这本书的出版。因缘际会，我们因石刻而相识，也因石刻而成为莫逆之交。

最后要感谢我的家人。谢谢你们的理解和支持，使我可以将自己的时间和热情毫无节制地倾注在这些冰冷的古代器物上。

石刻，如此沉重又如此灵动。
北朝，短暂而又永恒。

2016 年 5 月 3 日于深圳